Poverty and Promise

Just One Voice

Poverty and Promise:
One Volunteer's Experience of Kenya

Cindi G. Brown

Just One Voice
Surprise, Arizona USA
2008

JUST ONE VOICE

Published by Friends of TICH Worldwide
Friends of TICH Worldwide (USA) Inc.
15852 W. Desert Mirage Drive, Surprise, AZ 85379
Visit our website at www.justonevoice.org

First published in 2008 by Just One Voice

LIBRARY OF CONGRESS CATALOGING-IN-PUBLICATION DATA

Brown, Cindi G.
Poverty and promise : one volunteer's experience of
Kenya / Cindi G. Brown.
p. cm.
LCCN 2007939918
ISBN-13: 978-0-9800620-0-7
ISBN-10: 0-9800620-0-4

1. Africa--Economic conditions--1960- 2. Africa--
Social conditions--1960- 3. Africa--Biography--
Anecdotes. 4. Brown, Cindi G.--Travel--Africa.
5. Voluntary Services Overseas.   I. Title.

HC800.B76 2008   338.96
                                  QBI07-600325

Printed in the United States of America
Interior design by Ignacio Pintos
Cover design by GraphHik Illusions

For my children, Jaime and James, and for our children of the world. May peace and good health envelop you.

And for Jennifer, with her soft strength and unending goodness. May you always reap the kindnesses you sow.

Foreword

Rewards are not possible without risks.

This book reveals the risks Cindi took when she decided to leave her life in America and volunteer in Kenya. It reveals the risks she took each day as she worked side-by-side with us. When she first came to Africa, Cindi was brand new to the idea of development and knew little about non-government organizations (NGOs) operating in third world countries to eliminate poverty, hunger and disease. Cindi was relatively green.

I, on the other hand, was anything but. Born into the Luo community and raised in Saradidi, a tiny village on Lake Victoria's edge, I was cared for very well by my parents. My father, Jaduong' Clement Seje, and my mother, Mama Stella Anyango, tilled the land and raised livestock to provide for our family. However, as a child, I was quite sickly and needed regular treatment to sustain my life, so a local retired nurse took care of me for much of the time. On several occasions, my father had to carry me on his back, walking 18 kilometers to a clinic where I could get more sophisticated care.

As a devout Christian, my father did not leave the care of his children to my mother but, instead, took an active role in household chores, including childcare. My father often described opportunities he missed as a young man to become better trained in the medical field. His regrets and my early experiences influenced my desire to become a medical doctor when I grew up.

This vision came under threat during my high school years, when our school stopped offering a course in biology due to a lack of resources. My dream compelled me to study biology on my own and to sit for the exam. This earned me scorn from some teachers, as they thought I was arrogant in thinking I could study and pass in a subject as complex as biology without being taught by them. However, three of my teachers encouraged me: the Headmaster, Mr. Nathanael Oloo; David Kieffer; and Thomas Levit, an American Peace Corps volunteer who encouraged me to pursue a career in medicine or research. I passed biology, along with the other required subjects, and was eventually accepted to and finished medical school.

Although I enjoyed clinical practice, my mentors (Professor John Bennett, a South African, and Collin Forbes, a Canadian) urged me to contribute to a wider constituency by training other health professionals. My young professional life was well nurtured by my peers: Professor Harrison Spencer, the current President and CEO of the Association of Schools of Public Health; James Kagia, a resident of Washington who was the Chair of our Department; and Miriam Were, a senior colleague in the Department of Community Health, University of Nairobi. These and other great medical professionals gave me the momentum I needed to do what I do today.

While Cindi grew up hearing about people in need in Africa, I grew up in the midst of people in need in Africa. Early on, I understood how systems of colonization and post-colonialism hold countries like Kenya in a vicious cycle of poverty and ill health. I wanted to help change things, and found public health to be the catalyst for my personal growth as well as the growth of Kenya. After becoming a doctor, I specialized in tropical public health at the Harvard School of Public Health and studied theology in Vancouver in the 1970s. I then taught at the University of Nairobi, and later worked in Geneva as the Director of the Christian Medical Commission (CMC)—the mother of the Primary Health Care Movement, alongside WHO/UNICEF.

I returned to Western Kenya to found TICH in 1998. Even with my professional contacts around the world and the support of donor groups and UNESCO, building a private institute of higher education in a developing country involves great risks. In partnership with individuals like Cindi, who understand the connectedness of societies and economies the world over, and who want to be part of positive change, TICH focuses on enabling all households to enjoy dignified living. Our mission is to mold students into concerned and effective leaders who will transform health in the African context.

Africa experiences more than her fair share of the burden of poverty, disease and death. There are appalling disparities within and between countries, complicated by the attenuation of human resource capital through death, disease, civil wars and brain drain. Poverty compounds powerlessness and increases ill health, as ill health increases poverty. An estimated 54 percent of the total population in sub-Saharan Africa live in absolute poverty. Poverty eradication will require years of diligent hard work, with victories eked out in small bites. More than 40 years of multilateral and bilateral anti-poverty programs show that reducing rates of poverty is not an exact science.

We must think and act in the long-term. Three hundred million Africans living on less than one dollar a day cannot, by any stroke of economic or management genius, suddenly escape the cold hands of poverty. Social welfare programs of Western countries show that gains are incremental, sometimes intergenerational. Even then, these successful scenarios occur in environments where the policy is fairly stable, rule of law is present and most recipients can read at reasonable levels. This scenario is not applicable in many African countries.

The only realistic hope for making a dent in the extreme poverty of Africa is to have Western and African leaders on the same page. These leaders must agree on to how to end the choking debt burdens in Africa; how to end all forms of corruption and malfeasance in Africa; how to end trade inequities and agricultural subsidies in Western countries which impoverish African farmers; how to end the lack of genuine elections and democracy in many parts of Africa; how to end extrajudicial forms of justice in Africa;

and how to end the use of Western financial centers as the preferred end destination of misappropriated funds from poor African countries. In a situation whereby policy makers in the West and Africa reach abiding accord on these issues, the war against poverty in Africa can dramatically change.

Anti-poverty eradication programs in Africa must take advantage of the natural entrepreneurial spirit of its citizens. We like to trade on goods and services, and have done so for centuries. Creating opportunities for small-scale businessmen and women is critical. To make this happen, governments in Africa must create enabling regulatory environments that encourage budding entrepreneurs to push ahead with their ideas and that motivate large-scale entrepreneurs and foreign investors to plan for the long-term. Nurturing a sustainable private sector in Africa should also be a major strategic objective of poverty eradication programs in Africa.

At TICH, we have faith in the possibility of reversing today's trends in Africa. Our relative success so far is not based on the abundance of our possessions, but rather on the abundance of our hard work and faith. We refuse to believe our destiny is defined by the narrow limits of our existence. We dare to plan and act toward our dream, starting with small actions we can handle and improving toward the higher goals of our calling, until all poverty trends are permanently reversed. We are joined in this effort by people like Cindi, people from other societies who share our dream. We will all invest without reservation, because we have a passion and we believe it is possible.

Because of our intensive approach to learning at TICH, our graduates are highly prized by employers, including government ministries, universities and NGOs. Cindi shared with me her favorite aspect of TICH's education model: the "community college" we create in each partnership to share knowledge and skills with rural villages. Village members enroll and follow parallel programs developed to meet their specific needs using their available resources. At these colleges, everyone is a learner and a teacher. TICH students and staff view people not as vulnerable, powerless or sick individuals, but as partners who are already engaged, as my parents were, in solving their own problems and transforming their own situations.

Cindi has a unique capacity to listen. She listened to us and wove her contributions around our strengths. That is why every initiative she started at TICH continues today. She cross-fertilized our ideas and was comfortable recognizing our expertise and leadership. When Cindi left Kenya, she did not leave hope behind. Instead, she left determined to continue supporting TICH through the foundation of a non-profit called Just One Voice (www.justonevoice.org). We were encouraged that she would spearhead an entity in the United States to support our work, by sharing our stories and spreading the legacy of our efforts in lifting Kenya and Africa out of poverty.

TICH exists because we take risks every day, and because intelligent people around the world take risks to dedicate themselves to improving life in developing countries. In this book, Cindi highlights the efforts made toward development by the people at TICH, and she recognizes the promise of Kenyans. As we all take risks to improve our ways of life, no matter which country we live in, we might stumble. We might even fall. But we continue risking. It is the African way. It is the human way.

Dan Keseje
Director
Tropical Institute of Community Health and Development *in Africa*

CONTENTS

Prologue

*A*fter being in Kenya for two months, I come to realize the love sent by family and friends is my secret weapon against the hardships of living in Africa. Their love for me is the sap in my spine, straightening me, keeping my head level, keeping my mind perpendicular to the floor. No tilting.

Family and friends give me strength, and I must be strong, because there is so much need here. So much need.

I recently sent my friend, Jennifer, a note saying I maintain a balance of being open while protecting my personal boundaries with Kenyans who constantly approach and ask for things; a job, money, food, shoes or to be taken to America.

Who am I bullshitting about balancing openness and personal space in Africa?

Me, that's who.

Then a creak, a pop, like tons of ice shifting down a mountain.

A tilting.

Living in Kisumu, seeing poverty, walking around with an open heart (yet having little to give but myself) is heartbreaking. Each day in Africa brings a thousand heartbreaks. But I ignore the heartache and go to a funeral.

Maybe it was spending the day at Eric's funeral, where dogs are kicked and drunks are hit ("It is the African way") and young men drink while burying their friend and women wail. Maybe that's what led to the tilting.

While walking home that evening, two brothers, Churchill and Andrew, run down the darkening Kisumu street to catch up with me, claiming to be taking a pleasant stroll, but I know they have run just to talk to me, to be my friend, to go to America with me. They run in the dark, pretending to be casual, and they're very polite, but I cannot be every Kenyan's friend! And don't they realize I might be frightened when people run to catch me on darkened streets?

Flashback to last week's journal entry:

Sometimes I grow tired of being in Kenya. Like today. I get tired of smelling hot smoke from yard fires and from wringing heavy clothes by hand. Sometimes when I hear a rooster crow I want to scream. There is constant noise; people shouting, dogs barking, gates banging opened and closed, cars crunching down dirt roads, people worshipping through loud song and clapping (for hours and hours), hammering everywhere and bizarre, terrifying calls from huge birds. I get tired of not being able to walk down the street without someone (typically a man) introducing themselves and wanting to be my friend, or wanting to tell me their dreams. I long for my own space, my own home to decorate and run naked in if I please. I resent rocks in the road that make it impossible to walk without looking down, rocks that tear up a pair of good shoes in one trip. I want a refrigerator so I can have cold milk instead of room temperature milk on cereal, and mayonnaise for sandwiches. And so bread will keep for more than two days. But mostly I grow tired of Kenya because it causes me to feel too much and think too much, with orphans in our yard and funerals every day. I want to stop feeling and stop thinking for just a little while, for just a few hours.

And then I break down.

It begins Sunday afternoon, once I've washed two tubs of clothes and hung them on the line outside the kitchen window. After I read Faulkner's *As I Lay Dying*, I suddenly feel tired and sit on my bed, under the mosquito net, and ache to hold my daughter, Jaime. I cry for Jaime, silently, so no one will hear, because all the windows are open and all the household children -- Paul and Mercy and Joyce and Modis -- run hither and thither, mostly past my bedroom window. I rock on the bed, aching to hold Jaime, and lift my arms, imagining her in them, crying silently.

Could this be hormone-induced? There certainly is a strange, hollow feeling in my gut, near my ovaries. I cry and rock and wonder at the source of the pain until I sleep. Monday morning, I wake and find I don't want to get out of bed. Don't want to lift my head from the pillow. Tired. Immense headache. I text the reverend and say I won't be in to work, and then I curl up and cry and sleep. Chris from VSO calls and wakes me and I say I'm home with a headache and he says it could be malaria, and to go to Dr. Sokwala for a test. I go back to bed and read and cry and feel disoriented, thinking 'maybe it is malaria.'

I grab my pack with the emergency medical card and flag down a boda boda, pointing to Dr. Sokwala's address on the card: Ogada Street. The driver doesn't know it, but I climb on the back of his bike anyway and we head to town. I stare at the ground, sort of despondent, though I don't really know the definition of despondent. Suddenly I don't care... about a lot of things. I don't care that I'm not looking and smiling at others. I don't care that I'm not at work. I don't care that I've put the burden of finding Dr. Sokwala on this nice man. I don't care that I don't care. I'm very peaceful in my not caring. It is the African way.

I'm wearing my glasses, but cannot focus my eyes. From nowhere I hear the words, "the truth will set you free" and scenes flash through the sunny haze. My father, drunk, in the middle of the night, taking every bottle out of the cabinet and smashing them onto the Formica kitchen table, cursing all the while. Ketchup, mustard, mayonnaise and broken glass commingling in front of my sleepy four year old eyes... Waking one morning with a breast infection, the sickest I've ever been. I'm nineteen, and Jaime is two weeks old, and I can't lift my arm to hold her, to nurse her. Overnight, my left breast becomes hard and red and hot to the touch. I call Daddy in the next town, crying, saying "Please take us to the doctor because Jaime is so tiny and hungry and I can't lift my arm to nurse her." Daddy comes for us... Granny banging the piano with her fat fingers, me sitting next to her on the stool, my feet just touching the floor, Uncle Bill standing over us as we all sing, "Surely goodness and mercy shall follow me, all the days, all the days of my life." Uncle Bill, my father's brother, Billy Joe Brown, puts his hand on my shoulder as we sing and when we're through, he says, "Cindi, honey, you have a very nice voice." I smile down at my feet just touching the floor. I remember his hand on my shoulder again when I was reading Mama's email three weeks ago saying Uncle Bill had passed away. Uncle

Bill passed away… Uncle Bill passed away and I'm half a world away. I swallow the news, swallow the grief, swallow hard, sending it down down down to the hollow in my gut near my ovaries. I can't lift my arms to feed her. It's the African way. The truth will set you free.

What is my truth? I feel unloved, uncared for. Not my truth with a capital "T," just my unfocused truth on the back of a boda boda headed some place we don't know how to find. What's my other truth? I CANNOT CARE ABOUT EVERYONE IN KENYA AND REMAIN WHOLE.

We see Daktari's office. I enter and sit on the right, facing other patients. The room is 12 feet deep from front to back door and about 8 feet wide. Five people are ahead of me. I stare at the floor and seep weep. I avoid looking at the others because I cannot stop seeping weeping. The tears roll until I pull the travel pack of Charmin toilet paper from my bag. Jaime and James gave the Charmin as a gift. A very wise gift for Africa. I miss them and look at the floor, seeping.

The receptionist says, "Madam, you can go in now." So I rise and walk through the door with a wet face and Dr. Sokwala is surprised by my tears and almost hides it.

"I'm sorry" I say sitting across from her. "But I can't stop crying." She offers a box of tissues.

"What's wrong?" she asks.

"I have a headache since yesterday and I'm disoriented and tired."

"What anti-malarial do you take?"

"Lariam."

"What day of the week do you take it?"

"Tuesday."

"Do you feel this way every Tuesday?"

"No."

Never…

"Lariam's most common side effect is depression," Dr. Sokwala tells me. "We may want to switch your medication. But I'm going to send you for a malarial test, okay?"

"Okay."

She asks me to rest on the examination table while she checks my liver, kidneys and glands for swelling. Nothing noticeable. She avoids the hollow space near my ovaries.

"How old are you?" she asks.

"41."

"Oh, you can say *only* 41 because you're young. I'm 56." She works to level my brain, un-tilt my mind with her soft laugh.

"You'll get the test results and bring them back to my office this afternoon. I think they'll come back showing nothing, and then we can talk about changing your malaria medicine."

They take my blood at the lab at the Nakumatt plaza. An hour later, I pick up the test results and return to Dr. Sokwala. She reads the test results and says, "Are you happy?"

"Yes, it's not malaria."

"I think," she begins, "that you're not sick, you're adjusting. Everything here is new; new food, new climate, new friends, new language. Your friends are far away. It's very hard and if you don't admit it's very hard, then the stress will manifest itself physically. Some people get sick, some people cry."

Admit it's hard? That's the cure?

Ahhhhhh.

This shit is hard.

I tell her everyone approaches me, asking for things – money, jobs, food -- and she says, "Give it back to them. Tell them you're not a tourist, you live here! You're a volunteer and you don't make any money and you're helping through your work and then, you'll see, they'll turn around and will begin to sympathize with you! Stop being a victim."

There it is.

My Truth with a capital T.

I created this victimhood. Now I must un-create it.

The tears stop. The tilting slows, and then reverses, and once again my mind is perpendicular to the floor.

But despondency scares me – whatever its definition – and in the very early African hours with crickets popping and in the late Kenyan hours with thunder slapping, I think 'This shit is hard, this shit is hard.' Admit it and despondency will leave my hollow gut.

No more bullshitting.

No more victomhood.

This shit is hard.

Introduction

K enya was the region's (maybe Africa's) most stable country since its independence from Britain in 1963. The world watched as Kenya's December 2007 democratic election approached, knowing this would test the country's ability to hold legal and fair elections. Instead of a free and fair election, Kenya suddenly became home to carnage acted out in rage against supporters of the incumbent presidential candidate, Mwai Kibaki. With questions about vote counts, and Kibaki and Odinga appearing exceedingly close in the outcome, Kibaki forced the electoral commissioner to name him winner of the presidential election, ignoring voting fraud protests and denying the presidency to Raila Odinga, leader of the Orange Democratic Movement opposition party. Kibaki called for a swift and secret swearing-in ceremony, which caused people throughout the country to scream, "The election has been rigged, the rightful president is Raila, Kibaki has stolen the presidency." They were enraged, and for good reason. Their votes and voices were ignored, dismissed and trampled on.

Kibaki went on to seat many cabinet posts and made the third-place candidate his Vice President. Odinga refused to serve as Kibaki's Prime Minister. Odinga's camp garnered the powerful seat of Speaker in Kenya's unicameral parliament, but Kibaki could refuse to recall parliament for 12 months, which would make Odinga's position as Speaker one of impotence. When the people spoke out in rage against Kibaki's sly-handedness, Kibaki used police force to mute them. The BBC reported bodies were piling up in the morgue at the Provincial Hospital in Kisumu, the city I lived in. I know this hospital and this morgue. You will read about the Provincial hospital and morgue in this book. The thought of nearly 100 bodies lined up on the bare concrete floor, some half-clothed and others naked, some women and children, brought my heart low. I wondered if I knew any of the people.

Why Kisumu? Why so much violence in the western provinces? Because Raila Odinga is from Kisumu. His father, Oginga Odinga, was a hero in the independence struggle against Britain and was Kenya's first vice president, serving with Jomo Kenyatta, before Odinga broke away from the party and its divergent ideology. The main street through Kisumu is called Oginga Odinga Street. Raila Odinga can now influence Kenya's future, positively or negatively, by his action in this political standoff where more than 1,000 people have died in post-election violence. On his party's website, Raila says Kenyatta's 1963 government wanted to retain the colonial status quo, which has hampered Kenya's development in the last 45 years. Raila writes of Kenya's first elected government:

> The new government's policies were based on maximising growth immediately and taking care of equitable distribution later. This meant investing in those parts of the country that were already prosperous, due to their proximity to the centre of colonial power. The policy was justified with the explanation that, as the nation became more prosperous, the benefits would trickle down to everyone. The promised trickle-down effect has never happened. Families who were poor then have become poorer. Millions of Kenyans have since been born into poverty – grinding poverty that defines and dogs their lives from birth to death, and from which there appears no chance of escape. (www.odmk.org)

Binyavanga Wainaina, the Kenyan-born editor of Kwami?, a literary magazine, offered insights in a New York Times editorial, dated January 6, 2008, into the political forces driving much of the violence. Wainaina espouses what many Kenyans feel; that politicians manipulate their communal identities to gain political power, which ultimately divides ethnic groups, not along historical lines of hatred or folklines, but along political power lines.

Reading each day's news reports, I worried about my former colleagues at the Tropical Institute of Community Health (TICH), who are working hard to help the poor Kenyans described by Raila. Dr. Dan Keseje, Director of TICH, emailed me from Kisumu and reported on the staff and students. He wrote, "We have been preserved so far, although the government is using undue force to contain an impossible situation. The people are too angry to be intimidated by guns and so they end up being killed, as they attempt even peaceful demonstrations. We are paying too expensively for greed and lust for power by a few."

Security forces clamped down across Kenya as protestors tried to leave slum areas and assemble, so they could be heard, saying "No Raila, no peace," and "Kibaki step down!" Police used water cannons and tear gas to stop the crowds of mostly young men who had no other way of being heard. Businesses were looted and destroyed throughout the country, especially in Kibera, the country's largest slum area in Nairobi and the parliamentary constituency of Raila. A church in Eldoret, in the west, was burned, killing 50 people, mostly women and children seeking refuge from angry mobs.

Oginga Odinga Street, the main street through Kisumu's business district, was burned out, most stores down to Lake Victoria's edge in ruins. Street children, mostly boys, were more exposed than ever, even as they were reported to sift through the ashes of businesses on Oginga Odinga Street. Most Indian residents, who made up a large percentage of merchants in town, fled to Uganda, leaving Kisumu a ghost town. American Peace Corps volunteers were evacuated from throughout Kenya to Dar es Salaam in Tanzania. Nyalenda, the slum area of Kisumu, experienced its share of violence. Only two blocks from TICH, and from where I lived, Nyalenda stretches for five or so miles along Ring Road and is home to many people, mostly those from rural villages who come to the city looking for work. I suspected many of the bodies in the morgue were young men from Nyalenda, who are often out of work with little prospect for employment. Men in Kisumu were saying they would never surrender their quest for political right, while other men called for guns. TICH, in the midst of the violent aftermath and on-going tension, sought to assist the residents of Nyalenda. Dr. Dan Keseje wrote:

We wish to make a meager contribution to the healing among the people of Nyalenda, where neighbors have destroyed each other. Post-trauma management is essential as we seek to prevent more violence by promoting discussion among the residents. However, to those who have been bodily hurt and have had shelter and possessions destroyed, mere discussion is not enough! We are seeking a way to be with those who are suffering right next to us.

As the days went by and talks between Kibaki and Odinga broke down, new spurts of violence erupted across the country. Those feeling helpless attacked anything they thought might send a message to Kibaki, who remained tucked away safely in his mansion, avoiding the media. He seemed to be sitting quietly, waiting for the protestors to wear themselves down. However, they did not wear down within a month, or within two months. They ripped up miles of the railroad running from the coast to Uganda. They burned out businesses and pulled down streetlights. They burned cars and homes, and set up roadblocks to extort money, and to screen passengers and kill people from other communities. Luo men living in Kibera told reporters they attacked Kikuyus because they could not talk with Kibaki, so killing Kibaki's people was the only way they felt they could reach him.

Men used machetes and bows with poisoned arrows against their former neighbors, driving them away or killing them. Families and communities were now severing intertribal marriages once accepted unquestioningly. Fearing for their lives, an estimated 600,000 Kenyans fled their homes in areas where they were in the minority. International aid organizations had difficulty delivering food and other essential supplies to these displaced people. Aid as well as commercial supplies arrived in the port city of Mombasa and stayed there. The trains could not get through and companies would not risk their vehicles and cargo to travel through the many roadblock gangs. Food, fuel, medical care and other essentials did not pass through Kenya to Uganda, Rwanda, South Sudan or the DRC, crippling the region and causing prices on most goods to double and triple.

After weeks of angst, displacement, suffering and uncertainty, there remained hope of a unity government. Yet, many Kenyans felt the situation could not be resolved because of arrogance, myopia and greed. Then, Mugabe Were, a newly elected member of parliament from the opposition party was murdered in his driveway. Two days later, a police officer at a roadblock in the Rift Valley killed David Kimutai Too, another newly elected member of parliament from the opposition party. Clearly, these were political assassinations, though a rumor circulating said Too was murdered because he was having an affair with the wife of the officer who shot him.

I, along with many others around the world, grieved for the injured and the terrified and the dead, for the children who saw and heard and felt the tragedy, and we grieved for how greatly this post-election carnage set Kenya back on many levels, especially economically. In this book, you will read about the successful flower and produce industry near Naivasha. Planes carrying tourists back to Europe typically carry millions of cut flowers and tons of fresh produce, but because tourism to Kenya has evaporated since the election, the flowers and produce are staying in Kenya. Tourism was Kenya's economic engine driving growth, which has been around 5% annually for the last few years.

The people I met while living in Kenya were doing well if they could attain the basics, like shelter and minimal nutrition, and if they were able to feed their children and perhaps send them to school. Barely getting by. That is how most rural Kenyans and slum-dwellers lived. They had been looking for that trickle-down of economic prosperity and it had not come. They possessed only their freedom to vote for their choice of leader, and suddenly, with the election, that freedom was taken away, too. As you read this book and notice the daily struggles of Kenyans, know their lives are even worse now. As Dr. Dan Keseje says, many only have their life, which they are willing to give to fight a police state masquerading as a government.

Former United Nations Secretary General Kofi Annan has worked as negotiator to bring Kibaki and Odinga together, to bring peace to Kenya. News reports say Kibaki and Odinga have agreed there is a need for a new constitution and an independent review of the election, both issues at the center of their dispute. Many of us are holding our breath to see if the leaders will do what's best for the country and to see how Kenya will evolve.

Kenya's National Anthem says, in part, "Justice be our shield and defender. May we dwell in unity, peace and liberty; plenty be found within our borders." Like all other citizens of the world, Kenyans deserve justice, unity, peace, liberty and plenty. With each passing day, I continue to read the news reports with a heavy heart and look for a glimmer of hope that Kibaki, who is 76 years old, will tire of being a tyrant and Odinga will bend for the good of the people. I read the news reports each day with a low and heavy heart and hope Kibaki, who is hiding safely behind his money and high walls, will look beyond his personal quest for power to allow Kenyans access to what they deserve; freedom and prosperity.

Chapter One

Nairobi

We are training in Nairobi, this newest influx of Voluntary Services Overseas (VSO) volunteers. Our employers sit with us through classes each day as we learn about development issues particular to Kenya and the regions where we will work. Reverend Boniface Obondi, director of Finance and Marketing at TICH (and my new boss), has a quick smile and great mischievousness behind his eyes. I'm nervous, wanting to make a good impression on him this first week. Immediately, it's apparent the reverend is a dear and is equally anxious to make a good impression on us.

One evening, our large group of nearly 50 people goes to dinner at The Cellar, a restaurant built under massive trees behind a high wall just across the street from the Methodist Guest House where we're staying. It's dark when we scurry from our guest house to the gate at The Cellar, where armed guards allow us entry and make us feel safe again. We are volunteers, employers and VSO staff enjoying a meal together.

After we eat, Pushparaj, a fellow VSO volunteer, takes charge of the entertainment and invites us all to stand around a fire built next to our dining tent. We're handed a glass bowl filled with folded pieces of paper and told to pass the bowl as Pushparaj plays "drums" on a metal plate with a spoon. When the drumming stops, we are told, whoever holds the bowl selects a piece of paper and does as it instructs. For an hour, in a circle around the fire, under a tree with the bright moon peeking through, we all laugh and clap and sing traditional songs (sadly, this even includes "YMCA") and dance tribal dances. Filipinos, Ugandans, Americans, Canadians, Dutch, Kenyans and Britons are all connected through playfulness.

During our week of training in Nairobi, we receive instruction in Kiswahili, Kenyan culture and what to expect from VSO and our employers. We are also briefly introduced to life in Africa; Dave and Barbara, a couple from Canada who have been in Kakamega (north of Kisumu) for 18 months, kindly give me the name of a hair stylist in Kisumu who can cut "soft" hair.

VSO (www.vso.org.uk) was voted the top international development charity in the International Aid and Development category at the Charity Awards of 2004 for its work in promoting innovative approaches to globalizing volunteering. Their tagline is "Sharing Skills, Changing Lives." VSO currently has 1,500 volunteers in 34 countries working to tackle the root causes of poverty. The average age of a VSO volunteer is 38 and the majority come from skilled, professional backgrounds. Since its inception in the UK in 1958, VSO has sent more than 30,000 volunteers to work in Africa, Asia, the Caribbean, the Pacific and Eastern Europe in response to requests from governments and community organizations such as TICH. Their vision is a world without poverty where people work together to fulfill their potentials. Instead of sending food or money, VSO sends human currency—women and men from all over the world.

Our group of volunteers is diverse. Pushparaj is the first VSO volunteer from India; he now lives in Mombasa. At 34 years of age and schooled in gender studies, Pushparaj understands better than most of us how difficult life is for women in Kenya. Vini is also from India but has lived in the United States for a while. She works in a village in east Kenya and is accompanied by her partner, Dawn, who is from Austin, Texas. Gelasius, from Uganda, works with an orphanage and school in rural Kenya. He is tall and lean, his face well-structured and gleaming. Gelasius gave four cows to his wife's family as dowry for her hand in marriage. They have four children—three boys and a girl—and their family is pressuring them to have more. To rural Africans, respect increases with the number of children a couple has. Gelasius and his wife believe they can do more for their family by stopping at four.

The newest volunteers are me and Ian from North America; Tom, Heidi and Frank from the Netherlands; Hilary from the UK; and Lino, Mila and Sandra from the Philippines. Ian will also work at TICH as a finance manager. We'll share living space in Kisumu.

Tom is an engineer who will work at APDK to improve the process of designing and producing wheelchairs. Heidi will work at the same organization training speech therapists. She is currently the only speech therapist in Kenya; her goal is to train a corps of therapists to carry on the work after she leaves. Frank is also from Holland. He's quite handsome. The women take to him because of his dark curly hair and blue, blue eyes. He genuinely delights in life and is eager to get to the small hospital in Ndhiwa where he will act as administrator.

Hilary is from the UK, although she was born and raised in South Africa. She'll work as a physical therapist at a center in Dagerotti, a suburb of Nairobi. We room together during training and both of us find it difficult to talk about racial issues. Hilary grew up in South Africa before the end of apartheid. I grew up in the American South, a spot rife with old hurts and continued tensions. Neither of us is proud of the heritage of our homelands. In fact, we both carry guilt about the way blacks were and are treated. We find it painful to discuss, so we don't speak about it, just nodding in total understanding and looking away when the subject is broached.

Lino, from the Philippines, will work as the administrator of a drug and rehabilitation center. He left the Catholic priesthood to volunteer. Lino spends a good bit of time with his iPod, listening to all types of music and singing off-key. He especially loves Madonna and Michael Bublé. Mila will work in a remote area of west Kenya. Her location is so remote, she'll need to learn to ride a motor scooter, or Picki, as VSO calls them. Sandra, like Lino and Mila, is also from the Philippines and will work in business management in west Kenya. Although she is quiet most of the time, Sandra loves music and has no reservations about singing aloud when so moved.

Training ends on Saturday with a prayer from Reverend Obondi. We collect our certificates for completing the training and admire the group picture on the front, rows of intermingled white and black smiling faces. Our group is splitting up, heading with our respective employers to destinations all over Kenya.

Kenya gained independence from Britain in 1963. All too often, outsiders don't take time to consider the lingering effects on peoples once ruled by a foreign government; their religions have been annihilated, their languages suppressed and natural clan or tribal areas bisected by colonial borders. Many volunteers are aware of these effects on countries, but we're now going to experience them on the ground and learn how the average citizen is impacted. Most of us realize that in a state of post-colonialism, newly-independent countries lack internal structures, institutions and good governance. They often experience human rights violations and, most visibly to the rest of the world, are left with an uneven distribution of resources, which can lead to corruption. We've all asked ourselves if we can accept corrupt practices we might encounter in our jobs. Most volunteers agree a little corruption won't cause them to give up their ideals of making a difference. But knowing how colonialism leaves many countries bereft of natural resources and without people skilled to organize and govern its citizenry, we must really ask ourselves how much corruption is too much?

Chapter Two

Nuances

*L*eaving Nairobi with the reverend, Ian and I follow his lead through the hectic streets to the Akambe Bus station. We drag our bags, containing all we were allowed by airline weight restrictions. My luggage includes a large duffle bag and suitcase and my backpack. Ian has two large suitcases and a backpack. Even with the three of us, we have to work to make sure our luggage is watched throughout our six-hour bus ride to Kisumu. The bus is ratty and the heat is almost unbearable, even with the windows down. The seat cushions no longer cushion. Faded, worn curtains fly in the breeze. However, the views are spectacular as we climb the Rift Valley Ridge and descend and cross the valley floor. Mount Longenot, a volcanic relic, stands tall and handsome in the distance.

Baboons lounge on the side of the road and zebra are plentiful. Midway, we stop at a station and use the public toilets, which are pit latrines like most of the toilets in Africa. Also like most toilets here, there is no running water and no toilet paper. (I learned the importance of carrying a small roll in my pocket while climbing Kilimanjaro. I also learned to hold my breath and not mind the flies.) Often, in the countryside, even pit latrines are not available, so using shrubs and rocks as shelter becomes commonplace.

Ian and I have agreed to share living space even though we only met for the first time last month in the UK. We share the wing of a house in Milimani, a nice neighborhood in Kisumu. Our wing consists of two bedrooms, a living room, toilet room, shower room and kitchen with a walk-in pantry. Our house is walled in with a courtyard and gate, which is manned by 10-year-old Paul, an AIDS orphan. In addition to letting folks in and out of the gate, Paul sweeps the yard at 6:00am and again at 6:00pm and boils our landlady's water on a fire outside their back door. He sleeps in a storage shed behind the main house. Phoebe and Joseph, our landlords, have raised five children and have also taken in Paul and two teenagers, Boniface and Joyce. All three children are orphans, their parents having died from AIDS.

Although Phoebe says Paul attends the primary school next door, we never see him in uniform and he's always at home during the day, usually in the tree outside our kitchen window, watching over the schoolyard wall as the other children play.

We live next to Lake Victoria, the second largest freshwater lake in the world (Lake Superior is the largest). Yet only 40 percent of Kisumu residents have piped water, and even the piped water is unsafe to drink. We can shower in it and wash our clothes with it, but we'll invite certain unsavory waterborne diseases if we drink it.

We buy a gas cooker from the Ukwala supermarket on Oginga Odinga Street, the main street in Kisumu named after Jaramogi Oginga Odinga, a local hero of the successful Kenyan independence struggle against the British. We also buy a set of pots for boiling the water. Even though it's 34 degrees outside (100 degrees Fahrenheit!!), we boil pot after pot of water, pouring it into our VSO-issued water filters and allowing it to filter overnight.

It is hot in Kisumu in February and March, the height of summer here. Dancing around 100 degrees Fahrenheit each day, there is no relief and no air conditioning. Walking to town or to work on the red, dusty roads leaves our feet and shoes coated in dirt. All windows are kept open at home, at work, in shops and in hotels; when cars speed down the unpaved roads, dust clouds travel indoors where we smell and taste it. I keep my computer in its case and zipped in the backpack to ensure it remains dust free. To keep my feet clean even in the house, I have taken to wearing rubber sandals. The dirt washes away in the shower and I am temporarily relieved by the cold water (we do not have hot water at home). But as soon as I dry off, the heat returns. They say things will cool down when the long rains start.

The equatorial sun beats down most furiously between 1:00pm and 3:00pm. Adding to the intense heat is the smell of fire from nearly every yard. People burn their trash and leaves, generating thick smoke. Walking in the strong sun and smelling fire is like being in a tolerable hell. Even though the dirt roads will be especially muddy and messy when the rains come, I'm looking forward to daily rain showers.

My first day of work isn't spent at the college but at the New Gulfstream Hotel, where TICH is hosting a two-day Leadership Retreat. Board members and key personnel are gathered—19 in all—to assess TICH's current status and to determine areas of improvement. Everyone speaks of the director, Dan Keseje, with great respect; they are dismayed he is not available to open the retreat. Instead, Reverend Obondi opens the conference and we sing hymns and pray. We're on the second floor of the hotel looking out onto the dirt road leading to my new home.

Fans mounted high on the wall oscillate, reminding me of being in Eureka Baptist church in South Georgia. A rooster crows nearby. The muezzin calls Muslims to prayer.

Parliamentary procedure runs the meeting. The master of ceremonies introduces the co-chairs of each section, who then introduce the speakers. Permission is sought and granted to contribute and everyone graciously acknowledges each person's contribution. All is very formal and polite and time-consuming. But the content is good, giving me a background on the institute, its programs and its progress. I meet many coworkers from TICH.

We're several hours into the retreat when there's a bit of a buzz, as if a celebrity has walked in. The director, Dan Keseje, is at the door. Everyone stands while he enters and takes his seat. He's gentle and respectful, maintaining the reverence in the air. This kind of ambience is fitting, as this gathering contains many of the men and women who worked hard to make TICH an institute of higher education. They are professors from other universities who were able to excel in a country where options are limited. They've held and hold positions in government and private businesses. Many have lived abroad and received their educations in Europe or the United States.

Dan speaks to the group, thanking them for taking time from their busy schedules to explore ways to make TICH better. He acknowledges me and Ian. Dan puts a little humor into his talk before he turns it back over to the meeting chair. His manner is not overbearing but one of a moderator. It is immediately clear that Dan values every person's opinion, no matter their position, and he strives for consensus by allowing everyone to have input and buy-in before decisions are made. He's not afraid to speak up and make suggestions, to show other perspectives. Within a few minutes of being in his presence, I know why everyone trusts his guidance.

Dan is a Harvard-trained scholar, an Anglican priest and a medical doctor. In the 1970s, he specialized in malaria, a field that continues to need much attention today. He has also lived in Vancouver, Boston, Geneva and South Africa. Like all great philanthropists, he uses his network of supporters from around the world to attract donations to TICH. Many of his friends and supporters teach at universities in Europe, North America and Australia. They often travel to TICH to teach, to help develop specialized courses and to share their public health research at conferences.

"I believe in hard work because of my very poor background," Dan tells the group. "I had to change primary schools several times to get my education and when it became too difficult for my parents to care for the entire family, I stayed with relatives to complete my schooling."

Dan worked as Director of the Primary Health Care Programme of the Aga Khan Health Services of Kenya (AKHSK) between 1975 and 1988. The organization sponsors health services to reach the poorest and most remote populations of Kenya; Dan contributed substantially to its methodologies for reaching those most in need. Dan acted as a senior lecturer in the Department of Community Health at the University of Nairobi, and, in 1979, he and a colleague established and managed a community-based health and development project in the Siaya District of Nyanza Province. The project, funded by the World Health Organization (WHO), was so successful it became a learning site for community based health care and development in Kenya, eventually expanding to Kisumu District. This project was the seed that would sprout as TICH in 1998.

As his career progressed, Dan served as the Director of the Christian Medical Commission (CMC), World Council of Churches from 1989 to 1992. While there, he enhanced the capacities of churches to interact with national governments, as well as with the WHO and other international organizations in promoting health care and education for the disadvantaged. Between 1992 and 1996, Dan brought together the Health Department, International Federation of Red Cross and Red Crescent Societies to address the needs of populations in distress from various forms of violence and despair.

I soon learn Dan also has experience in management by crisis. In 1998, Dan evacuated students from war-torn Congo's Great Lakes University of Goma and brought them to this peaceful academic environment on the shores of Lake Victoria, an action that instantly transformed the lives of many paramedics who would later become leading African peacekeepers. As founder and Director of TICH, Dan created a satellite college to the Great Lakes University of Goma. His education model integrated Kenyan public health students and nurses into the university system, making certificates and diplomas available to them and changing the core functions of their work as paramedics. Previously, the public thought paramedics simply shuttled patients between hospitals and markets, dealt with opportunistic diseases and consulted for HIV/AIDS projects.

Dan continues to make huge contributions to Kenya and Africa even today. He knows what universities in Africa must do to help the continent develop. At TICH, he reaches beyond the usual campus-based education and research to include the communities of Kenya and Africa. He believes in coalitions of universities, corporate sectors and communities that will directly engage those in need in the process of advancement, making them full partners in change rather than simply recipients of aid.

"As you know," he tells us, "TICH is a community university founded to pull the community out of health disasters through public health education. I do not own the school, but the community contributes local funds to develop a sense of need and ownership. Membership is open to all. Thank you again for joining us to strategize about improving our processes."

TICH's objective is to improve the lot of Kenyans, who cannot seem to catch a break. It often appears everything is working against them: lack of safe water, lack of health care, lack of markets for their goods, lack of political will, inaccessible education, very limited resources, corruption, civil war and the infiltration of terrorists. The list goes on; poverty leads to infections, insufficient nutrition and frequent pregnancies. Newer influences, such as smoking, eating too much refined sugar and vehicle accidents, are also working against Kenyans. Even the smoke from wood fires in their huts increases the risks of children contracting some types of meningitis and acute respiratory infections (ARI). But Kenyans persevere, and so does TICH.

Looking around the room, I can see how colleagues and students at TICH are absorbing Dan Keseje's values and the processes for using those values in meeting the challenge of creating health and human well-being for Africa.

A photographer takes candid photos during the two-day retreat and offers them for sale. This is a common practice; freelance photographers show up and snap pictures at all Kenyan gatherings, and most people buy the photos as mementos. I'm hesitant to buy the photo of myself, but when Dr. Stephen Okeyo, who heads up TICH's Health Sciences Department, asks me, "What will he do with it?" I give the photographer 50 shillings.

We break into small groups to discuss a variety of issues, and I'm placed in the Institutional Development group. We move our discussion to the hotel's deck during the hottest hours of the day. Sweat pours down my legs and soaks my skirt. With Dr. Okeyo in our group, we manage to agree upon the need for more facilities and leadership development for staff and managers. It's our last task of the day and we'll recap the group's work in the morning.

TICH spends a good deal of money to meet the requirements for becoming a university, as mandated by the Commission of Higher Education (CHE). At this time, TICH is striving to earn a Letter of Interim Authority from the CHE, which will give the college actual university status and allow it to begin nursing classes and a master's program in Community Health and Development. Until then, their master's program is offered at TICH through the Great Lakes University of Goma. Management worries about the college's ability to pay for the CHE requirements if accreditation isn't awarded soon.

Both days of the retreat spotlight the issues TICH faces. These issues aren't taken lightly, because TICH teaches rural people the necessary skills for farming and husbandry—as well as other skills to produce a steady income—through its academic programs. The school directly impacts villagers living in poverty while training students in establishing health and income programs.

After dinner in a small room on the hotel's second floor, a security guard escorts Ian and me to our house a couple of blocks away. He's an old man half my size and he carries a fat, wooden stick. As he heads back to the hotel alone, I worry for his safety.

I awaken at 6:00am to the scratch of Paul's broom outside my window. The school bell is rung by hand at 7:00am. Children's voices pray and sing. I taste dirt drifting into the house.

After walking to the hotel for breakfast and the second day of the leadership retreat, we are surprised to find only 10 attendees. Others had to return to their homes and jobs. Even with the smaller group, we begin with a devotional, singing and prayer, followed by two minutes of silence to confess our sins to God.

We present our group assessments before breaking for tea. Our group leaders consolidate the objectives from all group presentations. Each objective is assigned a team, a team lead and a deadline. Overall, it is an excellent culmination of two day's work.

We're given the rest of the day off to set up our house.

The first day I actually go to work at TICH, a driver picks me up at home. He tells me this ride is a privilege for today only. I'll have to walk from now on. As a volunteer, I knew there wouldn't be enough money for a car or a cab and fully expected to get around on my own. TICH is only a mile from the house, so walking provides exercise.

TICH's building is very attractive and well-maintained. My office, on the second floor, has a number of windows and the view is astounding, looking out over flowering trees and lush vegetation.

Dan Keseje's house is next door, separated from the school by a wooden gate. Chickens, roosters and sheep wander from his yard into the school grounds. At morning devotion, Reverend Obondi mentions that Dan's house was ransacked by "thugs" the day before, as were a few other local houses. Everyone seems saddened, but not surprised, and almost resigned to such misfortunes.

Devotionals at 10:00am mean hymns to sing, prayer requests and vigorous hand-shaking. Drinking a cold Coca-Cola after the devotional, when coworkers gather for tea in the common room, reminds me of home. The geographical distance is vast, but the human difference is virtually nonexistent.

Elizabeth, the librarian, asks if I'd like a tour of the library. It is much like libraries I have visited in the past, but the books are not catalogued online (they're working on that). They are still catalogued on cards and sorted alphabetically and by author. Elizabeth also introduces me to TICH's student hostel where lunch is served. Prices are reasonable. For 100 shillings (or about US $1.25), you get talapia, rice or ugali and a side of greens. The café is really a cement floor with a tin roof and open sides. Pots of food are set out on a table and dished up by the cooks.

I'm very much at home eating Kenyan food, even with my hands, because I grew up eating fried chicken and ribs. Like people from the American South, Kenyans like to cook their vegetables with meat. Sukuma wiki, a sort of green, reminds me of the turnip and mustard greens we eat at home. Sukuma in Kiswahili can mean to lift up or to stretch, and wiki means week, so the name refers to the greens' ability to help stretch the household budget to the end of the week. Ugali, made from ground corn, is cooked to a stiff consistency. We pinch a piece of ugali and wrap it around a piece of meat with sauce, or around sukuma wiki. Ugali reminds me grits, just a more firm version. I'm very much at home with the tasty food here.

After lunch, I spend the rest of my first day meeting with various coworkers. I learn I am to attend a 4:00pm meeting for the upcoming Annual Scientific Conference. Dan Keseje puts me in charge of the communication committee for the event's planning. To accomplish this, I'll work with Rose in our Nairobi office.

On the equator, Kenyans use Swahili time, a 12-hour time-keeping system. Throughout the year, the sun rises around 7:00am and sets around 7:00pm each day with very little variation. In Swahili time, 7:00am, when the sun first appears, is considered the first hour of the day, or 1:00 o'clock. The people I work with never mention Swahili time. Maybe it's so obvious to them, they think everyone else knows. But the difference in the two time systems is apparent when we schedule meetings and someone doesn't show.

"Where were you?"

"Oh, you meant European time instead of Swahili time, huh?"

1:00 o'clock in the evening, the first hour of night, begins at 7:00pm when the sun sets.

Primary school children are required to learn English. The first words they learn are "How are you?" and "fine." These are often the only English words young children know. As I walk through Kisumu, there are constant "How are you" questions coming at me, yelled with a clip: "How. Are. You?!" When I respond, "Fine, how are you?" they fall apart giggling. Sometimes, before I utter a word, they chime in with their "fine," which makes me laugh.

People, both children and adults, call white people "mzungu." A boda boda (bike for hire) driver trying to sell me a ride might even simply say, "Hey, white lady, let's go." Children in their yards will run to the gate and yell "mzungu!" as if they've made a brilliant discovery. It's nice to be discovered and my response is a big smile along with the expected, "How are you?"

No matter where you are, in the city or in a village, in a store or in a home, there is always a rooster crowing. It doesn't matter if I am in the middle of a meeting at work, reading in the living room or walking into town—a rooster is trumpeting. This is not the only soundtrack to my days; early in the morning, while it's still dark, when the city is quiet and even the roosters are sleeping, the song of the Muezzin will float across town. It arrives from Mosque Road, over our back wall and into my bedroom window. His ancient song is soothing, rousing the Muslims to prayer.

People sweep their yards every morning and evening, piling up leaves and seeds. Push brooms are uncommon. Instead, they use a bundle of sticks tied together. These are handmade and can be bought at street markets and department stores. Paul sweeps our yard daily, bending low to pull the branches across the drive. It takes countless swings of his small arm to clear the yard.

Each morning at TICH, another Paul, a grown Paul, mops the painted cement floors of the school. He mops inside and out, although "inside" is "outside" here. The two intermingle, because windows are almost always open, walls rarely reach all the way to the ceilings and doors don't have seals. The crimson cement floors shine with Paul's mopping. His movements, swishing in the bright morning sun, are reassuring.

Chapter Three

Wailing

W ould you like to go to a funeral today?" asks Ogutu, a coworker who usually bubbles with joy. "You should learn how
the Luo bury their dead."

The deceased, Lorna, is the sister-in-law of Dina, another coworker at
TICH. To reach the funeral we drive far from town to the ring of mountains circling Kisumu and Lake Victoria. The ride grows bumpy in the back
of the TICH vehicle as the road narrows. The farther we drive, the more
pregnant women I see; and the younger they are. After riding an hour and a
half and stopping several times to ask women and girls if they know where
Dina's father lives, we arrive at the compound where four houses form a U-
shape. The funeral is set in the middle of the compound, under blue tarps
tied to trees and houses. The coffin, hand-made and stained mahogany,
sits toward the front. It is surrounded by several Anglican ministers—both
men and women—in full robes.

A choir dressed in white sits to the left. Chairs of every sort, as well
as church pews and prayer benches, are lined up under the tarps. We approach from the back and several men stand so we can sit in the shade.
People move about outside the tent, going into the houses, carrying food
and pots. Young children from the community wander through. I sit next
to a very tiny, black man.

An older black man stands next to the coffin, his hat crushed in his hands as he gives testimony about Lorna. Since he is speaking Dholuo, I have no idea what he is saying. Although English is a national language in Kenya, most rural Kenyans never attend school, the primary place to learn English. Many do not even know Kiswahili, the other national language, and only speak their local, tribal language. After the old man finishes, a young man also gives his speech in Dholuo. He is followed by each minister. The lead minister appears to be 50 years old. He reads from Genesis, Chapter Six, and then preaches. Every once in a while, he'll switch to English.

"For 20 years," his anguished voice proclaims, "people have been dying of this cursed disease. For 20 years. Because they have sinned."

Lorna was 32 years old. She died from AIDS. She contracted it from her late husband, who died five years ago. The disease is hitting young people aged 18-30; an age when people are normally at their most productive and earning money. But those suffering from AIDS are too ill to work and the usual outcome is death. In addition to the obvious medical repercussions, the economy also takes a hit, and the children are left for relatives (usually the grandmother) to care for.

"Redemption," the minister says.

He raises his arms and talks of redemption while the choir stands to sing for 15 glorious minutes.

"Please pass and pay your respects," the minister instructs in English. While the choir sings and a drum sounds, visitors pass the casket for a final look and to deposit an offering in a plastic bowl. Ogutu and Liz, a coworker, debate whether I should visit the casket.

"Do you have any money?" Liz asks.

"Yes," I say.

The choir and the congregation sing "Onward Christian Soldier" as we walk to the front. Near the coffin, an old woman sits and shakes hands. I turn to look into her face and her eyes light up. She smiles and I notice she is missing three front teeth. Taking my hand in hers, she clasps her left hand just below her right elbow, a sign of respect. I do the same. She pumps my arm in rhythm with the hymn and we look at each other until the line shifts and I'm forced to move on.

The coffin and Lorna are tiny. Glass encloses the casket top, revealing Lorna's torso. She wears a white lace dress and her face looks surreal, almost plastic. She certainly doesn't resemble the full-faced young woman in the photo held by a young man stationed at the casket's head. I drop coins into the red bowl on top of the casket.

Several young men answer the call to carry the casket.

"Would you like to stay and see the coffin buried?" Ogutu asks.

It only feels right to say yes. The choir walks and sings, followed by the young men who slowly carry the coffin out into the sun. The crowd, with me in it, moves solemnly behind. Between the houses, we pass through a gate into the backyard and across a small field. Beneath a stand of trees, with the mountains looking on, the hole that will become Lorna's grave is surrounded by two mounds of black dirt.

The ministers stand at the foot of the grave while two young men jump in to receive the coffin. The entire group struggles with the weight of it. The coffin bobs and slides, often off-kilter, and my heart goes out to these young men working so hard to place the coffin carefully in the hole. The minister asks family members to throw a handful of the dark soil into the grave. What a heavy, hollow sound the dirt makes on the casket. Then, as the choir sings and drums, men grab shovels and spades, swinging them furiously, pushing and pulling the soil into the hole.

They work quickly and with strength, fighting to keep their footing in the loose dirt as their sandals slip about. As each one grows tired, a new man steps up to take a shovel or spade, swinging in tempo with the choir. They all work earnestly to move the soil back from where it came. One man, tall, skinny and probably in his mid-20s, begins sobbing out loud. He will not be comforted. Soil lands on the casket in this backyard where mountains rise and sobs echo above the falling dirt.

A man speaks to Ogutu and Liz, telling them our presence is requested in Dina's father's house. We enter the walled courtyard and see a square house with a tin roof.

Inside, the walls are painted shiny turquoise, the cement floor painted brick red. The low ceiling is covered in a shiny material with embossed fleur de lis. Old photographs hang on the walls and a wooden plaque of a forest scene tells us to "Find a place you love and go there." In the corner, a table is set with chicken, stewed beef, cole slaw, and piles of steamed rice and rice pilau. A warm bottle of either Coke or Fanta Orange sits at each place setting. They insist we sit and eat. Ogutu had warned us about the Luo, how they treat visitors as special guests; to refuse their food would be considered rude. We wash our hands and dig in, eating with gusto.

"I didn't expect to see so many of you come to say pole," Dina says.

"Pole" means sorry.

And we are.

On the way back to TICH, I sit in the front of the truck with Liz and John, the driver. Several local people from the funeral ride with us, so we stop frequently along the bumpy dirt road to let them out. As we travel, Liz shares with me that she has a four-year-old daughter.

"Why are you volunteering?" she asks.

Liz is the first person to ask about my previous life and my personal background. I feel like I'm connecting with Liz as a friend, moving from "stranger" status to something warmer, closer. In this foreign land where funerals are common, I need to feel a connection.

When Kenyans learn I'm from the United States, they almost always ask about the weather and how it compares to Kisumu. Differences in finances are also a pretty common issue.

"How much would that white car cost in America?" they ask as they point. They all want to know the cost of air fare from Kenya to the United States.

Street children ask me to take them to America, and grown men want to know if we have lions and cows and giraffes as they do in Kenya.

"What about these secondhand clothes," one shop owner asks, "do people sterilize them before they're sent to us?"

The United States is the land of milk and honey to Africans. I know why, after seeing the poverty, and especially when a merchant asks if people back home are as poor as the people in Kenya. Before he asked, I had somehow managed to avoid thinking about the disparity.

"Not even close," I answer.

No matter how little money someone may have in the United States, everyone has access to emergency medical care, even if they can't afford it. When disaster strikes, they have somewhere to go in the middle of the night, and they usually have the means for transport. In Kenya, most rural people have no money to pay for any kind of health care, and they can't even afford the cost of a ride to get to where help is.

TICH works with rural communities to provide medicine and to train local women as Community Health Workers (CHWs) who can dispense medicines to their neighbors. Working closely with communities is the heart of TICH's partnership model, which focuses on partnering with communities to meet the needs of the most vulnerable. Through the partnership department, TICH aims to ensure that all households have access to food security, income, shelter, water, sanitation, health care, education and personal security.

TICH has partnership sites in 14 districts, and each district engages approximately 400,000 people. TICH aims to impact 20 percent of every district. The hope is for the changes to spread throughout. In total, TICH's partnership department covers a population of about two million people. This approach has so far succeeded beyond TICH's expectations because the Kenyan government has adopted the model into a government policy implemented country-wide. National, regional and district teams have been trained in the partnership approach.

Some of the training allows for communities to use evidence-based information to discuss issues affecting them (such as health, education, environment, nutrition and food security). This is evident during our visit with the CHWs in the Bondo district. The CHW women farm for a living, so the work they do in the community pharmacy is voluntary.

We visit the community pharmacy in Abom, Bondo District, during the weekly partnership field trip. Alice, a coworker and student at TICH, works with the community as research for her master's program. To reach Abom, we ride with other coworkers who are going to rural villages in the area. After driving for two hours, we cross a field and are dropped next to four mud houses, which make up the compound owned by the community's leader, Alex. Each home is for one of Alex's three wives and their respective children. The vehicle leaves us to take the students and staff to the next village.

It's quiet here in the country except for goats bleating and children talking as they play. The pharmacy, a round mud house with a thatched roof, sits near a huge mango tree on the edge of the compound. It's incredibly neat inside the hut and cool compared to outside. Chickens and their offspring walk into the room, peck around, and then tumble over themselves out into the yard. Several wooden fold-up chairs stacked in the corner appear to be handmade. Flip chart pages cover the walls and show the community's animal and farming projects: their objectives, goals and results in graphs and photographs, everything seen in the boardroom of a major U.S. corporation (except for the little chicks pecking at our feet).

One flip chart shows a list of the most common illnesses for the people of Abom: malaria, diarrhea, cough, common cold, headache, fever, rashes, backaches, worms, wounds, scabies, measles, stomach aches, cholera, swelling body, typhoid, asthma, ulcers, amoeba, TB and Virus (HIV). Another poster shows the project's membership broken out by gender. In 1998 (their first year), 10 members were male and 20 were female. In 2005, there are 50 male and 65 female members. Their various projects include activities like animal feeds, pest/insect control, vaccination, soil conservation, water harvesting, soil improvement, energy saving, food processing, kitchen gardening, bee-keeping and tending to dairy goats.

Two men from the area sit under the nearby mango tree. They called a community meeting to inform everyone of their rights to participate in directing how their tax monies are spent. Projects will begin soon, and the men want the people in the area to set priorities for what should be done. One man tells me he was a schoolmate of Dan Keseje, TICH's Director, when they were small boys.

Lucas, Alex's 18-year-old son, takes me across the path to his father's houses. Lucas' mother is the first wife, and he is her only child. His father's second wife has borne three children: Alfred, 14; Vivian, 7; and Zyron, 3. Lucas' aunt and uncle died, so their two children, Cathy and Fin, also live in the compound. Lucas calls them his sisters. He has his own house next to his mother's.

Phelesia, Janet and Priscah are the three trained CHWs for all of Abom. Phelesia looks old. She's a Traditional Birth Attendant (TBA), more commonly known in the Western world as a mid-wife. With eight children of her own, Phelesia has delivered 20 babies in her neighborhood in the last seven years. When I ask if they discuss birth control with their neighbors, especially the 16-year-old girls who have just given birth, they giggle.

"Yes," she says through Alice's translation, "we can discuss these things with the women, but it is still the man who wears the pants in the family. He decides if they use birth control and if they have more children."

By now, Alice has completed her work, giving us time to relax in the hut's coolness while waiting for our coworkers to pick us up. The women are bright and energetic, bringing us tea and tiny bananas. Alice refuses to drink tea until they bring cups for themselves. She translates into Dholuo and English so we can all share stories with one another. Though we don't speak the same language, I feel a kinship with these women.

Our car arrives so we say hasty, but sincere, goodbyes. We go to pick up Charles Wafula, TICH's accounting head, at the church where our colleagues are training women in counseling techniques. On the road back to Kisumu, 11 of us pile into the back of the truck, hold on and talk.

"I remember in 2002 and 2003," Charles says, "traveling down this same road, and every 100 meters passing a group of people waiting for a body to be delivered. So many people were financially ruined by funerals. Their wealth, their animals, were being slaughtered and served at the funerals. Most people who die in the city are brought to their home places, the villages they grew up in, for burial. Everyone wanted to have their funerals on Saturdays so bodies were delivered on Fridays. Some villages had as many as three funerals on a Saturday."

"Yes," George Nyamor, another passenger, adds, "there were so many funerals that only people who had large families were buried on Saturday." He says with a bitter laugh, "Young men with no wife or child would be buried during the week since they didn't expect a big crowd."

"This region has the highest percentage of the virus," Charles says. "We can probably predict the day and hour when the last Luo will die."

"That's a morbid thought," I say.

"Perhaps Luos need to hear something like that to snap them into the reality of AIDS," answers Charles.

Before going to work one morning, I go out back to find Paul. He is crouched next to a fire, boiling tea in a pot. Porridge boils over a second fire. Peter, a neighboring teenage boy, walks up and we greet each other. Peter is friendly and his English is very good.

"He doesn't speak Kiswahili, does he?" I ask Peter about Paul.

"Yes, he does," Peter says, putting his hand on Paul's shoulder, a familiar movement an older brother might do.

"He's quiet then?" I ask.

"When he gets used to you," Peter says, "he'll be talking to you all the time."

I like that prospect, but will definitely have to learn more Kiswahili to keep up my end of the conversation. I pull a pack of colored pencils from my back pocket and hand them to Paul. He is pleased. Peter laughs out loud and pats Paul's head, instructing Paul to say "asante" (thank you). Paul is shy and offers his response while looking up at Peter rather than me.

"I'll get him a drawing pad over the weekend," I tell Peter. He shares the news and Paul laughs. There is genuine affection between the two boys. I can't help but feel that Paul, who spends much of his time sweeping the yard and boiling tea outside, is treated like a yard slave.

Ian and I walk to the Police Officer's Mess, a bar-like place close to our home. We enter the dim interior to find two men sitting at the "bar," which is more like a store window than anything else. Two other men sit at a white plastic table watching television and drinking beer. Overhead, two fans stir the air. I'm cheered to find moving air and a television. The beers here are a mere 60 shillings, the cheapest price in town.

We watch Manchester United play an Italian team, followed by motor-bike trials and a show on female runners. After a little more time, "Flying through Time" comes on, depicting Boeing building their 747 in the late 1960s, complete with scenes of the United States. I feel a little homesick, even if the U.S. footage is from the 60s. I enjoy this show, enjoy seeing flashes of the stealth fighters and Harrier jets that I've actually seen up close at air shows in Warner Robins, Georgia.

Both my parents worked as civilians at Robins Air Force Base, so we visited frequently and attended annual air shows. My mom worked as a scheduler for the maintenance performed on F-15 Eagles. These planes are returned to Robins every six years from wherever they may be in the world. They are then disassembled and rebuilt, which is where my mom's scheduling came in. She worked with the mechanics to document the rebuilding process and to have new parts manufactured if needed. It was always an amazing sight to me, walking into a vast hangar and seeing those machines, stagnant and wingless, lining the walls.

Watching the Harrier take off vertically was thrilling. The vibration of the jet pulsated into the ground, running up through my bones and veins until my heart was ricocheting off lung and rib. I can understand why men (and women) become addicted to fantastic flying machines. Being close to such earthshaking intensity is intoxicating.

After the Boeing show back in Kenya, the local news comes on the KTN station. I complete my usual (one beer), and Ian finishes two. We head home in the dark, walking down a divided street with neat homes tucked safely behind high walls, noticing how close and plentiful the stars are.

"KTN shows movies at 8:00pm every Saturday night," I tell Ian, "we should come back next week to watch a movie." He agrees. I miss things like movies and planes flying overhead. The other night, I heard a plane in the distance, the only plane I've heard since being in Kisumu. At first, I thought it was thunder.

I must be losing my plane sensibilities. Growing up in Warner Robins, planes and jets were constantly streaking the sky. Sonic booms were common place, occurring almost daily, and I learned not to flinch as the shock wave landed on our house, rattling windows and doors. That is, until just before I came to Kenya when I was sitting across from Mama in her living room in Warner Robins, chatting. Suddenly, the French doors in her dining room seemed to come into the house, forced inward by a horrendous racket. The pressure subsided but left me shattered.

"What was that, Mama?"

"That's a sonic boom," she said, looking at me a little oddly. I could almost hear her thinking, 'Don't you remember?'

There's quite a bit lately I'm remembering I remember.

Elizabeth, the librarian at TICH, has taken huge stacks of neglected books and organized them into a beautiful symphony of literary opportunities, filling shelf after shelf. Most of the books are old. I'm reading *Emma* by Jane Austen, a paperback edition published in 1964—only one year younger than me.

As I check out my latest two choices, Dennis, the library assistant, reaches for his bottle of paper glue. He smears the glue on a piece of paper and presses the form into the back of the book. He then checks the calendar next to his desk, looking ahead one week, and adjusts his date stamp.

As Dennis stamps the date onto the paper, a smile spreads over my face. Just the thought of taking that book into my hands brings me joy. It's not a new book. It possesses yellowed pages and an ancient smell, but it's new to me. Knowing I have only one week makes me want to scurry away, to devour this goodie before it expires. There are many, many other yellowed pages on Elizabeth's shelves for me to turn while the turning is good.

On the way to lunch, an older woman stands in the road and stops each passerby. She tells them she has a stand just around that corner (she points), asking them to please stop to see her Maasai-made goods. She is not easily put off and I admire her marketing technique of standing at the intersection of two dirt roads and taking folks to her "shop." Wanting to be considered a neighbor and not a foreigner, I like to support local merchants. As I pass her, I learn her name is Priscah. I tell her I'll stop by on my way to work the next morning. And then I forget.

As I'm writing a workshop proposal in my office, Eric comes in to tell me I have a visitor. Upon arriving at the gate, I recognize her face but can't quite place it at first.

"Oh, Priscah," I say, "I'm sorry I forgot."

"It's okay," she says, holding onto my arm.

"Can I meet you at the guard gate tomorrow at 12:30pm, so we can walk to your stand and see the Maasai-made goodies?"

"Yes," she says turning to pick up her bag and still holding my arm, "that will be nice."

In the evening in town, I stuff my backpack with cereal, milk, peanut butter, bread, potatoes, carrots and bananas from the Nakumatt, a sort of very tiny Super Wal-Mart, and start walking home. At the end of Oginga Odinga Street I come upon a young man. Because we're walking in the same direction at the same pace, trying to avoid the same speeding cars in the dark, we begin to talk.

His name is Walter Odede and he started a non-profit called Pambazuko Youth AIDS Link Project three years ago. Pambazuko means "new horizons," which is what he's trying to offer street boys. Once a victim of drugs (those are Walter's words), God spoke to his heart and told him to help others. His type of organization is called a "briefcase NGO" because it is operated without office space and lacking other assets like computers, business licenses or marketing materials and credentials, such as degrees.

Walter pulls an introduction letter from his pack, fills in my name and signs it as chairman.

"Are you single?" he asks as he signs. I laugh out loud. No one else has cared to ask that question since I've arrived in Kenya.

"Yes, I am," I tell him, "and you're the first person here to ask me that."

"Well," he replies, "you'll continue to be single whether I ask you if you are single or not. So I ask you."

Like most Kenyans, Walter sees my white skin and thinks I can turn his organization into a top performer. If I don't give money, then perhaps I'll know how to write a proposal or get my friends to give money. He doesn't say it, for they seldom say it, but I know what he's thinking.

Although I want to contribute in some way while I'm here—maybe with money, maybe with my time, maybe with writing proposals—it's important to me to assess each organization. I want to make sure it is managed efficiently and the monies go directly to those who need it most. I ask Walter if he will take me to the slums one day, so I can meet the boys he is helping. He readily agrees.

I don't want to go to the slums, but must. Otherwise, I'll never know how I can help. We part company in the night, on a dirt road with dim light barely showing his face. I will definitely meet Priscah tomorrow to view her wares, and I will definitely email Walter so we can walk through the slums.

Deep down, I don't want to. But I must.

Chapter Four

B r a v o !

We're sitting under a tin roof, supported by beams of tree branches with the "walls" open. Paul is in a chair with a worn sheet wrapped around his 10-year-old shoulders. I sit on a stack of loose rocks, and Joyce, Paul's "foster sister," sits opposite me on stones. Today is the first time they've left our yard and ventured to town with me. Paul doesn't seem to mind this break from his gate-guarding duties. A "barber" clips and clips, shearing away the one-quarter inch of growth on Paul's head. Occasionally, I see Paul squeeze his eyes, as if in pain. And some cord, attached from his flinch center to my viscera, causes me to feel it, too.

"Does that hurt him?" I ask the barber, who is young and considerate.

"I'm sorry," he says, "I do not understand you."

"Is it painful?" I clarify.

"No," he says reassuringly, "it is not painful."

Next door, about 40 feet away, an old man works under a tree, making furniture. On the corner next to his shack sits a grove of trees under which boda bodas congregate to lube their bikes and fill their tires. Foot traffic passes on the road more than cars. From the house next door, a man pushes his wooden handcart loaded with 12 black water containers. On top sit two boys, grinning. When they stop in front of the furniture maker, the boys jump off and run back to their yard. The man rebalances his load and turns toward town, using his upper body as leverage to steer.

The barber asks Paul where he's from. "Unatoka wapi?" When he doesn't get a response, he asks again in English. Paul is shy and answers, speaking in a low undervoice. When Paul doesn't respond to a question, the barber asks Joyce. She replies, but also in a low voice. At 15, Joyce is shy, too.

We've just come from town, me, Paul and Joyce. Our destination was Black Berry Enterprises, a school uniform shop. Paul will begin attending school soon. After telling the sales girl the name of Paul's school, Central Primary, she assesses his size and heads to the back. As we wait, an attractive woman walks up and greets us as though she knows me. It's not uncommon to run into friends and colleagues in town, so I look closer to see if I've met her before, but I'm pretty sure I haven't. I greet her warmly just the same, and shake her hand as she says, with much heart, "Thank you so much for helping him. It's so wonderful and we're very appreciative." Her remarks embarrass me.

"No thanks are necessary," I assure her, "the thanks are all mine because Paul is such a fantastic kid."

The sales girl brings back a shirt and pants. Gently, she guides Paul into the dressing room, where he tries on his new clothes. Joyce points to the wall behind the counter and says, "bika." I follow the direction of her finger and see some very lovely lingerie bikas hanging overhead. They're shaped like shorts with lace trim on the legs. Local women wear them under their pants and skirts. We ask to see their bika selection and Joyce picks out a pair. About the same time, the sales girl escorts a nicely dressed Paul to us. I check the fit around his waist and find the suit fits nicely, with a little room for growth. Paul is quite thin.

"He's missing one other thing," she whispers. I'm puzzled until she says, "He was missing something when he tried on his clothes." So I ask how much boy's underwear costs and we settle on a pair, which she takes into the dressing room with Paul. We also buy a pair of socks, part of the uniform.

"Can he try on a pair of these shoes?" I ask her, "I didn't bring enough money today, but if we know what size he wears, I can run by next week and get them."

We remove Paul's shoes, a black pair so worn the sides and back droop. The soles, smooth from wear, no longer display the size. We hold the old, ratty shoe up against the shiny new ones. She hands Paul a plastic bag to put over his foot while he tries on the shoe. I remind her that we're buying the socks, so she can let him wear them while trying on the shoes. She refuses for some reason I cannot fathom. Size three is a bit snug, so we decide on four. They're handsome black leather shoes, very well made, but I can't help but feel he needs some tennis shoes, too. His only other shoes are red plastic flip flops that sell for 59 shillings, or about 75 cents. Perhaps next month we'll buy sneakers.

As we exit the store, I ask the kids if they'd like a Coke baridi (cold). Paul grins and shakes his head no.

"No?!" I respond, teasing him, "what do you like then?"

"Fanta," he says. We go to the Somi Snacks, a vegetarian shop operated by Indians, and sit at a table. The waiter brings menus and we each order a cold Fanta orange along with three samosas. The television behind me is playing an Indian movie. It's a musical scene in which two attractive stars sing to each other, standing close among beautiful landscapes. The woman's colorful sari blows sensuously in the wind, its loose movements juxtaposing the couple's sexual tension. Paul is mesmerized. He sips Fanta from the straw in his bottle, nibbles on the samosa and never removes his eyes from the screen. I'm a little embarrassed at the intimacy portrayed between the adults on screen, but cannot help but grin at Paul's face, turned toward the television, eyes wider than usual. We linger so he can take it all in.

I suggest we run into the Nakumatt, quickly, so I can buy mazewa (milk). Paul shakes his head no again. I laugh, because I'm not suggesting he has to drink the milk. We grab the milk and head to the checkout, where I encourage them to pick out a candy bar. They both select a Cadbury with nuts. I get a Twix. We head home, munching our candy bars.

We pass through town and head toward our neighborhood when Paul sees the barber under the tin roof and trees. He tells Joyce he wants a haircut, and she repeats the request to me.

"Let's see how much it is," I say.

"10 bob," Joyce says, using the more common term for shilling. That's nothing really, but when I ask the barber his price, he tells me it is 30 bob.

"Wow," I say, "we were expecting 10." I look at Joyce, who also indicates the price is too high.

"Okay," the barber says, "I'll take five shillings."

"Five!" I say.

I don't understand why he lowered the price to five, a figure much lower than I am willing to pay. So often, things happen here that I don't understand. Like many things, I accept it, hoping with time to learn the cultural nuances.

The barber sits Paul down and begins working diligently. Once he's clipped Paul's hair, he unwraps a brand new razor blade and very, very carefully shaves a tiny path around Paul's head, making a straight hair line, even over Paul's ears and neck. Paul looks very sharp. I'm impressed by the amount of work required as well as by the barber's compassionate treatment of Paul, so I give him 20 bob. We're both pleased.

As we walk home, Paul and Joyce cannot know how much pleasure they have given me, allowing me to take them to town, to buy them needed clothing. It's something I did weekly when my children were young, and I miss that part of parenting. There's nothing quite like making sure children have what they need. Not necessarily what they want, but what they need.

It's a rainy night in Kisumu. Around 7:45pm, thinking the evening's storm has passed, Ian and I walk to the Police Officer's Mess, hoping to catch the Saturday night movie and drink a beer. I plan to order a whole chicken just for myself, I'm so hungry. We use a flashlight to navigate mud puddles and dirt paths. It's a bit trickier than I imagined and I regret being out here, afraid of the speeding cars on roads with no street lights. Only the thought of chicken and ugali keep me moving. A car flies up behind us, going too fast. It brakes suddenly and slides, the horn blaring. There, frozen in the middle of the road, is a boda boda. The car stops just short of hitting the man, pausing only to steer around him.

"What the hell is that guy doing?" Ian asks.

The man and his bike do not move. As we approach, the boda boda driver attempts to pedal away, but he hits the edge of the road, his tires sliding out from under him. Afraid he'll be hit if left lying half in the road, I cross and lean over him. He's in his 20s and very, very drunk, his legs entangled in the bike and his seat now twisted sideways.

"Are you alright?" I ask, gripping his arm and feeling the mud.

"Yes, Mama, I'm alright. I'm alright."

He tries to right himself but is pinned by his bike and his blurred senses.

"Pull the bike away from him," I tell Ian, "so he can stand." Ian lifts the bike slightly while I assist the boda boda driver out of the mud puddle. His back is wet and his breath is loaded. I fear for him trying to make it home in the dark on his bike.

"Do not ride your bike," I tell him sternly, "walk your bike. Stay off the road. Go straight home."

I can tell that if he didn't sober up when almost hit by the car, he needs to sleep this one off. I repeat myself as though I'm his mother, emphasizing every word, realizing my heart is pleading with him while my voice reveals nothing but a command.

"Yes, Mama, thank you very much. Have a nice evening, Mama."

He shakes my hand, then Ian's, and pushes his bike in the opposite direction, shakily.

It's a rather disappointing evening at the Police Officer's Mess. They don't serve food inside, just outside, and even then only if you've ordered ahead. To make matters worse, there is no movie on, just a Latin soap opera dubbed in English by people from the UK. It twists my brain to hear British accents coming from beautiful Latinos. I get a bag of crisps and devour them while watching the very masculine men and ultra feminine women working at a Brazilian coffee plantation.

The guy who owns and runs the farm in the soap opera looks like Fabio. While his long, wavy hair hangs across his face and flows over his shoulders, he broods about being impotent. We audience members are forced to wonder what could be weighing on him to cause this problem. We are then introduced to the very spirited, very shapely, almost angelic-looking female laborer, who fights tooth and nail to ward off unwanted sexual advances from her fellow laborers. The Fabio-hero intervenes and quiets her feistiness. The way he looks at her says he wouldn't experience his "problem" with her. It's all gloriously stereotypical, but not quite interesting enough to keep me from walking to the door occasionally to see if it's still raining. I feel caged by the night.

We finally leave around 9:40pm to avoid watching "The Nutty Professor." It's drizzling. We turn down a side street, and from the dark a voice says, "Why are you walking at night?" A security guard approaches, an automatic weapon hanging from his shoulder.

"The bad boys of Kisumu are about," he tells us. I just want to be home, out of the drizzle, to wash the mud from between my toes and to read *Emma*.

"It is not safe for you," he reconfirms.

"What should we do?" Ian asks.

"From now on, when it's this late, take a taxi," he says, turning and walking back into the darkness.

"The bad boys may not want to be out in the rain, our natural defense," I say to Ian.

I've never been so happy to see our locked gate. I wash my feet and climb under the mosquito net, opening the book to read about Emma's family and circle of friends, safely tucked away in their English village, threatened by nothing more than an inconsiderate remark.

I hope the drunken man is home now, sleeping, perhaps dreaming of daylight and dry roads.

Casmos, a local man who looks to be about 40 years old, sits next to me at the cyber cafe, waiting for a computer. Although we have never met he asks me where in the States I am from, just like that.

"How did you know I'm from the States?" I ask, "don't I look the least bit European?"

"I could tell by your face," he responds.

Casmos tells me his brother lives in Houston, and he wants to go there. He is very animated when he talks, sounding much like a Westerner with only a slight Kenyan accent. We each get a computer and start to work away in our own separate spheres, but when Casmos is leaving, he stops by to give me his business card. He asks if I'd like to get a coffee when I'm done. "I'll be here at least two hours," I tell him and give him my email address.

Sunday morning, I'm back at the cyber cafe when Casmos stops by.

"I sent you an email asking you to meet me here last night for dinner."

"This is the first time I've checked emails," I say.

"Would you like to get a coffee?"

"I'll be here at least two or three hours," I say.

He says he'll check back around 1:00pm. Casmos dresses very nicely, has a relaxed manner and his business card says he sells medical equipment. He wears sunglasses pushed up on his head and nice athletic shoes. Casmos is not in any real need, but I can tell he thinks I can get him to the States.

Albert, the security guard at Kisumu Hotel, stops me as I walk home from the cyber cafe. We've never met but he says he'd like to discuss something with me and wants to know when I will be by again. I tell him I may be by the next evening, wondering briefly what it is he wants to discuss.

After I leave Albert, a young man catches up with me and introduces himself as Victor. He's 18 and walks beside me, matching my quick pace.

"My father passed away Friday and we need money for a coffin," he tells me as casually as if he'd told me about a sale on eggs at the Nakumatt. I stop walking and grab his sleeve.

"Your father passed away this past Friday?!" I exclaim, letting it sink in. My heart goes out to him.

"Yes, and we still need 1,500 shillings for the coffin, to get him out of the morgue."

Victor's request for money is very quick; he allows me no time to digest the news. His eagerness causes me to doubt his story, but he appears earnest, so it is with great pain that I tell him, "I cannot help you. I'm sorry."

He then tells me how thieves broke into his home and, when he woke up to discover them, they threw fire on him. He pulls up his left sleeve and shows me a horrendous scar on his forearm, massive and raised at least half an inch. It is difficult not to be moved by such obvious suffering, but I can tell the wound has been healed for years. Victor is using his full arsenal to pull at my heartstrings. When I commiserate about his troubles, he says, "I do not want your sympathize."

This remark amuses me slightly because getting my "sympathize" is obviously the persuasive tool he is using to get my help. But I honestly don't have the money. Fifteen hundred shillings is about US $20, which is a lot to me.

"Can you help me with the means to get back to my father's village tonight?"

"Sorry, no."

"I've never slept outside and I'm scared to be out alone."

"No," I say nicely.

Victor has walked with me about one-half mile and I worry he might follow me home or become angry, maybe even hit me. The thought passes quickly, however, and I walk confidently on, saying goodbye and turning left when he turns right. He says goodbye and moves away.

Casmos, Albert, Victor.

The hits just keep on coming.

Victor's request for US $20 is indicative of the nation's economic status and the desperate measures people will take to be able to eat. Each year, the United Nations releases the Human Development Index (HDI) focusing on three measurable dimensions of human development: living a long and healthy life, having access to education and having a decent standard of living. In 2006, Kenya's rank fell to 152 out of 177 countries. In 2004, the country was 148 out of 177 countries. Norway ranks number one, Iceland ranks number two and the United States ranks number eight.

The poverty line in Kenya is US $17 per month per adult in rural areas and US $36 per month per adult in urban areas. More than half of Kenya's population (56 percent) lives below the national poverty line. If the current trend continues, this percentage is projected to increase to 66 percent by 2015. Poverty remains a major impediment to the fulfillment of basic needs, especially for women and children. The average life expectancy in Kenya is just 45.2 years.

In the past few years, the UN created eight Millennium Development Goals intended to coalesce the objectives of governments and aid organizations in all developing countries. The goals they hope to accomplish by 2015 are to:

❯ Halve the proportion of people whose income is less than $1 per day.

❯ Ensure children (boys and girls) will be able to complete a full course of primary schooling.

❯ Eliminate gender disparity in all levels of education.

❯ Reduce the number of children who die under the age of five by two-thirds.

❯ Reduce the maternal mortality ratio by three-quarters.

❯ Halt and reverse the spread of HIV/AIDS; halt and reverse the incidence of malaria.

❯ Integrate principles of sustainable development into country policies and reverse the loss of environmental resources.

❯ Develop a global partnership for development.

Kenya adopted these goals in 2000 and is currently tracking the nation's progress. Half-way to 2015, many of these goals appear to be unreachable, and critics of the MDGs say they're a waste of time. For people on the ground, though, MDGs provide focus and create strength in the number of organizations tackling the same issues simultaneously.

Saradidi (pronounced Saradeedee) community is an hour and a half drive from Kisumu, heading north and then west, skirting Lake Victoria. The lake lies silent just a mile away from the church where we have gathered. Our mission today is to meet with 70 community health workers (CHWs) for their sixth weekly session of counseling training.

These women come from near and far for the event. They're amazing— simply wives and mothers who elect to volunteer time to their community and their neighbors. (I shouldn't say they are "simply wives and mothers" because being a woman in Kenya is not simple. Plus, two of the students are men.) What these people are doing for their neighbors is quite extraordinary. Several of them have babies—some only a few months old—that they nurse as the need arises, passing them to a friend when it's their turn to role-play.

One child is exceptionally cute at three months of age. I can't resist putting my finger in his firm grip.

"What's his name?" I ask.

"Dan Keseje," she says.

I think I've heard wrong and I ask again.

"Dan Keseje," she says again. I am awed. This child's name is a testament to Dan's dedication to rural communities and their acknowledgement of his hard work. In fact, she went into labor when she was attending a class here at the church and Dan was the instructor that day. The baby was born the next day.

Kenyans have a tradition of naming babies for great people and current events. Whatever is in the news and the talk of the nation is fodder for naming. Many babies born these days are named Senator Barak Obama, who is a hero in this part of Kenya. Senator Obama's father is from a tiny village outside of Kisumu and his grandmother still lives there. At Pandipieri, where a colleague named Ed works, I visit for lunch one day and a baby less than six months old lies on a cot next to the table where we eat. He cries until his mother picks him up.

"That's Senator," Ed says, "Senator Barak Obama."

This is the sixth and final session of counselor training provided to CHWs from the area. Local children come to the church where we're holding class and position themselves outside of the door to look at me. I go out to say hello and they appear scared, shifting as though they'll run. One girl is brave and stands her ground, taking my hand to shake it. I snap their photo on the red, dirt road to Lake Victoria and show it to them. As a response, I get lots of giggles and pulling at the camera so they can peek at themselves again.

After photographing the girls, I return to watch the women (and two men) prepare for their role-playing by selecting a problem one of their neighbors might have. Sitting under the trees in the churchyard, they prepare and gossip and laugh. They then practice their counseling skills in front of the trainers, my coworkers from TICH. The ladies speak English and Kiswahili and Dholuo, and even though I can't always tell what they're saying, I always want to stand and applaud their magnificent acting skills.

"Bravo!!" I cheer to myself. These ladies can act!

In these remote Luo villages, there are a variety of problems to be enacted by the groups. In one, a mother-in-law dislikes her new daughter-in-law, who lives at the family rural home while her husband works in Kisumu. The new daughter-in-law eats too much food and doesn't share any of the monies her husband sends. In another, a woman who has been married for five years has not become pregnant. Her husband beats her regularly and threatens to take a second wife, who will surely produce a son for him. The groups of CHWs are commended by their trainers for picking such real issues.

Next week, the ladies will again congregate at the Saradidi Church. They'll bring their packed lunches and one or two live chickens with their feet tied together to sell at market. The women will throw the chickens into a corner of the sanctuary and then spread their colorful kangas under a shade tree, where they'll sit and gossip and laugh easily. They'll take the written exam, the culmination of their training. If they pass, they'll receive a certificate proclaiming them to be professional counselors. I suspect these women (and two men) are already excellent counselors. Certainly they are gifted actors, every one.

Chapter Five

Holiday

S everal VSO volunteers from across Kenya meet at Lake Naivasha Lodge for Easter holiday near Hell's Gate National Park. We begin walking to the park's entrance, hoping a matatu will come by, when a private car stops and the driver introduces himself. Patrick, who lives in Durban, South Africa, is in Kenya working with the Mamias Sugar Company. He gives us a ride to the park, which is about 10 kilometers from Lake Naivasha Lodge. As we cruise along the lake's rim in Patrick's company car, he says, "You are about to see some of the worst roads in Africa." Soon the road becomes a checkerboard of pocks, large and small and deep and wide. The road is so bad that many vehicles leave the road entirely and ride along the side (if there is a shoulder to ride on). We bounce and jar, ever cognizant of other cars also bouncing and jarring—often straight into our path. The jostling goes on for four or five kilometers and is all the more remarkable because along the road are nurseries where flowers are raised and exported to Europe.

This area hosts multi-million dollar horticultural industries. Homegrown, one of Kenya's largest growers, exports more than 50 million flower stems to the UK each year. Someone told me a flower can be cut in the morning and arrive in Holland the same afternoon. It's hard to believe transport is so quick with these roads.

Because of the number of horticultural farms and their contamination of the lake with pesticides, environmentalists managed to get Lake Naivasha listed as a Ramsar Site. In recent years, the growers have started to show an awareness of the dangers of pesticides for workers as well as the lake, which is a wetland of internationally recognized ecological importance. Measures are being taken (such as not cultivating within one kilometer of the lake to prevent runoff) and health checks are becoming required for workers. Still, the danger of chemical use is pervasive in its way of settling in soil and water and living tissue. In her 1962 book "Silent Spring," Rachel Carson describes the impact of pesticides in the United States after two decades of use, showing how the chemicals seep into groundwater, soils, and the bodies of fish and animals, even humans.

Even with awareness concerning pesticides, the future of Lake Naivasha is uncertain. 350 species of bird, hippopotamus and other wildlife in the area are threatened with extinction and the Lily-Trotter, Crested Helmet Shrike and Great Crested Grebe have practically disappeared.

As we skim the lake in a fiberglass boat, I peer at the hippos and flamingos through binoculars, knowing the nearby horticultural houses go on for miles and miles. But in my view, the landscape rolls away in layers, with a wall of hills followed by a wall of mountains ringing the valley. Looking at the shoreline and beyond through the binoculars is like watching a National Geographic special. There is so much beauty in the grass at the water's edge, in the furred and un-furred animals, in the feathered creatures only yards away. I feel my heart expand into my throat as the waterbucks graze and the pelicans preen. The beauty fills me.

The delicate, delicate beauty fills me.

───────────

Hell's Gate is one of only two parks in Kenya where people can walk and see animals. All other parks require guests to be in a vehicle, but here we rent bikes just outside the park's entrance and cycle through, rolling past zebra, warthogs, baboons and wildebeest, Cape buffalo and gazelles. At one point we actually stop as we cycle past the buffalo, out of fear they might attack us. Stopping is precisely what you don't want to do in this situation, because these young and frighteningly large buffalo are just as curious about us as we are about them. When they start staring and turning toward us, taking an occasional step out of curiosity, we turn back. Quickly. A British couple comes along in their red four-by-four and offers to drive ahead to scope out the herd. They return to tell us the buffalo are actually young and we can safely cycle by if we just keep on cycling. We follow their advice, albeit with a bit of trepidation; as we pass the massive animals, we are surprised to find them turn and run away from us.

Geothermal pools run underground throughout this area. At the park's lower gorge, a power station has been constructed to tap into these pools with minimal impact to the area, boasting pipes of all sizes zigzagging in earnest. Experts predict the station will eventually supply half of Kenya's electricity. The super-heated underground water can reach 304 degrees Centigrade, one of the hottest sources in the world. On our hike through the gorge, our Maasai guide, Jackson, shows us the hot water running down the walls and over rocks, steam rising. Shells lay on the ground where someone has taken the challenge to poach an egg. The water is so hot it appears to bubble in a small, bowl-like rock.

Hilary, a volunteer from the UK, Heidi, from Holland, and I take a break from biking in the park. The sun is severely hot, so close overhead, and the roads are dusty. Sometimes, the deep sand in the road's grooves causes our wide, knobby tires to scoot out from under us.

"I don't find Kenya beautiful," Hilary says cautiously, peering as though she is waiting for a backlash from me or Heidi. I glance at the walls of the gorge rising straight up for hundreds of feet, showing off their stratifications, their lovely geometric fissures, their strength in standing for eons and eons.

"I think I'm spoiled," Heidi remarks, "because I've traveled to so many other beautiful countries in Europe and Latin America."

I want to say, "Beauty is in the eye of the beholder," but I know it's trite and not nearly powerful enough to express what I see when I look at Kenya: beauty and ugliness and sometimes beauty in the ugliness. I see more than dustiness, more than landscapes made hazy by the sun's glare. Sometimes I'm not exactly sure what I see. Other times I see beauty so exacting my breath catches at the bottom of my lungs, trapped, until my brain furiously registers the sights and smells of a million grass leaves and pine needles and feathers floating, past and present, landing on lion tracks pressed into soft sand, landing on zebra carcasses with faded stripes of decomposing flesh stretched against dried bone. Arresting beauty, heartbreaking beauty, beauty especially poignant in its ugliness.

I guess I know what Hilary is saying.

I find beauty in the strangest places. One such place, Nyalenda, is a slum in Kisumu. Just as I promised when I met Walter on the darkened road that evening, I follow through with my plan to visit the slums. I email him and we arrange to meet at TICH at 8:00am on Wednesday morning. My initial concerns about this man I met on the street soon subside. As it turns out, Walter grew up in Nyalenda with Tonny, a coworker and friend of mine. It seems everyone knows Walter and thinks of him as a fine man.

On Wednesday morning, Tonny, Walter and I walk ten minutes along Ring Road to Nyalenda, turning into their neighborhood at the water source: an open stream. Tonny still lives in Nyalenda, though he has a university degree and works in IT at TICH. He's a role model for the children.

Tonny and Walter have huge hearts. They know the people we pass on the streets and speak to them with warmth and coded handshakes and smiles. Their plans are huge, too: Get the government to change plastic pipes to metal pipes running from the stream to the houses. Build a well at the back of the slum, creating a single, treated water source for everyone so they aren't bathing and washing their dishes or putting their toilet-contaminated feet into the stream. Build pit latrines for those who now use "flying toilets" (plastic bags filled with feces and tossed along with hundreds of other feces-filled plastic bags into piles near the stream). Construct a tin-roof structure under which they'll gather the neighborhood children to teach them ABCs and 123s and about children's rights, because so many of them are orphans living with guardians who do not care if the children are educated or even if they are loved.

Walter and Tonny also plan to create income-generating activities for the widows of the area. Activities such as weaving mats from Papyrus, which grows along the river, and fishing can go a long way here. We talk with one widow who looks like a teenager but who has six children. She makes the local alcoholic beverage, illegally, and sells it to feed her children. Tonny worries because she drinks much of the "illicit brew" herself. We walk through and they introduce me to their neighbors. We talk to the older woman at the back of the slum who currently has the land rights to where the water will be collected into a single, treated well for everyone. I marvel at the children who are naked, who have runny noses and crusty eyes, but who have incredible light shining out of those very same eyes.

There's a light that emanates from most young Kenyan eyes. This beauty, always captivating, especially grabs my attention in the slums of Nyalenda. It is an energy. Amongst the mud and the hogs wallowing in the mud, alongside the dogs chasing goats from between thatched houses, there is this happy energy. It is excited shouting and frenzied hand waving. It is a bright intelligence. I see it in children of all ages in Kenya, this potential. They are all pregnant with promise.

To me, the most amazing thing about being in East Africa is the thought of this area as the birthplace of humankind. The earliest evidence of human existence has been found in East Africa, north and south of the equator, from Ethiopia to Olduvai Gorge in Tanzania. I visited Olduvai Gorge on Christmas Day in 2004, as we traveled through the Serengeti, a wide space of grass, zebra, hyena, Thomson's gazelle, wildebeest and an occasional lion pride.

We turned off a major dirt road onto a minor one that ended abruptly at Olduvai Gorge, the archaeological workplace of Mary and Louis Leakey.

In Olduvai Gorge, the Leakey's discovered Homo habilis, the first hominid with a brain larger than a chimp's. Homo habilis, a new genus that appeared in Africa 2.5 million years ago, was the first toolmaker, using stone tools, such as sharp flakes of rock. Their direct descendent is Homo erectus.

During our Christmas day visit, our group of eight joined many other people from Australia, Canada and Asia making their way through Olduvai Gorge's two-room museum, where artifacts lay within touch, not separated by glass. On display, in addition to stone tools and fossil skulls, was a recreation of the fossilized footsteps discovered at Laetoli, a site not far from the museum. Mary Leakey was in charge when these fossilized footsteps were uncovered. They were created more than 3 million years ago when rain showers mingled with light ash falling from nearby volcanoes. The mixture of ash and water turned to mud that, when walked on, captured the footprints of more than 20 different animals of all sizes: cats, hares, giraffes, rhinoceros, elephants, hyenas, antelopes, pigs, baboons and even the hipparion, the ancestral three-toed horse.

The trail left by the three hominids is nearly fifty meters long. It shows they walked north toward the plains of what is now Serengeti, away from the puffing volcanoes. These three individuals—two adults and one juvenile—walked together, leaving their prints alongside those of the animals. I stand and stare at the reproduction of the footprint scene in the museum. Nearby, children run and scream; parents talk and read exhibit signs loudly to their kids. I work to block out the noises, to imagine what it was like for these small people to walk through this valley millions of years ago.

The Great Rift Valley is the only geographical feature of the world visible from the moon. The Rift runs like an inverse scar from Africa's coast, near the Saudi peninsula's attachment to the continent, down through Ethiopia, Kenya and Tanzania. It is dotted with ancient volcanoes like Mt. Kenya and Mt. Kilimanjaro, along with dozens of other equally beautiful volcanic mountains rising from the plain floors. The first time I see Mt. Longonot on the road from Nairobi to Kisumu, I want to climb it. The Maasai name "oloonong'ot" means "mountain of many spurs." Those jutting spurs along the crater rim, crown-like, create its royal beauty. Longonot is not an extinct volcano; the puffs of steam rising from its interior give it the classification of "senile."

I travel home from Lake Naivasha on Easter Sunday, crossing the Great Rift Valley, and John, my matatu seat mate, points out the rice project in Ahero. He tells me how it failed, although many of the people still, of their own initiative, farm their plots of flood plain to raise rice. I tell John about my conversation with Heidi and Hilary, how we discussed the beauty and promise in Kenya. I tell him of the potential I see in all Kenyans—in Kenyans of every age—but especially the street boys. John agrees. He's headed to his home village north of Kisumu. John lives in Nairobi and is doing well for himself, but he can see the need of his fellow Kenyans. If only they had the resources, if only the government made sure everyone had clean, piped water, if only there was available electricity. If only every child could go to school.

If only.

Back from Easter break, I visit Nyalenda again. As we walk through the slums of Nyalenda, meeting people and discussing their daily struggles, Walter and Tonny ask if I mind visiting Eric, a friend of theirs. We cross the creek and pass two mud houses with thatched rooftops to where Eric's mud house sits. They show me the thatching, made from stems of Papyrus. We hear singing and hand clapping, a rather mournful sound.

"Eric has AIDS," Walter tells me. Eric is 26 years old and has been showing signs of the illness for several months. He has been bed-ridden for a few weeks, but his family is in denial. They believe demons are visiting him. Their spiritual leader is here, exorcising the demons with songs and prayers and hand clapping.

Walter and Tonny visit Eric often. They work diligently to convince him to go to the Voluntary Counseling and Testing (VCT) Center to be tested for AIDS. But the stigma of AIDS is still too strong. Eric can see no benefit in telling everyone he is infected and actually thinks it will cause people to shun him, despite the fact that Walter and Tonny accept him. They know how Anti-Retroviral (ARV) drugs can impact Eric's quality of life. The drugs are now being given free by the Kenyan government; they can restore health, cause weight gain and prolong life.

While we stand outside the mud house, in a compound in the heart of Nyalenda, Walter and Tonny decide we should come back another day. We settle for a week later.

Walter pops his head into my office, a lovely surprise in the middle of a busy day. He's looking for Tonny but cannot find him. Walter shakes my hand, gives me a hug and takes a seat. He's preoccupied.

"Remember Eric?" Walter says.

"Yes," I say, "we're still going to visit him tomorrow, aren't we?" Walter rocks in the chair and makes a tsking noise with his tongue. He tells me he's just been to the hospital and Eric is dead.

Walter tsks and rocks and repeats, "Dead. Dead."

"I'm so, so sorry, Walter," I say, watching as his mind throws thought on top of painful thought. Eric, part of Walter's non-profit organization, was dedicated to improving their neighborhood and the lives of their neighbors. Walter talks about Eric's intelligence, his widowed mother who is now left with one son. They'll probably take Eric back to their home place to bury him. The body will be at the morgue soon, he tsks.

"Dead."

I suggest that Walter name the shelter he plans to build for the children in Eric's honor. He nods agreement.

"This is a lesson to me," he says, leaning forward, "I won't wait with my other friends; I will insist they go for testing and medicine."

"Do you have many other friends with AIDS?" I ask.

"Several. Too many."

I'm called into a meeting so Walter and I walk to the front. I tell him I'll let Tonny know the news as soon as our meeting is over.

"Please find out about the funeral arrangements," I say.

"What about the camera?" Walter asks in a panic, "will you bring it tomorrow?" The three of us had already discussed documenting the slums' water source and latrines, the children and widows, so I reassure Walter I'll bring the camera.

Walter is tall, about 6' 2" and slim. He leans in with earnestness and says, "We missed an opportunity." I instantly know he is talking about Eric. One more day, just one more day, and we would have had a photo of Eric.

Walter needn't worry. I'll bring the camera tomorrow and we'll photograph the neighborhood and its people, his friends with AIDS. We'll photograph all of them, too many of them.

On our next tour of the slums of Nyalenda, Walter wants to show me the interior. Tonny is in town uploading the latest version of the TICH website, so he's unable to join us. In the interior, garbage dumps sit on paths between the houses. These dumps contain human waste as well as household waste. Chickens and goats climb on the mounds, digging and pecking. The stench is overwhelming. Garbage pits are okay if they're dug below ground and filled in with earth, but these are simply piles of trash and waste sitting outside someone's front door. With the camera, we document the dumps, the defunct latrines left standing near the water, the minnows from Lake Victoria spread to dry in the midday sun as hundreds of flies turn the fish from white to black, two boys drawing water from the stream, women at their fruit stands and widows with their children at play.

The children pose for pictures like professionals. Walter asks a group of women for their permission to be photographed. They ask for something—maybe money—in return. Walter speaks with the woman who runs the fruit stand, explaining what his organization is doing in the community. He explains to her she'll see long-term benefits, not just a few shillings for the photo. But the talk turns somewhat heated and while I can't understand what's being said, I understand what's going on. When Walter says we should just move on, I listen and move.

As we change directions, an older woman walks up and speaks in English. She shakes my hand, welcoming me and inviting me to stop by any time. She is Mama Ogai, the village elder's wife. She tells us to photograph her with another woman selling corn. As we set up the shot, the woman from the first group who wanted to be paid tries to sneak into the frame. Our corn seller uses her entire body and three "nos" to push the woman out of the picture. I grin from behind the camera.

The woman's corn is in a wheelbarrow. She digs a container deep into the corn, dramatically, while Mama Ogai flourishes her basket out for filling. The basket is almost flat and made of woven straw covered in dried cow dung. Corn floats kernel by kernel into the cow-dung basket.

It's understandable why the people of Nyalenda expect payment. They see so many groups come through, so many people with cameras who promise more this and better that. Then they never see the visitors again. Some people use the slums and its inhabitants to raise funds from donors, and then skip out with the monies. It's hard to believe, but I try to reserve judgment. With such poverty everywhere, any amount of money is tempting to people. In the end, it's just one more symptom of the extensive corruption in Kenya, beginning at the very top and trickling down. The government is trying to tackle corruption through transparency, but it is slow going.

We visit the older woman who owns the land where the common well will be built. She's sitting just outside her door in the same chair she occupied on our last visit. She's been ill, perhaps tuberculosis, and doesn't move around a lot. Most of the people I meet are ill, close to death. They're not always ill with AIDS: there is cancer, diarrhea, TB and typhoid (which is common in the slums and deadly for small children). Several toddlers, between 18 and 24 months old, sit naked in brightly colored plastic pans, an older child soaping and rinsing them under the bright sun.

The last time we visited, almost all the children were terrified of my white skin. They screamed and ran into the house. This time the reactions are less extreme, although one four-year-old girl sitting under a fruit stand begins to cry. As usual, the ladies laugh and I back away saying "pole" (sorry). The mother yells at the child and throws a flip-flop at her legs. It only makes the child scream louder. I back away as quickly as I can, distressed. The rest of the children simply look at me with curiosity.

We stop to visit Mama Eric, but she's not home. In East Africa, a mother and father are named for their children; Eric's mother is known by the name of her first born. Walter opens the door to Eric's house and leans in, but only slightly, enough to determine Mama Eric is out. He spent quite a bit of time with a bedridden Eric in this room. A framed picture of Jesus hangs on the wall, above two wood-carved chairs with red velvet cushions. Eric has only been gone for two days. We stood in this spot last week and heard the singing prayers and clapping hands. Today we hear nothing.

No longer able to bear not hearing my children's voices, I go to town during lunch to buy a mobile phone, the first in my life. I don't even know how to turn one on. After going through all my choices and finally settling on a phone, I don't have enough money on me. I go to the bank to exchange U.S. dollars to Kenyan Shillings and am astonished to find that they've closed my account.

It wasn't easy to open that account. I had to show a letter of introduction from VSO and have my supervisor, Reverend Obondi, stand next to me at the time. In addition, they needed to see my passport, my Kenyan ID and a passport photo. A month ago, when first opening the account, I tried to deposit money, but Robert Matete, the "personal banker," said I'd receive a note at TICH's P.O. Box letting me know when my debit card was ready for pick-up. I would be able to put money in the account then. What he didn't tell me was the account would be closed if monies were not deposited within five days. I never received the notice. Today he tells me the account is now closed and we must go through the entire application process again.

"But you made copies of all the paperwork," I say.

"Those papers have been sent to the Nairobi branch," Walter replies.

"Didn't you keep a copy of the papers here?"

No answer.

I'm mad. I stare out the window and state the obvious.

"I'm mad," I say.

Robert agrees with me, saying, "I'm sure you're mad at yourself."

I'm not mad at myself; I'm mad at the bank's restrictions and mad at Robert for not telling me about the five day deposit rule. Barclay's bank does not operate in any way like banks in the West. They don't even take a customer's home mailing address because the postal service doesn't deliver to homes—only to P.O. Boxes. Robert writes my address down as

"Milimani Road behind the Classic Guest House." They'll send a letter to TICH's P.O. Box when the debit card is ready. Barclay's doesn't send out monthly statements. You have to go to the bank and stand in line to get a copy of your bank statement. I'm determined to get this account settled today because it's needed for payroll deposits. I get on my bike to peddle home and get money and my debit card for my U.S. bank account, plus all the paperwork.

I peddle back to the phone store, where it takes an hour to buy the phone. Afterwards, I go to the bank and wait for one of the "personal bankers" to assist me. The first one free is a sour looking woman. She calls me over, saying, "You want something?" rather snottily. I wonder if she thinks I like waiting around banks for hours on end. She looks at my documents for what seems like forever with her face all screwed up tight, finally saying, "This is a copy of the introduction letter." I tell her the original was sent to the Nairobi branch by Robert. For effect, I point to Robert, who is sitting at the next desk. He's with a customer. She tells me to wait for Robert because he saw the original.

Eventually, Robert opens the new account and sends me downstairs to get a counter deposit slip, which he and I must sign. At this point, we both want money deposited into this account so the same thing doesn't happen again. It's now 2:25pm. He hands me the slip and tells me to go to the cashier and bring a copy of the receipt to him. I'm fearful he means for me to stand in the line in the lobby.

"You mean the cashier downstairs with the long line?"

"Is the line long?" he asks innocently.

The line is always long. It's long inside and it's long outside at the ATM. I have no choice but to stand in line. There's a horrible American movie on the lobby television that I can't stop watching. At 3:00pm, the security guard closes the front doors. I step up to the cashier's window at 3:25pm, take the receipt to Robert, and head downstairs to leave. Unfortunately, the security guard is not around and the door is locked from the inside. Everyone is just sitting or standing, complacently, waiting for someone to let them out. Ten minutes later, the guard arrives, all smiles, and sets us free.

I travel to campus on a bike with a flat back tire and arrive at 3:50pm, only to be told that the director just called a meeting of the Scientific Conference committee. I attend the weekly meetings, usually held on Fridays, because I head up the communications team for the conference. But I'm hot—hot and thirsty—so I ask Apollo, an intern in the computer lab, to get me a Coke before going to the meeting. We walk to the break room where Apollo removes the padlock and chain from around the cooler to extract a Coke. It costs 20 shillings and is worth every one!

Luckily the meeting is not long. Several of us confer afterwards to fulfill some tasks, and I go to my office to write a piece for the website about a new East African cooperative that's starting up. Once it's written, I take it to Tonny, who will load it to TICH's website. He tells me there is something he meant to tell me, but can't remember. As I turn to leave, he yells out, "Oh, yes, Walter wants us to meet him at 5:30pm downtown." Even though it's my internet cafe night, I figure we can meet Walter for a few minutes. Tonny and I make plans to leave campus together on our bikes.

As the time for us to leave approaches, Tonny gets held up a little. Remembering that my back tire is flat, I go to Fred at the guard stand and ask if he can show me how to use my pump. He does so quickly and cheerfully, and I'm very grateful for the assistance. Mobile once again, I'm ready for the end of the work day. I wait in the cool shade of a tree for Tonny and our trip to town—my third one for the day. It's 6:15pm.

Tonny and I cycle into town and lock our bikes together around a sign post. We walk to where Walter sits, displaying his handmade wares for sale to passersby. He has a spot near the entrance of a shopping center, along with other men who hawk their goods on the sidewalk. Although I'm impressed with Walter's handmade flower vases and clocks, it's now after 6:40pm and I can feel my internet cafe time slipping slowly away. Communicating with family and friends keeps me going and I feel desperate at the thought of not hearing from them this evening.

Walter packs his merchandise in a giant, faded cardboard box that no longer stays closed. He ties it up with rope and puts it behind the sliding locked gate of the center, where security guards will watch it until tomorrow morning. As he's working to box up his stuff and Tonny is on the phone, two street boys come up to me with their hands out. Tonny begins talking to the boys in Dholuo. Walter calls the boys over to a woman sitting on the curb selling bananas and oranges. Each boy picks out an orange and begins to eat.

Tonny gets off the phone and talks to the first boy, who is hiding a plastic bottle containing glue. Tonny exchanges the bottle for bananas, warning me to never give the boys money because they will only use it for glue.

He holds the bottle out for me to sniff. When I do, all I can say is "dang!" It's much more potent than I imagined. When we were growing up, we used it to put model airplanes and cars together. It's been a long time since I smelled airplane glue. Suddenly, I can see other boys carrying their bottles of glue wherever I look. I wonder how I've missed it this long.

I feel foolishly naïve. Didn't I see boys at the matatu station fighting over what appeared to be an empty plastic bottle? At the time, I couldn't understand why they were tussling over a bottle. It occurs to me now that this is how they spend their days, sniffing and looking through hazy eyes with their hands out.

Walter and Tonny know these boys better than the boys know themselves. They know because they've been there. Although they may have never lived on the street, they know what it's like to be from the slums, hooked on drugs and with little hope for the future. When Walter and Tonny talk to these boys, it is with compassion and firmness. They get tough when they have to and use kindness when they don't. They calm the boys and talk to them like the human beings they are. This means a lot, especially when you compare them to the many people who are afraid of boys on glue, or any street child who asks for money. Sometimes people hit the boys. Sometimes policemen hit the boys.

Walter and his organization, Pambazuko, plan to build a shelter to house their program next to the main water source in Nyalenda slums. The stream of water separates Nyalenda A from Nyalenda B, a rather strange division created by the municipal government. The location for the shelter is ideal for bringing street children and widows together for income-generating programs, education on children's rights and AIDS prevention, as well as training in water sanitation.

Walter, Tonny and I get together to look at Walter's drawings of the building sketched in pencil in a spiral bound notebook. We've already determined that 30,000 Kenyans shillings (or about US $350) will buy all the materials needed for the shelter. Labor will be provided by community members, many of whom are members of Pambazuko and lifelong friends of Walter and Tonny.

Tonny worries about not having the landlord's agreement in writing. He wants to know why they can't just sign a formal lease or even a lease to own contract, but Walter assures him the landlord is committed to Pambazuko's cause. Walter considers the landlord's word as good as a contract.

"Just the sight of building materials being delivered to this little parcel of land," Walter tells us, "will be enough to lift the spirits of Nyalenda's residents."

In Kenya, road detours are called diversions. Leaving town, I decide to take a diversion along Ring Road, the front line of Nyalenda slums. I pass row after row of wood kiosks and shacks. I pass sewing shops with colorful cloths draped on open doors and ladies sitting behind Singer sewing machines, pumping with their feet to move the needles up and down. Butcheries pop up occasionally with huge meat chunks hanging in the day's heat. Beauty salons are frequent, as are video stores with movie dialogue blaring from a back room. People call out to me: "Hello!" "How are you?" "Hi, Madam," and "Hey, white lady."

One very large man, big enough be a bouncer in a nightclub, calls to me, "Madam, will you greet me?" I step off the sidewalk to shake his hand. Several men stand nearby, watching me closely. My new friend has a white cap that fits snugly on his head. He tells me they are gathered here for a funeral, and I notice the truck parked on the sidewalk, ready to take the deceased to the family's burial place.

"Pole," I say. While still holding my hand, the large man tells me his name is Godwill and the deceased is his cousin's sister. My first thought is that such a relationship should make her his cousin, too. But I know in Kenya, "Sister" means different things. It could be a biological sister, someone from the same community or even someone from the same church. I can smell alcohol on Godwill's breath and see in his eyes he has a good buzz going. But he's not quite drunk. Yet.

"Will you pay your respects to the deceased woman?" Godwill says.

I nod yes.

We walk away from the road, down a dirt path for nearly 100 yards. Because I've been in this neighborhood with Walter and Tonny, I am comfortable following Godwill into the slum. He tells me the deceased woman's name is Susan. We come upon a group of people under a tarp strung between two houses. A woman is standing and speaking in Dholuo. It's strange to me to approach a group of mourners I don't know.

People tend to welcome outsiders just because their skin is white. I'm becoming more comfortable with being the person with the white skin who is afforded the honor of paying respects to deceased loved ones. Everyone is watching me as I follow Godwill through the crowd, past the woman who is speaking and into a narrow doorway. The room is dark and the casket is on the ground. I grab Godwill's arm at the sight of Susan. She seems tiny; her simple coffin is small, less than half the size of caskets in America. The dead women always seem so small.

I kneel by the casket to get a better look and notice how young Susan is. Perhaps in her late 20s, she's wearing a white lace dress. There is no glass separating her from the dimly lit room. Susan is leaving behind three small, fatherless children. I stand to follow Godwill back to Ring Road.

"Here's the father of the deceased, will you greet him?" Godwill asks, pointing to an elderly man.

"Pole for your loss," I say and shake the man's hand.

He returns my grip and smiles. I find it hard to understand why he's so kind to a strange white woman pulled off the street while people eulogize his daughter under a nearby tarp.

As I turn to leave, Godwill tells me he is a "business man," with a clothing store just back on Ring Road. He wants me to visit his shop, so I tell him I'll come by another day.

"Tomorrow?"

"I can't give you a definite day, but I'll be coming by here regularly," I say. He thanks me and shakes my hand, giving me the coded handshake for intimate friends.

Chapter Six

Peace

*A*s the marketing and communications adviser at TICH, I've been busy creating a marketing plan that targets TICH's niche markets of students, partners, donors, and members. As I work on the plan, I learn most TICH staff members have lived and studied abroad. Luckily for me all meetings, classes and communications at TICH are in English.

Most people, including slum-dwellers, are well-versed in development vernacular: "People living with HIV/AIDS" (PLWHA), "vulnerable persons," "capacity building." The Mamas in the slum can talk to you about the psycho-social needs of orphaned children. Women in rural communities know how to "mobilize" their neighbors into taking action to increase their crop and animal husbandry yields.

Students planning to work in the health industry to help these "vulnerable persons" come to TICH for diplomas and degrees. TICH continues to grow. Two programs in Community Health and Development—a PhD and a master's program—have been approved and will be launched when the Commission for Higher Education awards TICH university status. Students follow a rigorous coursework curriculum and experience hands-on practical training by going into the field every week. These field visits are performed by students and staff members, who work in partnership with community members to determine which programs will most benefit the community. Students collect data for baseline surveys, write their reports, guide the communities in implementing recommended programs and follow up on the community's progress, all of which is documented in their research papers. Through this partnership program, students learn theoretical and real-world concepts, while communities receive the benefit of shared knowledge and techniques to improve their health and agriculture.

TICH has friends around the world. They will all come to Kisumu later this month for the Annual Scientific Conference, co-sponsored by UNESCO, a division of the United Nations. This year's conference theme is "Linking Research to Policy for Evidence-Based Action towards the Realization of the Millennium Development Goals (MDGs)."

It's quite exciting to be part of the conference planning committee. University professors and guest speakers will join us from Ethiopia, the UK, Tanzania, Australia, Uganda, Canada, South Africa, Botswana, the United States, France and Holland. Already, preparations are under way at TICH. Our water system is being repaired with a new tank and piping. The old well in the central courtyard, once covered with wood slats, has been demolished and filled with dirt. New gravel is being laid and floors are being painted. We're even ordering a screen for the LCD projector (it seems someone complained last year when the presentations were projected onto the bare wall).

Everyone here is busy working on their research projects, preparing class materials, developing the Enterprise Department (five chickens arrived this morning, huddled into one corner of a cage on their way to the field), making travel arrangements for our conference guests, preparing the conference agenda, printing banners and moving computers to a new e-center. In addition to the three-day conference, we'll host several workshops before and after the conference. An Israeli organization and TICH are co-hosting a four-week workshop in entrepreneurship. Visiting academics will convene to optimize TICH's master's degree program. Three editors from African peer review journals will conduct a one-day workshop instructing attendees in writing research for publication. And, finally, two workshops will be held to explore social determinants of health status and tackling health improvement through community partnerships.

Dorene, a graduate of TICH, stops by my office this morning to ask about our upcoming scientific conference. She'd like to present her study on the psycho-social needs of orphans. Dorene tells me every orphaned child she interviewed cried at some point during their discussion. Her work demonstrates that even orphans who are cared for by relatives are suffering from a lack of love and emotional support. They may have food and a bed, but they are usually treated as unequals to other children in the family. Oftentimes, they clean and do chores while the other children just sit.

Dorene tells me about two sisters, 9 and 11 years old, who are living in their father's house, being cared for by their aunt and uncle. The girls sleep on the floor while their uncle takes their father's bed; the house and bed they technically inherited from their parents. Meanwhile, their cousins bathe with soap while the orphans do not. Her work has led Dorene to become an advocate of counseling for these girls and other orphans growing up without the love of parents.

After being in Kenya five weeks, I realize I need my own private living space. The wing of the house Ian and I share is too small for two people who do not know each other. Elizabeth, the librarian, tells me about Sam, a man who "finds places." Sam found Elizabeth an apartment in the home of an Indian woman just around the corner from TICH. He's not a real estate agent, this Sam; he's just a guy who makes money connecting landlords with tenants.

"How much do you pay him?" I ask Elizabeth.

"Oh, I bought him a Coke."

A large Coke goes for 30 shillings.

Sam shows up at TICH one day while I'm hosting a meeting in my office. It's hard to tell his age; perhaps late 30s. He has a bare spot near the center of his head as though someone swiped his forehead off with a sword. He stands in the hall beckoning to me.

"I have a house for you to see," he says. He promises it is nearby, in a good neighborhood and with good security. After work, we walk over. It's actually on my way home, just around the corner from TICH. I've walked past this house every day on my way to work. Sikh Indians live in the main house. The guard lets us in and we sit on the deep veranda with the landlady, Mrs. Ruprah, who is waiting for her husband.

Neighbors stop by. Sonya, the Mama from the house across the street, is with her husband, father-in-law, two daughters and a nephew who looks like a girl. (Sikh males wear their hair long and wind it up under turbans.) This little boy looks about two years old, with his hair pulled into a ponytail, wisps floating around his face. Sonya is kind to me and tells me if I move in, I am invited to her brother-in-law's wedding celebration in a couple of weeks.

Mr. Ruprah comes out to join us. We talk price and he tells me the place will come fully furnished. Anything I need is "no problem. Is no problem." He says this phrase a lot, and I like hearing it. I also like the little carriage house (actually the servant's quarters) with its openness and brightness. It needs painting inside and out.

"Is no problem. We paint. What color?"

I want to live here. I want to sit on their veranda drinking tea. I want to go to wedding parties.

We negotiate a price both he and VSO can agree upon. We shake hands. They'll start painting the interior tomorrow, no problem.

They paint, two coats, and it's lovely, lovely, lovely.

Eric is being buried in Seme, a community 40 minutes from Kisumu. I meet Walter at 10:25am in downtown Kisumu, and we walk to the matatu station. He carries a bouquet of fresh flowers with ribbons, placed tenderly in a plastic bag and sprinkled with water, and stops to buy two trees to plant as memorials near Eric's grave.

We seek out the matatu going to Seme. Out of the corner of my eye, I see a street boy shadowing us. Walter, without a word, hands a Coke vendor 20 shillings and points to the boy, who gladly takes the Coke. Once the matatu fills up, we climb aboard and head north around Lake Victoria.

Seme is located next to Kit Mikaye, a giant natural rock sculpture made of three huge, stacked stones. Kit Mikaye means "first wife," an appropriate name since the structure does resemble a woman's figure, large and powerful, who might dominate her husband's second, third or fourth wives.

We alight at Kit Mikaye along with a man named Tom, who lives in Nyalenda. We walk back along the red dirt "highway" until we hear music. About 200 yards from the road, a red tarp is strung between trees; energetic, modern music bounces out to meet us, as though there's a festival in the bush. Mama Eric once had a mud house here, but it crumbled. Now only bits of wall enclose bushes where rooms once enclosed people. A temporary "house" has been constructed from tree branches and grasses. In the doorway stands Mama Eric. Just outside the hut, Eric rests in his coffin, a woven mat protruding from the roof shading Eric's glass-encased face.

A scrawny dog sleeps in the shadow of the coffin. We stop to view Eric while Walter says a prayer. Though only 26, Eric looks like an old man. He died Tuesday a week ago, 11 days before the funeral. His family didn't have money for the coffin or for transporting the body from Kisumu, so the funeral was postponed while money was raised. Eric's body was kept in the city morgue.

We step under the tarp and are ushered, encouraged, to the front—the very front, where cushioned couches wait. Taking the most comfortable seat doesn't seem right, but they insist on the mzungu sitting up front. I don't want to offend. I actually just want to melt, invisible, into the furniture, but that doesn't happen—could never happen.

Several men from Nyalenda are there and we shake hands. Walter walks away to photograph Eric. As I'm sitting, looking at Kit Mikaye across the field, I hear a toy whistle being blown above the music, which comes from a boom box powered by a car battery. The whistle is blown incessantly. Wondering if this is part of the ceremony, I look to see a tall, thin young man—clearly drunk—stumbling through the dusty bush toward the tent. He grins and stops in front of me. But he doesn't really stop because parts of him, mostly his head and shoulders, keep moving in circles. He shakes my hand and speaks to me in Dholuo. One of the ladies sitting behind me throws a stick at him to scare him away. His hand, covered in dirt, deposits soil into mine. As he jerks away, blowing his whistle, I notice dirt and dried leaves clinging to his back.

The tradition at Luo funerals is for friends and family to speak about the deceased before the clergymen take over. Walter is the first person to speak. He talks for 15 minutes, followed by a young woman, followed by an old woman, followed by an even older woman—Eric's tiny, creased grandmother. It's all in Dholuo, though Walter occasionally translates, such as when to stand and when to sit.

The choir arrives. It is made up of ladies of all ages, each one wearing a white lacy scarf tied around her head. They sing and clap with fervor, one solitary voice ringing out the verse while all other voices meld as backup. It's quite lovely and uplifting. The dog keeps coming into the inner circle between our front seats and the reverend's table. At first, Walter throws dirt clumps and sticks at the dog to move him out of the "sanctuary," much as the ladies tried to scare away the drunken young man. As the elders of the church arrive, the reverend announces that the choir will go to the road to escort them. The choir sings and claps, walking in unison to the beat. They surround the elders and start heading in our direction. All of a sudden the reverend, just behind me, pulls back his right foot and lets it fly into the dog's backend. There's a shrieking howl and I jump. The dog runs from the tent. I feel his shock, feel it for awhile because the reverend didn't care about the dog being in the center until the elders were approaching.

Seven elders stop in front of Eric, serenaded by the choir. The leading man raises both hands, a Bible in his left, and yells out a prayer. The preachers take their places in front of us, on cushioned couches, as young men from Nyalenda lift Eric's coffin and bring him under the tarp, lowering him onto a coffee table. The ground is uneven, so someone places a stick under the table leg. Now Eric is with us, only inches away. And his mother weeps.

Each preacher gets up to deliver a sermon; every one of them speaks in Dholuo, never a word in English. The choir sings as the men take turns preaching. One man, a small guy in short sleeves with a belt buckle that reads "Ford," gets up, clutching a Bible wrapped in bright yellow oil cloth. Each preacher has a Bible that looks as though it's been read at least four million times, any previous color worn away by sweating hands. The short preacher puts on a performance, practically screaming his message, spraying me with every word. At first, I turn my head because his voice is so loud and its intensity offends me (and I can't, just can't, watch any more spit sailing my way). Just when it seems the protruding veins in his neck and forehead will surely burst, baptizing us all in his blood, his face goes completely slack, with a slight smile, and he says "Hallelujah." The crowd immediately answers with an "amen." He continues his sermon with the same intensity, but every time I'm sure he's about to explode, as I feel his spittle hitting my face and knees and shirt, he steps forward with his slight smile and softly says "Hallelujah."

"Amen."

I want to walk away to protest his very obvious performance but instead sit quietly. The man goes on and on and jumps and jerks his arms and spews on more people in the audience. The choir members are rocking and holding their faces in their hands and speaking in tongues. Well, they're not actually speaking in tongues—just Dholuo—but they're each saying their own personal prayer in response to the frenzied, spittle-filled words being hurled at us.

Finally, the short preacher stops and asks the choir to sing. He moves back to his spot next the other preachers and I hope and pray he doesn't talk to me after the service.

Mama Eric stands to speak and a heavy-set woman stands next to her, for physical support. Mama Eric's grief slaps me like the reverend's foot on the dog's rear. Tears form and roll from my eyes. She is a mother who just lost her oldest son, and I cannot imagine the pain she's in.

During her speech, Mama Eric says the word "mzungu" repeatedly. It is only later that Walter tells me what she said. It's seems because Kenya was a British colony, Kenyans think wazungu, or white people, know how to do everything. They also think when a white person says he or she will do something, it will get done. Mama Eric was comparing Eric to wazungu, because any time he told her he was going to do something for her, he did. Mama Eric's voice catches and she sobs, though she's working hard not to. When she hesitates, to reclaim her calm, the woman at her elbow begins to sing; the choir joins and soon everyone is singing, giving Mama Eric time to compose herself. She does. But she doesn't speak much more before sitting down again.

Robert, a young man from Nyalenda who I met in the slum, stands in front of the group in a very white long-sleeve shirt and dark slacks. He begins to speak in English.

"There is someone with us today who cannot understand anything that is being said."

The ladies in the crowd shout at him, telling him to speak in Dholuo. He responds in Dholuo and begins to speak to me directly, in front of the group, in English, thanking me for being there and for everything I've done. It's too late for melting into the furniture. I'm ashamed to be thanked simply for showing up.

"Will you greet the crowd?" he asks. I stand and pivot and cannot believe the number of faces turned toward me. Over the last couple of hours, more than 200 people slowly accumulated under the tarp. Walter says he will translate.

"I'm honored to be with you today," I begin, "but I'm saddened to not have known Eric. Walter and several young men in the congregation have shared with me what a wonderful man Eric was." I pause to allow Walter to translate.

"I look forward to getting to know Eric better by getting to know you, his friends. Thank you for allowing me to join you on such a sacred and solemn occasion."

The faces looking toward me are upturned, many leaning forward, intent on what I'm saying. I see compassion and recognize genuineness. One young woman's face tells me she finds me sincere. I love her face.

It's time to give contributions, so space is cleared in front of the coffin. The choir sings and everyone lines up to pass Eric and drop money in a plastic bowl. It takes awhile for everyone to pass, but once we're out of our seats and standing in the sun, the reverend calls several young men to lift the coffin, to carry it the 12 feet to the grave. The young men scramble into position, gripping the homemade handles and lifting Eric. The choir surrounds the men and the preachers take their places at the head of the grave. After placing the coffin on the ground, some of the young men leap into the hole to receive the box and lower it. The hand-off isn't smooth. It can never be smooth when the grave is barely wide enough to hold the box. The men brace their feet against the grave's walls, hovering, to bend and lower the coffin. They have to tilt it back and forth to get it into the people-free space.

Lowering a casket is never smooth.

Mama Eric sits in a chair next to the grave, her ever-present friend at her side and Walter's bouquet of flowers on her lap. The choir sings. Men leap up onto the dirt mound, swinging shovels and their contents toward the coffin, flinging red dust onto Mama Eric. Women begin to wail. Several women. Many women. Walking and wailing and with tears flowing, they lean forward and speak of their agony between their cries, marching to the choir's tune.

As I feared, the small preacher in the blue short-sleeve shirt stands before me with a big smile on his face, pumping my hand. He tells me his name, but it doesn't catch. Behind him, on the other side of the grave, I hear loud and quick bursts on the toy whistle. As I look into the short preacher's face, I hear the women wailing and the whistle blasting and cannot concentrate on what he is saying.

"We heard there was going to be a white man here today," he says. I could swear he's salivating, as though he's picturing me as a cooked and stuffed turkey.

"You have come here to preach God's word?" he asks. The whistle blasts three hard times.

"No," I say, waiting for him to release my hand, "I'm here as a volunteer at a college."

It's no use. I cannot pay attention to his dancing, happy eyes when women are in pain a few feet away and a drunken guy is tripping over the dirt pile, blowing his whistle and being rejected by the men who shovel.

"We would be honored if you would visit our church," the preacher tries again, "because when people hear a white person will be there, it draws a big crowd."

The drunken guy wants to shovel, but they brush him away—sometimes gently, sometimes not—and keep throwing dirt into the hole. As the dirt piles up over the coffin, Walter and his friends from Nyalenda plant the trees. I take photos of the group bending and packing soil around the tiny trunks. Walter says a prayer over the trees, blessing the locale with prosperity.

The drunken man breaks branches from a bush next to the grave and pokes the branches into the dirt. Someone lays the floral bouquet at the head of the mound. These are the only markers for Eric's grave. A few older people want to be photographed by the grave. Then a few more, including Mama Eric. Then younger people want to be photographed, and when they see the digital image on the camera, they all laugh out loud and press their heads together to glimpse the tiny screen. Robert, who thanked me for being there, is standing at the head of the grave, waiting to be photographed with a few young women. The drunken guy steps up behind him but is brushed away. He is persistent and doesn't go away, so Robert pulls back his hand and slaps him across the neck and face. I stop breathing. My eyes widen and I want to speak but don't. Can't. And I don't take the photo. Walter is nearby, so I call him over and say, "Robert just hit the drunken guy."

"That's the African way," Walter says with an apology in his voice. I must be shaking my head from side to side.

I take the photo and as the group disburses, Walter calls to the drunken man, motioning for him to stand by the grave to have his photo taken. He stands at the head of the grave, alone, with a smile.

It's time to eat, so we pack up the camera and walk about one-half mile to the next group of houses, where Robert grew up. Under a huge, spreading Mango tree, eight couches are placed in a giant square. A coffee table sits in the center. People coming from the grave site carry couches, chairs and cushions over their heads, placing them in the shade of houses and trees. Under the giant tree sits a group of about 30 men; most of them are from Nyalenda and most are drinking. After Walter introduces me to each one, we go into a small house across the way. It's just me, Walter, two boxes to serve as chairs and a coffee table.

Robert brings in a tray bearing dishes of fried calf liver, dried fish, shredded and steamed cabbage, ugali, sukuma wiki, stewed chicken, rice and goat. It is a beautiful spread of food just for me and Walter, and we dig in, eating with our hands from the tray and from the bowls. I'm very hungry and very grateful for this delicious food. They bring us water to drink and water with which to wash our hands afterwards. The 30 or so men from under the tree start heading back to Kisumu, a few of them on bicycles, which will take about three hours. We say our goodbyes and walk to the road to hail a matatu.

Trucks carrying soldiers pass by, headed back to Nairobi after providing security for the president's visit. Kenya's President Kibaki was the great hope for Kenyans when he and his rainbow coalition party were elected in 2002. While they promised to stop corruption, little progress has been made since then. People feel the corruption is still just as bad, or that it could return to the extreme very easily. Each day, the newspaper headlines call for Kibaki to dismiss his cabinet.

Overhead, two helicopters buzz, carrying ministers of this and that—possibly even the President of Kenya himself. Matatus going to Kisumu are packed with people who came out to see the president.

We finally squeeze into a matatu. It's not long before we stop to let a passenger off. I recognize the place; it's the town where George Nyamor, a coworker, grew up. He pointed it out to me on one of our weekly field trips. On an impulse, I look for George down the center street, even though the chances are slim that I'll see George. He lives in Kisumu and rarely goes home.

George is one of my favorites because his eyes always twinkle and his voice is soft. He teases that his last name means the roar of a lion, which is the opposite of his gentle nature. I'm missing George and my other co-workers from TICH and would love to see one of them right now. Wishful thinking.

The first man I see on the street is facing away, but his build is like George's, his gait leisurely and sure. The woman to my right wants out, so I exit the matatu and look back into town, to see if it actually is George.

My impulse was right! George looks up to the road before I even have the chance to shout at him. He sees me immediately. I wave and he waves back, smiling.

"Where are you coming from?" he calls. I can't answer because I'm being commanded back into the matatu.

"I was looking for you," I yell, "because this is your home. It's good to see you! See you Monday." I watch George turn behind a house and am happy to see him glance back once more before he disappears. After this hard day, I am elated to see George's friendly, familiar face looking back at me.

I walk to the main road looking for two strong boda boda drivers. I explain I'm shifting house and ask if they'll help.

"20 bob," one guy offers.

"No, you'll get more than that for moving heavy stuff," I respond.

They come home with me. I bring out my suitcase, duffle bag, box of books and a bag containing the water filter. They work to balance it all on their bikes, securing it with rubber straps.

We walk to the Ruprah's house. I'm carrying a box with a bag over my shoulder and the bigger man is telling me his story. He struggles with English but tells me he was orphaned young, has two children, has a hard life, he's trying, trying to get by but it's tough. I listen, nod and agree. We drop off the goods and I pay the men 200 shillings each.

The first night in my new home, Mrs. Ruprah sends Samuel, the guard, to fetch me. I find her sitting in a white plastic chair on their driveway, just down the steps from the marble-floored veranda. In her lap is a huge mound of white netting, collected around an iron hoop. Very exotic.

Mrs. Ruprah is lovely. She wears traditional Sikh attire, a Punjabi suit with a long tunic top covering loose pants. Each day, I look forward to seeing what she'll be wearing. The fabrics are all beautiful: some glittering, some with beads, mirrors and sequins sewn on. I'm in love with the Indian fabrics.

Mrs. Ruprah hands me the massive net as well as a set of embroidered linens to drape over the velvet couch and chair. There is so much pleasure piled in my arms. I immediately hang the net and drape the linens. The net stretches over the wide, wide bed, forming an erotic, gossamer canopy, perfect for frolicking. Climbing inside, there is so much room: room to stretch and room to play. The high wattage bulb is bright enough to read by. I can even sleep with books on the bed instead of having to untuck the net to deposit the books on the bedside table.

A cool breeze steals in from outside. It comes from under the giant trees, slipping over my head and into the tent. Crickets howl and cars pass infrequently on the paved road just beyond the purple gate. I hear the television from the Ruprah's bedroom, faintly, and am content to lie in the cool tent and stare at the ceiling, to gaze at the roundness of the net's high gathering spot and to watch the occasional long, red ant crawl up the wall. I'm just relaxing and enjoying the space.

Content.

Chapter Seven

K i b o k o

*E*d and I cycle out to Kiboko Bay for lunch. Ed is a fellow VSO volunteer from the UK who works as financial adviser to Pandipiere, a Catholic center servicing the residents of Nyalenda slums. The bike ride takes about 20 minutes to the lake's edge, even though we have to stop at a fundi (handyman) under a tree to fix the chain guard on my bike. We cruise down paved streets until the pavement ends at the Impala Reserve opposite the Kisumu water works. We bump along on the rocky dirt roads, passing huts and cows and men weaving furniture from the water hyacinth that grows in Lake Victoria. We lock our bikes to a black fence and admire the new pool next to the restaurant, overlooking the lake, complete with lounge chairs "imported" from Nairobi. It is mostly white people reclining by the clear, cool water.

Ed and I sit on the patio and talk for hours. We're hoping to take a trip to the coast. Mombasa. Malindi. Lamu. All three cities appeal to us. But other questions remain. Do we want to travel by bus or overnight train? How much time can we take off from work for this trip? It's fun to dream of a trip to the coast in a first class train cabin, which will surely be better than a second class ticket for an uncomfortable chair with very little chance of sleeping. Two fellow VSO volunteers, Tom and Wendy, live in Mombasa. Surely we can stay with them and find inexpensive accommodations in the other towns.

When we finish talking and eating, we peddle over to Dunga, a fishing village. Cows stand on the dock. Fishermen sit under a pavilion where the fish are weighed. I take photos of boats, men, cows and mountainous shorelines. As we're on our bikes headed out of the village, a young man named Kennedy approaches and asks if we know about the mimosa plant. Or the sausage tree?

Kennedy tells us to follow him and we do, somewhat reluctantly, to a spot in the grass where a few mimosa branches are growing. They're no taller than the grass. He tells us the Mamas pull the branch from the ground, chop the root, boil it and give it to children with stomachaches. He reaches down and touches the delicate branches. Before our eyes, the tiny leaves fold up to meet in the middle, and the branch seems to press itself closer to the ground.

"If a fly lands here," Kennedy says, "the plant will fold around the fly and absorb it."

He then leads us to the sausage tree, so called because there are giant, flesh-colored pods hanging from the tree that look almost like fat, uneven sausages. There are only two sausage trees in the village, and it is taboo to cut them down. The pod fruits are fermented to make the local brew. The bark is boiled to make a stomach remedy. One side of this huge tree's trunk is stripped clean of bark.

"If I go out on the lake," Kennedy tells us, pointing to Lake Victoria, "and I drown, but they cannot find my body, they will bury these sausage pods in place of my body."

Kennedy shows us the jacaranda tree, with its milky blood. He beckons us past the huge trees and onto a narrow footpath running between houses. Have you seen the hammerhead bird's house? Come, come this way. Two men walk up from behind and pass us, going where Kennedy is leading us into the woods. I imagine they're trying to lure us behind the houses so they can rob us. Ed is hesitant, as well. We push forward, following Kennedy, without communicating our suspicions to each other.

I think to myself, 'We'll just jump on our bikes and ride fast if they try anything.'

I can't stop these thoughts because before we left on our daytrip, Mr. Ruprah, my landlord, mentioned that three people were recently shot near Kiboko Bay. Three men and three women in a UN vehicle pulled off the road to look at hippos in the water. "Thugs," as the local bad boys are called, surrounded the vehicle, robbed them and shot into the car, hitting three people. Luckily, none of them died, but I think about those thugs as Ed and I cycle to the bay and as we push our bikes on the narrow footpath behind Kennedy.

'How did I let this happen? There's no turning back,' I think.

Ed is pushing on as well, both of us trusting Kennedy. We turn a corner and he points up to a clump of rags and rope and plastic draped in the fork of two tree branches, about 25 feet up. It's the hammerhead nest and I'm relieved. Even more relieved when two children approach and Ed greets them in Dholou. The dirt road—our passage to safety— is only 20 feet to our right. Ed and I both visibly relax to listen to Kennedy talk about the hammerhead.

"They're very clever birds," Kennedy says, "while the outside of their house is ragged layers of cloth, inside the walls are smooth. And there are partitions sectioning the house into rooms. They are very clever, these birds." The bird house is a very large square and looks like a ragtag mess, as Kennedy says. What a sight it makes; a multi-colored and textured house sitting in the tree's crook.

Very clever birds, indeed.

I know Kennedy didn't give us this short tour merely out of the kindness of his heart. I ask if he'll take 20 bob for the tour. He says fine.

"Please come back if you want to take a boat trip or to arrange a guided nature tour," Kennedy says, "I'll take you all over the village and bay area, showing the trees and birds."

Later, when Ed and I are at my place enjoying a cup of coffee, I tell him I became scared when Kennedy was drawing us deeper and deeper into the bush and away from the busy lakeshore. Ed said he had the same thoughts and fears. We were both wearing backpacks and looked like tourists, easy marks for easy money. Except that we're not tourists and we don't have money. Throughout his tour, Kennedy kept a smile on his face and showed us everything he promised. As far as he was concerned, he was simply showing us an experiential brochure promoting a much longer and more expensive tour for our next visit.

He didn't even notice we thought he might kill us.

For the first time since being in Kenya, I dress up. No flat, wide shoes with thick rubber soles to navigate rocks. No hair pinned up to tame a mass of moist tresses. Make-up is carefully applied. A blue, silky skirt rests around my waist, caressing my hips and legs all the way to the ankle. I feel feminine—something I haven't felt in nearly three months.

Mrs. Ruprah is wearing a lovely black sari with shiny turquoise embroidery that catches and throws the moonlight. She asks me to clasp a black velvet choker around her neck. Her earrings shimmer, the bangles on her arm dazzle. She's wearing a bracelet of red cloth with tiny brass bells attached, a typical wedding ornament provided by the hostess to female guests.

Mrs. Ruprah jingles when she walks.

We're going to Sonya's house to celebrate the arranged marriage of Sonya's brother-in-law, Raju, to Goldie, a woman who lives in Nairobi. Goldie will not be at the party; she is in Nairobi holding her own celebration. She will arrive Sunday night, after she and Raju are married in Nairobi. She'll be brought to Kisumu, to the house across the street, where she'll live in a room on the second floor while Raju's extended family lives downstairs. Sonya's family lives across the street from the Ruprahs, in the corner house. They've strung thousands of lights, colored and clear, flashing and flickering in trees and on the rooftop.

We can hear drumming as Samuel escorts us out of our yard. We walk in the darkness to Sonya's gate, where a uniformed security guard allows us to enter. We cross the marble veranda and enter the house between thick glass doors. To the left, mattresses are side by side across a large room. Couches and chairs have been pushed to the wall. We move down the hall and out the back door, onto a covered patio surrounded by a wall. Beyond the wall, men have gathered, some sitting like Mr. Ruprah while others stand around a cooking fire. Raju, the Ruprah's son (who has the same name as the groom), is stirring oil and spices in a giant skillet with a spoon as big as an oar. The men toss in earth-colored herbs and spices as the mixture tries to boil. This is where the men congregate, so we return to the house, to the front room carpeted in mattresses, where the women gather.

We remove our shoes and step carefully across the mattresses, taking a seat on a couch. Stripped of my lovely shoes, I'm conscious of my deformed-looking big toes where my toenails have fallen off from climbing Kilimanjaro. The ladies enter, remove their shoes and manipulate yards of cloth around their bodies so they can sit comfortably in a tight group. We are practically shoulder to shoulder, facing a woman in the center who plays the drum. Some of the women look at me and speak. Others do not.

Lying on its side, the drum has animal skin stretched across both ends; one side is larger than the other and produces a deeper and richer boom. Opposite the drummer, another woman hits a spoon against the wooden drum, providing a higher pitched percussion sound. In Punjabi, they discuss which song they'll sing. There is laughing and teasing leading into song. Voices fall away as lyrics are forgotten. The drum beat slows then stops, followed by more talking and laughing and false song starts. I'm enchanted, watching the way these 50 or so women (they keep coming in and coming in and finding spots to sit amongst their friends, on the floor, on couches, on laps) act as though they're all sisters, as though they've known each other forever. They are easy with each other, with their head tosses and thrown comments, with a single conversation amongst the group instead of 20 conversations whispered to a nearby ear.

I'm told they're singing love songs and songs about marriage. Perhaps those are the same thing. Perhaps not. This is an arranged marriage.

I'm getting used to hearing strange words rapidly spoken (or sung)—getting used to not understanding, but also not necessarily needing to know. With so many new sensations and emotions swirling around, it's often a relief to not follow conversations. It calms me to simply sit and watch, letting words and laughter and hand gestures wash over me. It is amazing how—even without knowing words—it's so easy to tell if someone is earnest or playful, chastising or simply providing information. Dholuo, Kiswahili, Punjabi. Their sounds come in crescendos, softly, harshly, day and night, registering but not understood. And that's okay. For now.

During a lull in the drumming, we hear the front gate clang and women's voices, singing, move toward us.

"Jagoo," Mrs. Ruprah laughs and everyone hurriedly stands to put their shoes on.

"Juggle?" I ask, and they respond, "Jagoo!" We move to the front door and spill into the yard, propping against porch rails and cars as a parade of women come from the dark night beyond the gate and approach the house, led by a woman in red whose face is illuminated by her crown of flames (she has a circular tray on her head filled with colorful flowers and six lit candles). The parade grows and follows her under the color-strung trees, around the house and onto the patio where a DJ has set up 10-foot tall speakers. Four young men—black and Indian—crank up the music, an Indian rap with heavy bass beats. The ladies use the large patio as their dance floor. They perform traditional Indian dances as the flaming tray from the woman's head is passed from woman to woman, around and around, until the men move onto the dance floor, taking the flaming tray onto their heads. Then it is time for the young boys and girls to join.

We dance and eat delectable Indian food, even a little goat and chicken appearing in our meal. (Although Hindus are normally vegetarians, Sikh Indians sometimes eat meat—except for beef, because the cow is still sacred in India.) Nearing midnight, we prepare to leave. Before we head out, two ladies come by carrying a large tub from which they hand out brown paper bags filled with baked goodies that soak the brown paper with oil. Mr. and Mrs. Ruprah, Raju and I walk home under the stars holding our goodie sacks tightly. There are no cars and no boda bodas at this hour. We own the road and practically dance across it.

The wedding for Raju and Goldie was today. Many, many family members and friends loaded up in a coach early yesterday morning and headed to Nairobi from Kisumu. It is now evening and they return, tired but happy, bringing Goldie with them to her new home. She'll stay here two weeks. Then, following tradition, her father will come from Nairobi to collect her and Raju. They'll stay with her family in Nairobi for a week, after which she'll return to Kisumu to live with Raju and his family forever and ever. She'll return to live in Kisumu, to build a life with people she doesn't yet know, to bear children and raise them in Kisumu for the rest of her life. Just like Mrs. Ruprah did 35 years ago.

At 9:00pm, Mrs. Ruprah calls to me through the open windows of my little house. I dress hurriedly and we go to the party across the street, where Indian rap music is already directing our feet to meet the new bride. She remains upstairs until it's time to cut the cake. When she appears, she is very shy, looking down throughout the cake cutting and also while dancing with her new husband in front of the crowd. Couples take turns sandwiching the bride and groom, simultaneously feeding them cake.

Goldie is bedecked and bedazzling in her jewelry and ornamentation. Everyone wishes them happiness, forever and ever, in the upstairs room of this Kisumu hamlet by the shores of Lake Victoria. Happiness forever and ever, for their children and their children's children.

TICH's Annual Scientific Conference is underway on campus. Hand-made items are displayed on the second floor of our library. These items, made by rural women from our partner communities, include painted gourds from which to eat porridge, painted terracotta pots, homegrown Soya beans and rice, woven baskets and a rattan basket for cooking. This last item is especially interesting. It is essentially a fuel-saving device; when cooking beans or rice, the woman will cook them for 10 minutes, drain them, and then pour the food into this cloth-lined woven basket with a cloth-covered lid. The food sits for three or four hours and is ready to eat.

During the conference, Professor Violet Kimani from the University of Nairobi describes a study she conducted around Lake Turkana in northern Kenya. This area of the country is a no-go zone for VSO volunteers for two reasons: bandits frequently shoot at passing vehicles, and there is continued fighting in Sudan, which borders northern Kenya. Many of the tribes in the Turkana region are either nomadic or forced to become nomadic—typically migrating due to drought, war or bandits. Kimani tells us anthropologists and other researchers use the word "emic" to describe how the subjects define certain concepts. This is necessary because many researchers use Western and standardized definitions of things, skewing the study results if the people within a culture define a concept differently.

In Professor Kimani's study, when she asks the people around Lake Turkana what they call someone who has AIDS, they reply, "White Teeth." Asked why they would call a disease by the name "White Teeth," they explain that when people reach the final stages of the disease, they lose weight and their skin tightens all over their bodies—especially on their faces—pulling their mouths open to reveal lots of white teeth. They also use the term "Long Neck" because a patient's neck appears to grow longer as the patient loses muscle mass.

Conference attendees crowd our outdoor courtyard at lunchtime, lined up around the serving tables to receive their stewed beef, ugali, chicken, goat or rice. Sometimes green bananas are cooked with the goat or stewed beef; the bananas taste just like potatoes. Despite the delicious smells, staff members hang back to make sure attendees get fed first, just in case we run short.

Today, I'm standing in line behind Jack Bryant, a lovable, white-haired professor from the United States who has worked in development for decades. Jack comes to Kisumu every year to teach courses on many topics: ethics, equity, human rights, social determinants of health, benchmarks of fairness for health care reform, health system development for poor populations.

"You know," Jack says, "Jaap Koot had an interesting remark in his session today." Jaap Koot is a public health consultant from Holland. He's at the conference to present on community-based action research. Jack tells me that while Jaap was addressing the group, he asked those who live in rural areas to raise their hands. Nearly 70 hands went up because many CHWs from TICH's partnership communities are attending the conference. Jaap then asked the group to keep their hands up if their family has ever experienced the death of a child.

"When he asked them to keep their hands up if they had lost a child," Jack says, "nearly all the hands stayed up." Jack's voice catches on the word "all" and his eyes tear up. I grip his upper arm while he collects his emotions. "Jaap then said, 'I'm 52 years old and my family has never lost a child. Not my immediate family nor my extended family.'"

In a room full of 70 or so women, a room full of Mamas from the community who bear the brunt of providing for their families, nearly every one of them represents a family who has lost a child.

Later, as we wait for a party to start in the grassy yard of TICH's medical clinic, Jack and I sit side by side talking about his years working in development. After his stint as a World War II fighter pilot flying F4U Corsairs, he visited his "wingman's" family in Lebanon, where he fell ill. Jack was impressed with the Lebanese doctors who treated him and decided to become a doctor himself.

Jack's early academic years were focused on biochemistry, internal medicine and hematology, but his career veered toward international health when the Rockefeller Foundation invited him to participate in a study of health in developing countries. Two years and 22 countries later, Jack went to Thailand to write the book, titled *Health and the Developing World*, and to help start an institution established on new dimensions in community-based health care: the Ramathibodi Faculty of Medicine of Mahidol University.

After Thailand, Jack returned to the United States to the Columbia University School of Public Health, then onward to the Office of International Health in the Government's Department of Health and Human Services. In that capacity, he served on the Executive Board of the World Health Organization (WHO) and represented the United States at the International Conference on Primary Health Care at Alma Ata in 1978.

Jack's involvement in development continued into the next phase of his professional life (from 1985 to 1994) at the Aga Khan University in Karachi, Pakistan. He calls his time there "nine splendid years in the Department of Community Health Sciences, working on the development of health systems for poor populations and related education of health personnel, including nurses for community health leadership."

Today, Jack continues as Emeritus Professor of the Aga Khan University, in addition to serving on the faculty of TICH, Johns Hopkins University School of Public Health and the University of Virginia, School of Medicine.

It's obvious from talking with Jack that his career continues to be spent in true partnership with his wife, Nancy, who published a book entitled *Women in Nursing in Islamic Societies*. They both work with UN Habitat in Nairobi, Kenya, on an immense problem: the Millennium Development Goal of improving the well-being of 100 million African slum dwellers. UN Habitat insists priority be given to Orphans and Vulnerable Children, so Jack and Nancy are helping to develop the OVC Care Systems in those urban slums. Jack has a Fulbright Grant supporting the both of them as they work in the slums of Nairobi, developing what will hopefully be pilot projects for OVC care in slums across Africa.

Jack talks of other development veterans like Dr. Arole in Jamkhed, India. In the early 60s, Dr. Arole and his wife Mabelle vowed to use their medical degrees to work with the poorest of the poor in rural India.

"They've written a book about their community work," Jack tells me.

The next morning, Jack calls me into his temporary office at TICH and says, "I have something to show you." He holds up a book entitled *Jamkhed*. "Listen to this Jack says." He begins to read to me. I lean forward, my elbow on the chair arm, chin resting on my palm, soaking up each syllable spoken by Jack's voice: the passage describes a conference audience listening to a community health worker from a remote Indian village. She compares doctors to chandeliers, that require electricity, while community health workers are like candle lamps. Their light can be passed from candle wick to candle wick, lighting the way to better health for all.

Chandeliers. Inaccessibility. Lamps. Jack and I both laugh nervously to hide our tears. I think of the 70 women who live in rural communities within a two-hour drive of Kisumu. I see the light of their lamp as they pass it amongst their neighbors and fellow workers. I marvel at what TICH has accomplished: providing training in rigorous, scientific research to students while reaching out to educate the rural woman. It is she who plants crops and feeds chickens and hauls water and cooks and cleans and builds her house out of mud and dung to shelter her children. This conference is attended by professors in public health and anthropological fields, who sit next to bowed, weathered women with kerchiefs tied around their heads and shawls encircling their shoulders. We all learn from each other.

Later, I run into Jack in the e-center.

"I have something to show you," he says. This sentence is quickly becoming my favorite sentence in the whole world.

We walk to the front porch of TICH and nestle into the wicker chairs. Jack flips through his notebook and says, "I've written a poem entitled 'Africa's Orphans.'"

As Jack reads his poem to me, again I relax, letting the words flow over me.

Africa's Orphans

One large corner of our world
Casts a shadow over its children.
So many have lost a father
Or mother, and then the other,
And the children are left,
Often not knowing who they are.

Who can save them, give them a chance?
Grandmother near the end?
Auntie fading?
Who is left?

A widow, with two goats and a cow,
Willing to mother?
An adolescent orphan boy
Caring for six young ones?

Realities of African poverty and despair,
Aloneness on all sides.
Who am I? Who might I be?
Who hears? Who cares?

What do I need? Food? Shoes?
A bed instead of the sidewalk?
A smile. A loving hug.
A chance to learn.

A sense of myself as a person,
With hope for a tomorrow.

I'm floating in the hope his words create around us, around TICH, around this community stretching two blocks away to the slums of Nyalenda. Jack and I are moved by the thought of the orphans' bright eyes shining out of their dark lives, by the raised hands signifying so many children's deaths, by the passing of light from selfless health worker to selfless health worker. We are moved. And we are moved again each day.

Even after 40 years of working in developing countries, Jack is still moved.

Tomorrow is TICH's sixth graduation ceremony. It will be held here in the courtyard of TICH's student hostel. Tents are erected, food is brought in and, tonight, the famous Ahanglo band from the Sunset Hotel is hired to play for us. They typically play every Friday night to huge crowds, so we are excited to have them all to ourselves. The band sets up under one tent while we congregate under the facing tent. The food is set out and we eat: TICH staff along with our international guests, who are still here for the conference. We drink warm soft drinks and warm beer with our stewed beef and ugali.

After 8:00pm, the band plays traditional music. Folks waddle and stamp their way onto the grass dance floor between the two tents. Men with men, women with women, men with women. We dance and dance until nearly midnight, bonding as folks from Canada, France, South Africa, Kenya, the Congo, Ethiopia, Tanzania and the United States attempt to mimic the smooth dancing style of our teachers.

On the day of the graduation ceremony, TICH is recognizing CHWs with certificates of achievement in addition to handing out diplomas to the regular students. This is the first time CHWs have been included in the ceremony, and there are 83 of them! They've worked hard this last year attending training sessions on agriculture and husbandry techniques and learning counseling skills.

Graduation begins with a Thanks Giving Service which includes communion, hosted by Reverend Obondi and Director Dan Kaseje. There are prayers, followed by speeches. Graduates come forward one by one to receive their diplomas from Chancellor Designate Omamo, a giant of a man who is a former member of parliament. Dan adorns each graduate with a sash bearing TICH's colors: blue and green. One graduate is named top student, but he is not present. He passed away from AIDS two weeks ago, so his widow comes forward to accept his award.

Five CHWs receive honors. Four of them are each awarded a plow. As they come forward to accept their award, their husbands rush across the green lawn to assist. They all bow toward Dan and toward Omamo, to show respect. Some people in the crowd mumble and grumble that the women did all the hard work and the men come forward to absorb the credit. There may be a bit of truth in this assessment, but some of the men actually do appear humble and appreciative. One CHW receives a voucher for a he-goat. This is not just any he-goat—it seems to be a special breed from Naivasha. Dan encourages the winners of the plow and the goat to share their prizes with their neighbors, perhaps charging a nominal fee for the rental of the plow. He suggests the goat's seed be shared freely. Everyone snickers.

After the ceremony, our campus is full of graduates and international visitors. Not much work is being done, but there are plenty of laughs, handshakes and congratulations all around.

A catering team prepares lunch and tea each day of the conference for attendees. The crew is set up in Dan's backyard, next door to TICH. On the back patio of Dan's house they stew beef and fry chicken, and cook ugali, rice and sukuma wiki. A temporary shelter has been erected to shade them from the sun.

Chickens are shooed and flies are swatted as the crew cooks and hauls food, plates, silverware and clean drinking water to the school. I enjoy hanging out in Dan's backyard, watching the process. It's amazing how well they work together to produce such a large amount of various dishes. They also wash the plates and cutlery here. In the United States, food cooked in such an environment would not be suitable for serving. Here, these meals are luxuries.

The catering crew occasionally allows me and other staff members to make a plate of the delicious food. We sit in Dan's living or dining room and eat. It's a nice reprieve from the hectic conference atmosphere. Sometimes, I help them carry serving dishes heaped with chicken and ugali to the lunch tables under the trees of our courtyard. Being with the cooking crew in Dan's backyard is like being at a family reunion; relaxed, surrounded by wonderful aromas and a sense of belonging.

Director Dan Keseje asks me to visit him in his office. He surprises me by asking if I'd be interested in managing the Information Technology team.

"Well," I say, "could we call it more of a coordinator role than a management role?"

"Why?" he asks.

"Don't you think they may feel like I'm an outsider coming in to tell them what to do?"

"But you're not an outsider," Dan says, "you're an insider."

"Well, I like to think I'm an insider, and I feel like an insider, but I don't want to step on anyone's toes."

At the next meeting of the IT/Research/Marketing team, Dan announces that I will head up IT. Immediately following the meeting, Tonny and Elias, our IT specialists, tell me how pleased they are. We're all rather heady with ideas and dreams of making the e-center, our school's computer lab, optimal for students and staff.

We're also anxiously excited about purchasing a new file server and getting a satellite connection for our internet access. We want to make good choices in getting the right company to provide technical support. We also want to clean up the computer lab. Imagine two rows of hodge podge CPU's hooked up to monitors of all sizes, some with working CD roms and disc drives, others without working anything. Imagine, at the back of the room, more than 200 monitors, CPUs, printer bodies, keyboards and broken pieces of this or that all stacked and piled in an incredibly dysfunctional eyesore. Add in reams of "research" papers and it is one messy mess.

When our IT team visits the lab, we envision a room where two rows of computers have all their components working optimally, all computers are linked to both the internet and our internal network so folks can print and research on the net and all the computers are sitting neatly on the tables, their wiring embedded in the console and hidden from view. The consoles are free of soda bottle caps and scraps of paper. It is a computer lab cleaned and mopped every day, not twice a week. It won't be easy.

My vision for TICH is to have a computer on every staff member's desk and to have that computer connected to the internet all day long. Right now, we're on dial-up. The more people logged on, the slower the system runs. As a result, staff members are discouraged from getting on the internet. We are severely limited in accessing our partners and sister universities around the world. But all that will change. We have dreams. Next week, we're sorting the junk at the back of the computer lab. Some pieces will be discarded, some pieces will be donated to community-based organizations and some pieces will be stored for later use.

The junk that gets sent to Africa is absurd. Donors seem to use Africa as their dumping ground. For instance, a German organization donated 17 computers to TICH, but no monitors. (And the computers were outdated.) Frank, my fellow VSO volunteer in Ndhiwa, said he found a secret room at the hospital where he works. The room was sealed. When maintenance opened it, they found the room stacked with unusable stuff sent by donors. A B3 Hammond organ. Two microfiche reading machines, but no microfiche.

I'm still the marketing and communication advisor, but now I get to learn about the world of Information Technology. This opportunity would have never existed for me in America. Of course, in the United States, I'd have the opportunity to fill my belly with peanut M&Ms while drinking caramel macchiatos from Starbucks, things I miss. But in Africa, I get to fill my head instead.

Chapter Eight

Spirit

Samuel, the guard at the Ruprah's gate, works from early evening until 6:30am, when George takes over.

Samuel is kind and thin and strong. When he sits by the gate and reads his newspaper, he'll pause at any interruption and push his glasses onto his forehead. He wears a black and white loose-fitting shirt, frayed at the collar and wrists. One Saturday when I arrive home, he's wearing a yellow dress shirt with a tie. He looks very sharp, so I compliment him. He becomes bashful and tells me it's his holy day as a Seventh Day Adventist, and that he spent the day visiting people.

As I walk to my little house, it begins to rain. Within the hour, Samuel shows up at my door, speaking through the open window, "Ex-cuuuuuse me, sorry to disturb." I guarantee him it's no disturbance and open the door. He's moist from the rain and cold, his yellow dress shirt damp, and he asks if I have two or three matches to build a fire. I give him an entire box of matches. He puts both hands together, bows his head and touches his forehead.

About 3:00am on another night, I hear water pouring off the back roof. I worry the tank might be leaking so I slip into my plastic sandals, grab the headlamp and walk out to Samuel's guard shack. The tiny shelter is three feet by three feet without a door. Small pieces of wood sit on the walkway; inside, on the floor, sits a metal bowl full of burning embers, heating up the shack on this cool night.

Samuel is in a wooden chair facing the center of the space. He leans to the back of one wall, his head propped up on the Styrofoam block from the coffee maker box I threw away. Samuel is curled up, his knees to his chest as his feet dangle dangerously close to the embers. He is sleeping soundly.

A pair of athletic socks cover his hands and arms, keeping mosquito bites away. He wears a lightweight black jacket with the hood secured so tightly around his head it shields part of his face from mosquitoes.

"Samuel," I lean in and whisper. Nothing. I touch his arm and say, "Samuel." Nothing. I shake his arm and say a little loudly, "Samuel!" He opens his eyes and jumps to right himself.

"Yes?" he says coming out of sleep.

"So, so sorry to bother you," I say. I tell him about the water running from the back of the house and he says it's because the tank on the roof is full from the rain.

"It's not a problem," he assures me, "don't worry."

I cannot apologize enough for waking him.

Last night, I arrived home at 8:00pm just as it began to rain. Samuel was on the Ruprah's veranda. He ran through the rain, wearing a white dress shirt and a double-breasted black suit, to let me in.

"Oh my, Samuel," I exclaimed as we shook hands, "you look so handsome this evening." He became bashful as usual, smiling and looking down at the ground as he locked the gate. It was Saturday, his holy day, and he had been visiting.

"Stay dry, Samuel, and stay warm," I told him. I entered my little house followed closely by sounds of Samuel chopping wood and dropping it into his metal bowl.

Heading to my office, I bound up TICH's outdoor staircase at a fairly exuberant pace. However, I immediately slow down when I see a white face sitting in the computer lab. Like all the other offices on the outdoor corridors, the computer lab has a half-wall of windows with narrow glass slats, so I can see right in. The owner of the white face doesn't look up, she just types away at her laptop, sitting in the front row of the lab. She looks American. Without hesitating, I step to the window and say, "Hello."

"Hi," she says, turning toward me. I lean down to see more clearly through the open window slats, almost as though I'm hoping to lap up the invisible Western qualities seeping from her pores.

"My name is Cindi and I work here as the marketing manager. What are you doing here?" It feels a little awkward, seeking out a face simply because it's white. It feels even more awkward to be holding back the enthusiasm of seeing a white face and hearing an American voice.

"I'm Tracy," she says, "I'm managing a water project with the Atlanta Rotary club, the CDC and Emory University."

"Are you from Atlanta?" I ask, not really believing it's possible.

"Yes," she says, smiling.

"So am I!"

"Really?" she says, "isn't that funny?"

As we talk, Tracy tells me the Atlanta Rotary Club has raised two million dollars to dig wells in rural areas of Kenya and to act as vendor of a water purifier to rural women. She's been hired to manage the entire project with direction from the CDC and Emory University in Atlanta, where she received her master's degree in public sanitation. Her project works with a small NGO that supports women in rural areas. The NGO will provide Tracy with a network of rural women through which to channel the water purifier. (They're not giving the purifier away—they will offer it at cost.) Tracy could have set her office up with the NGO, but she chose to have it at TICH. It's now my job to get her first floor office wired for the internet.

Ed, Vincent, Diana and I meet in town and walk to the matatu station. Ed is a fellow VSO volunteer, and Vincent works with UNESCO in Paris. He is in Kisumu for the conference. Diana is a former intern at TICH who met Vincent when he was visiting before. The four of us are headed to Kakamega Forest, an hour-and-a-half drive north of Kisumu.

A heavy disco remix pulses as we settle into the matatu's back row. Our heads hit the metal ceiling a couple of times as we bump, accelerate and brake along the highway out of Kisumu. The matatu climbs the escarpment, gaining altitude and cooler weather as we marvel at the lush landscape rolling from mountain to flat valley. Houses poke out of corn fields and banana groves all throughout the sloping hills. Cattle munch in yards and women carry baskets, bags and wood on their heads. We pass a coffin maker shop with caskets on display. One coffin, covered in plush maroon velvet, catches my eye and I can't look away. We come to the Weeping

Stone, a huge rock formation that seeps water from the top. It looks like an eagle. We bounce by, getting only a quick glimpse through the dirty matatu windows that sport decorative tape designs on the outside.

"Can you imagine how nice it would be to travel these roads in a private vehicle, stopping to take pictures whenever you wanted?" I ask. Diana agrees it's a fine idea.

We pass a road where a crowd walks toward us, hundreds of men, led by a bull.

"It's a bullfight," Diana tells us.

"Is it a man against a bull or bull against bull?" Vincent asks.

Diana laughs at Vincent, saying it's bull on bull, of course.

"Well, I ask because in Spain bullfighting is between a man with a red cape and a bull."

"Oh," says Diana, "here, it's bull against bull and it's very popular, as you can see."

We catch another matatu to the north gate of Kakamega Forest. A young man in tattered clothes follows us from the main road, espousing his expertise as a forest guide. We're not interested in his services and try to ignore him. It does not deter him.

"Do you know who Tony Blair is?" Ed asks.

"Yes," the young man answers, "Blair's re-election is a good thing, unlike Bush's." We all laugh. People all around the world, in developed and developing countries, know everything that's going on in the West.

We pay our entry fees and follow the sign to the Kenya Wildlife Services office. Kakamega Forest, approximately 240 square kilometers, is the only remaining part of an ancient forest in Kenya that once covered the African continent along the equator from the Indian to the Atlantic Ocean. With the population explosion, and people cutting down trees for farmland and firewood, Kenya's forest is now in danger of being lost.

Though the government talks about preserving the area, people live on the forest's edge and continue to slash and burn for farmland. It's also said officials, elected to protect the forest, sell parcels to locals illegally, pocketing the money. An organization called Kenyan Environmental and Ecological Protection (KEEP) works to educate the locals on the importance of preserving the forest. They are holding a class for children when we enter their building. Henry, who runs the program, shows us their tree nursery, where they're raising seedlings to distribute to local farms. This will give the farmers a source of firewood so they will not enter the forest for fuel.

Kakamega is of interest to zoologists and botanists around the world as an example of how an isolated environment can survive being cut off from its larger body. This forest is home to more than 300 species of birds, snakes, reptiles, an unknown quantity of insects, nearly half of all known butterflies in the country and seven species of primates and other mammals.

Ifango, our forest guide, shows us a Ficus sapling enveloping a full-grown tree. It's a strangling Ficus, which takes nearly one hundred years to overtake a host tree and several more hundred years to kill it. We come upon one strangling Ficus that killed its host tree long ago. This giant tree, estimated to be older than 500 years, is massive, with roots standing more than a foot above the ground. Farther into the forest we see another strangling Ficus—this one in the early stages. We are told that bird droppings deposit the Ficus seeds in the upper brances of the trees. The Ficus then grows roots that reach the ground. In the meantime, the Ficus is also growing upward toward the sun and spreading until it overtakes and kills the host.

Ifango points out an Antiaris toxicaria africana, a tree indigenous to Africa. When its bark is scratched, milky poison oozes out. This "ooze" is used on spear tips to kill animals and enemies. If someone has a cut on his or her hand and the milk touches the cut, that person will be dead in 15 minutes. He shows us a plant that, when ground up, will kill within minutes. Ifango says some people will grind up the leaves, put them in local brew and serve it to their enemies. When the person dies, gashes develop in their torso.

After our hour-and-a-half hike, we leave Ifango and head to the overlook, where we climb a nearby hill and sit, snacking on cookies and banana chips and cashews. As we soak up the hills and trees and sky, a man approaches from below, followed by a local woman.

"You guys been up there all day?" he asks.

Judging by his loose-fitting jeans and baseball cap, I guess that he's American. A third man follows in a dress shirt and khakis.

"I think that's my friend Sweetie," Diana tells us. We don't believe it, so we all give a laugh.

It turns out that the local woman is Sweetie, so she and her companions climb up to join us. They are Hong and Goofa, two men who work for the International Center of Insect Physiology and Ecology (ICIPE). Hong lives in Buffalo, NY (I was right about his American clothing!), where he works for the State University of New York (SUNY), though he's originally from China. Goofa lives in Kisumu. He is also affiliated with SUNY at Buffalo and originally from China. They are both entomologists studying malaria control in Kenya. We are happy to meet them, so we discuss mosquitoes and genetics, standing on this hill overlooking the magnificent Kenyan forest and mountains.

After 30 minutes of talking, they invite us to ride in their vehicle to the waterfall. Diana and I catch eyes and grin.

To get to the falls, we go past houses and children waving and yelling. We see the houses and farms coming right up to the forest's edge, evidence of continued slash and burn techniques used to clear the forest. The path becomes narrower until it's only wide enough for one person. We climb out and hike down. With the recent rains, the falls are gushing brown water. We take photos and enjoy the sights. As we head back to the vehicle, I wonder if it is too much to hope they're headed back to Kisumu and will allow us to ride along.

They are very kind and insist we join them, saying, "How often do you get seven people from five different countries together?" We head home in a cushioned seat. I relax into the comfort, relishing the space and the feel of a private vehicle. Even with all the creature comforts, driving in Kenya is tough; after an hour Goofa asks if we mind taking a break. We pull off the road and stretch, munching on crackers and cashews. We watch the big trucks climb the escarpment hill at five miles per hour, chugging out giant plumes of black diesel smoke. Children gather across the road to look at us. Soon, even more children and adults gather on our side of the road. We draw quite a crowd before getting into the car and driving on.

We pass the Yalla River, the site where ICIPE is running a malaria control test. Malaria is more prevalent in Western Kenya than in any other part of the country. Hong explains that within a three to four kilometer test area, they have sprayed every house and provided anti-malarial drugs to all children under five. Because children under five are most vulnerable to malaria—many of them die from the disease—they want to find the best preventive techniques. Only certain species of mosquitoes carry malaria;

of those species, only the female bites. The males seem to be born only to share their reproductive powers and then die. When their Yalla River test is complete, ICIPE will know better how to prevent malaria in other areas.

"Your U.S. tax dollars are supporting this project," Hong says, "you should be proud." For once, I am rather proud. Most people have only negative things to say about the States.

"Here's the Weeping Stone," says Hong. I grab my camera and turn it on, prepared to photograph the rock as we roll past. To my delight, Goofa pulls to the side of the road and stops. I snap the picture.

"Looks like your wish came true," Diana says. I smile at her smiling.

"Ed, have you seen a burgundy velvet coffin on your side?" I ask.

He says no.

"People shouldn't have coffins any other color than brown or white," Diana says, "most people in our culture believe dead bodies communicate."

As an example, she tells us that if a family is bringing a body back to their village from town and they have mechanical problems, they'll ask anyone in the vehicle if they've had disagreements with the deceased. If the deceased disliked any of them in any way, the person will be forced out of the vehicle.

"I've seen it," Diana asserts, "one time, we were driving from Nairobi with a body when the car broke down. After checking the engine and finding nothing, the uncle said, 'I know what's causing it,' and he went to the coffin, opened it, and slapped the corpse twice, telling him to give it up and move on to the next world. The car started and never had another problem."

We see the valley containing Kisumu and Lake Victoria. Goofa pulls over for photos, and then we cruise down the hill toward town, all of us relaxed and happy and comfortable, with no mechanical problems to speak of.

Tracy has a deal through the CDC in which she can have packages shipped over at very little cost. When we came over as volunteers, we were restricted to the airline's weight limit, which meant two large suitcases and a carry-on. CDC employees can pretty much ship anything and not worry about paying huge costs or having to go through the Kenyan postal service, which utilizes its right to examine the contents of every package, no matter how small, while you stand there and watch.

Of course, most employees of the CDC are doctors. Even though they may be from other parts of the world, they most likely made their way to Kenya through the Atlanta CDC. I feel a natural kinship with them, except of course for the differences in our salaries. And our access to shipments. And our access to Japanese cars shipped to Kenya duty-free (another deal struck by the U.S. government to benefit CDC employees). The more time I spend with Tracy, the more I realize how divergent our views of being in Africa are. She's here drawing a full salary as part of her career advancement. I'm here volunteering. She has a driver from her partner NGO. I have a bicycle. Tracy buys fantastic pieces of art and handmade wares and ships them home. I'll travel home with the same two large suitcases and backpack I came with; collecting goodies to take with me is out of the question and shipping them home would cost a fortune.

"Hey, would you like to go out with the girls tomorrow?" Tracy asks.

"Yes," I say, without asking who "the girls" are.

"We're meeting for drinks at the Kisumu Yacht club and then we'll go to dinner in town."

"Sounds good," I respond.

Tracy and I leave TICH after work and walk to her house, where she deposits her bag and we walk to the Yacht Club. It's not a long walk, even though it does sit directly on Lake Victoria's bay with hippos living nearby.

The Kisumu Yacht Club is a simple building with a bleached, white knee wall separating its expansive lawn from the parking lot. There are a couple of pavilions on the lawn in addition to a covered patio. We have a beer while waiting for the others. A family of Mennonites gathers at a large table on the lawn. The women wear their traditional plain, long dresses with white aprons and white pleated caps.

The kids are busy playing European football when one of them rushes for the wall at the lake's edge.

"Do they see a hippo?!" I ask.

We leap out of our chairs and make our way to view the darkening surface of the lake. Sure enough, there is a giant of a hippo headed ashore, only a hundred feet away. Then there are two. We watch the hippos and the lake as night descends on the sky and the wind makes silver ripples on the surface.

After a little more time, Mary, a CDC doctor, arrives. She seems to be in a hurry. One of the first things I notice about her is the tiny, tight ball that protrudes from her mid-section. She and her husband, another CDC doctor, are about five months pregnant.

"Will you have the baby here?" I ask as soon as it's polite.

"No," she says with a smile, "I'll go back to the U.S. before the due date."

Even though I don't know her very well, the information is a load off my mind.

We get into Mary's Range Rover, which seems perfectly natural to Mary and Tracy, but unnatural to me. We drive through the streets as if we own them. As if they're our streets and do not belong to the people making their way on foot just inches away. I wonder if they can see into the car. It feels privileged to be resting in leather seats, chatting about kids and work as though we're in Atlanta or Sacramento or Houston. I feel more kin to the Kenyans because my funds and resources are more restricted here than at home. I try not to judge Mary for her nice things. Why shouldn't a doctor who dedicates her life to research in an African country not live with the same quality she would at home?

We pull into her drive and wait for the guard to let us in. He's all smiles. The house is two stories and slightly Italianate, with a curved half-drive up to the front door. The yard is landscaped. Mary's husband is outside with their 2 year old, a blond boy who's learning to string words. Her husband is kind and quiet, an intellectual.

The CDC keeps several houses like this one for its doctors. They pay very little rent, comparatively, to live here. Two of Mary's female friends, Meghan and Sally, meet us. They are both wives of CDC doctors. The five of us pile into the car and drive to the Green Garden restaurant in town.

Judith, a German woman about 35 years old, runs the restaurant. She's married to a Kenyan. They have a new baby named Lulu, which means "Pearl" in Kiswahili. Our hostess lingers and we talk about her baby and about our children, though I say little since my children are grown. The conversation naturally turns to men: boyfriends and husbands. We don't really talk about the difficulties of living in Kenya. Maybe we're avoiding the topic, or maybe they don't find it difficult. They live in beautiful homes with high walls and guards and perfectly safe cars to get them around town. Compared to them, I'm rather exposed.

The CDC performs a multitude of studies on diseases here in Kenya. TICH does its fair share of research as well. We collect health data from our community partners, and Dr. Henry Oyugi and his team input the data into statistical applications. TICH staff members write reports and conduct research commissioned by other African governments to determine the health status of citizens. All of this data is shared almost instantly in the hope that governmental policies will change to promote and subsidize health programs.

One of the best things about TICH's work is that the research is being performed by Kenyans, compiled and interpreted by Kenyans and provided to anyone interested. It's called Action Research, because the idea behind collecting quantitative and qualitative data is to take immediate action on the findings: to improve nutrition for children, to stop the spread of HIV infection and to prevent malaria, especially in children under five years of age.

But we discuss very little about health issues during dinner. Instead, we talk about men and Valentine's Day and raising children.

After dinner, we plan to meet other CDC colleagues at Mary's house. We enter through the kitchen, which is huge and has a full-sized (meaning non-Kenyan) refrigerator sporting magnetized letters for their child. Liquor and whiskey bottles line the counter and there are several opened bottles of wine. Twenty-five people mingle, two of whom are black. I look down the hallway leading to bedrooms at the back and see a metal bar near the ceiling.

"What's that?" I ask Tracy.

"Oh," she says, "that's the gate to their safe house. If anyone tries to enter, the secured gate will make the back part of the house impenetrable. The windows are already barred."

The walls are smooth and the floors are hardwood. I haven't seen anything like this in Kenya, where the typical construction is concrete walls and floors—or marble floors for the Indians. It's constructed like homes in the United States. As we walk down the wide hallway and I see an open dining room opposite the high-ceilinged living room, it feels as if I'm in Dunwoody, an upscale area of Atlanta. The large living room has American-style furniture, unlike any furniture available in Kenya. A large tapestry rug covers the entire floor space, and a bookcase the length of one wall is stacked with hundreds of books and CDs. There's even a patio with sliding glass doors—these are the first sliding doors I've seen in Kenya.

Mwairu, the one black woman present, is from Atlanta. She was born and grew up in Nairobi, but she went to the United States after finishing school in Kenya. She's been in the United States for 16 years, attending college and getting her medical degree. The CDC sent her to Kisumu and put her into one of the large, fabulous homes they own. Even though she's from Kenya, she's mostly American and is having a hard time adapting. We talk for a while about the difficulties of adapting to Kisumu, because I've been depressed lately, feeling pressure from people on the streets who always want something. Mwairu feels pressure from Kenyans who think she should automatically feel at home or understand things because she's from Kenya.

I come to a conclusion while looking at Mary's house and listening to the conversations going on in different rooms: the CDC ensures that the lifestyles of their employees will not be altered just because they're living in Kenya. Some have their favorite cereals and crackers sent over. Others have toilet paper shipped. Meghan recently ordered a beer-making kit off the internet for her husband, and she basically paid $110 for what she said was a bucket and a tube. Another man, Francesco, has been keeping up with the doll series of Lucille Ball collectibles, which he buys annually for his partner.

Yet, there are six-square kilometers of slum area just blocks away.

The conversation eventually turns to health. One woman from Boston, with a sturdy build and loud voice, says, "No one in Milimani gets malaria." (Mary's home is in the Milimani area, where I also live with the Ruprahs.)

"My landlord's son has malaria," I say, remembering Raju staying in for the last few days.

"Well, either it's not malaria or he's been hanging around outside Milimani," she says confidently. She is insinuating what many people say about Indian males; they usually have girlfriends from the local community but they would never be seen in public with them and they certainly would never marry them.

The Boston woman and her husband offer to drive me and Tracy home, and we gladly accept. We drop Tracy off first and wait to make sure she gets inside the gate. I direct from the back seat, showing them where I live. It's less than a mile from Tracy's place. We pull into the driveway and the woman suddenly says, "Oh, this is the house where Ben lived. He was shot right there." She points inside the gate.

"What?!" I say and lean forward to hear her better. Samuel shows up in the headlights and unwraps the chain from the gate.

"Ben worked with the CDC and lived here with his wife," she begins the story, and "they came home one evening and when the guard opened the gate, several thugs were already inside the compound. When Ben saw their guns, he hit the gas and drove across the yard there and around the house. He made a complete circle and came back to the gate. The thugs shot at his car and a bullet went through the door and hit him in the leg. He crashed the car into the gate post. They wanted the car, but since it was wrecked, they ran away."

"I've never heard that story," I tell them, understanding why Mr. and Mrs. Ruprah wouldn't have mentioned it. But feeling lied to just the same.

I certainly hope my presence here doesn't attract thugs. If any harm came to Samuel just because I live here, I could never live with the guilt. Instantly, I want to be invisible, so no one sees me coming and going from the gate.

Walter organized a crew to break ground for laying the foundation of Pambazuko's building in the Nyalenda slums. He began digging last week while Tonny and I were busy with the TICH conference. We're finally beginning to return to business as usual at TICH, so Tonny and I walk over to the construction site and take a couple of pictures.

Children call out "mzungu!" as we approach. People stare and congregate to see the white lady in their neighborhood. Two men call drunkenly to me from across the stream, wanting their photo taken. Two older men, village elders, ask Tonny for money simply because he is walking with me. Tonny explains how our programs will benefit children and widows. The men are satisfied, allowing us to move on.

On our way back to TICH, we run into Walter, who is accompanied by a man pushing a cartload of bricks. Walter is organizing his members for the next step in the construction process: the laying of the cement foundation. The joy is evident on his face as we talk. His vision and dream are being realized, step by step. We all get a little silly and laugh when we discuss the building and the widows and the children.

Walter must hurry along, to catch up with the cart full of bricks and to organize the men for the construction party. He runs with a bounce.

The Ruprahs host a party in their backyard pavilion. Raju and Goldie, the newly-married couple from across the street, are the guests of honor. They bring along their extended family. In all, there are 20 of us. Mr. Ubi, nephew of Mrs. Ruprah, cooks chicken in a pot over a jiko, a coal-burning stove. As usual, the women sit on one end of the pavilion and the men on the other while the children alternate between groups. Raju sets up a radio, tunes it to an Indian station and we listen to top "Bollywood" hits, tunes made famous by Indian films of the last 20 years.

Raju prepares calf's liver expertly.

"Sandy!" calls Mr. Ruprah from the men's end of the pavilion, "how do you like the Indian liver?!"

He laughs at his little joke, "Indian liver," which makes me laugh, too. I say it's delicious.

"Sandy," he yells again, "have a beer. A cold Tusker." I refuse because I'm sitting with the ladies (who do not drink alcohol), but Mr. Ruprah gets up and brings me the big beer and a glass, which I self-consciously fill, hiding the remaining beer behind the chair leg.

The newlyweds somehow find each other from their respective gender groups and make their way onto the Ruprah's roof for a closer look at the moon. They're away for nearly 20 minutes and I imagine they're making out on the open, flat rooftop. At least I hope they're making out on the roof, after entering this arranged marriage. I hope they make out on roof-tops forever! Eventually though, several curious children clamber up the stairs. The newlyweds rejoin the larger group, Goldie with the ladies and Raju with the men.

"Sandy!" Mr. Ruprah calls, "have another beer."

"Oh, no," I protest, "that's just too much." But I really do want another beer.

"It's okay," Mrs. Ruprah says at my side, "you're at home. It's okay to have two."

So I have a second cold beer. I'm at home.

Angela and Jackie, 21-year-old student nurses from Canada, arrive at TICH on a six week attachment. They will work and study at TICH and the district hospital to gain a better understanding of health issues in developing countries. Ed, Jack Bryant and I take Angela and Jackie into town to show them around. We walk along a paved road and pass cows. Jackie says she's not sure she'll ever get used to seeing cows on city streets. Or turkeys. But despite the animals running loose, bad roads and strange language, Angela and Jackie seem to be acclimating well. At least at first.

After two days at the district hospital, they look shell-shocked. Emotionally void. Angela says she's seen more people die in two days than she's seen in three years in Canada. Two or three people occupy each bed and there are no sheets or pillows. A pregnant woman, 19 years old, walks a day and a half to reach the hospital. She is malnourished. Her husband arrives at the last minute, just before the baby is birthed, with supplies required by the hospital: IV tubes, dextrose, syringes, needles, catheter, razor blade (in case surgery is required) and other miscellaneous items. The husband is 40 years old. He drops the supplies and leaves. The baby is born with cracked lips, a sign of malnutrition. The mother is afraid to breastfeed, certain she has no milk. When Jackie rolls the mother's nipple, colostrum streams out. But the mother is still afraid to breastfeed. Jackie thinks the baby will not survive.

Another woman gives birth to twins. Both are extremely underweight. One dies immediately, and the other is jaundiced. The district hospital has no treatment for jaundice. Jackie thinks the baby will die anyway simply because it is too tiny and malnourished. Angela has been working in the children's ward, which holds twice as many patients as it can handle. Children are sick with malaria, pneumonia, diarrhea, and AIDS.

They work for a government-run hospital. Here, many Kenyans blame the nurses and doctors for negligence, believing that the staff is there just to make money and not to care for the people. Some of these fears are founded; corruption exists in many hospitals. Equipment and drugs are stolen and sold. One doctor was recently found taking government drugs to his private practice. When people would show up at the government hospital, he'd tell them he had to leave but they could see him at his private clinic, where he would sell them the drugs at an increased price.

Corruption is a way of life for Kenyans, who are used to paying for services that should be free. It's engrained in the culture, and even has a name: T.K.K., Tai Kitu Kidogo, "Give Something Small." It's hard to imagine what would happen in the United States or another Western culture if children were crowded onto dirty hospital beds or forced to sleep on the floor, where they often die from lack of resources. The outrage would be swift, long-lasting and severe. Here, it's just the way things are, just another day.

Angela and Jackie say they'll take me to the district hospital one day. I tell them I'll take them to Nyalenda, to the slums, so they can meet the widows and orphans they've been hearing so much about.

It's a rather pitiable exchange.

I visit the Pambazuko building being constructed in the heart of the Nyalenda slum area. Walter is busy directing the crew in mixing cement and pouring the foundation with the help of a professional contractor, William, who is donating his time. Caroline and Karen, two women who are active with Pambazuko, prepare meals for the workers and bring water to the site for mixing cement.

The main water source for Nyalenda flows next to the building. Right now, it is clogged with plastic bags and other trash. I tell Walter we must clean the stream from Ring Road to Pambazuko's building and perhaps beyond; maybe all the way to the river. We will teach the community children to clean the area.

The elderly woman at the back of the slums, the one who owns a large plot of land next to the river, has agreed to allow Pambazuko to construct a water collection site on her land. It is here that water will be purified and made available to the residents of Nyalenda. Right now, hogs wallow in the water, pit latrines leak into the stream and it is constantly contaminated by people stepping in its flow after they've visited the bathroom. People simply bend down with a plastic Kimbo container and collect the water they'll use to cook and bathe with, even though a hog wallows a few yards upstream. We're still working out how to ensure residents take ownership of the purified water source and help keep the area clean. The elderly woman is also allowing Pambazuko to plant a garden on her land. This will give widows and children space to grow their own food for eating and selling.

A man who lives next to the construction site sits with the workers as they eat lunch. He's drunk and irritated, trying to provoke them, somehow angry that we are putting up a building. Walter talks with the man and invites him to be in some photos. The man lifts a shovel of mortar and throws it in the wood frame, smiling hugely at the camera all the while. He is now on our side.

I walk to town along Ring Road—the beginning of the slums—and two very small boys come up to me. They're probably four and five years old. They call me "mzungu" and want to shake my hand. The smallest one reaches out with both his arms, waiting for me to pick him up (which I promptly do). In the United States, picking up a child is practically taboo without the parent's permission. Here, I have a child with no obvious guardian other than his little friend, and I am able to simply pick him up and put him on my hip.

He giggles and laughs and I pretend I'll carry him home with me. I put him down and he continues laughing. He falls onto his friend saying, "Mzungu picked me up," very excitedly. My instinct since arriving in Kenya has been to hug every child I've seen. Usually I daren't hug them; I just gladly shake their slim, tiny hands when they offer.

Chapter Nine

Coast

*O*ur bus leaves Kisumu at 9:00am, heading over the escarpment and across the Great Rift Valley into crowded, muddy, hectic Nairobi, the first leg on our trip to Kenya's coast. It is a journey of about six hours to Nairobi. Luckily, the bus station is 200 meters from the train station (although it still takes great skill to navigate the people, matatus and mud puddles). Kenya has received a good bit of rain over the last month. I have to pull up my pants legs to walk, thankful my Chaco sandals are waterproof and practically indestructible.

Everything at Nairobi's train station is a throwback to colonial times, including the uniforms worn by personnel. Ed and I park our baggage in the train station.

We sit and watch the crowd get on the 5:30pm train to Kisumu. Most are traveling third class; they cram into the cars, standing on the outside stairs and holding the exterior handles. Once they pull away, our train arrives. We find our first class cabin and explore its full eight-by-seven-foot interior, which includes a sink with a cover, a water dispenser that does not work, a mirror and a tiny closet with hooks for clothes. Restrooms are at either end of the car; even then, there is no toilet to sit on, just a hole in the floor. Urinating into a pit on a moving train is a true test of balance and stamina, and it never fails to make me laugh out loud when managed successfully. Luckily, the bathroom is right around the corner from our cabin.

The dining car is just ahead of us and offers a nice, open space to sit and watch the landscape go by. It looks like a 50s diner with overhead oscillating fans and Formica table tops.

The train leaves the station as night falls. Ed brought the book *Stupid White Men* by Michael Moore to pass along to Julia in Lamu. I read the book until bed time. Ed takes the top bunk, so I spread a sheet on the lower bunk and nestle into my pillow, which I brought from home. We paid 1,885 shillings (about US $23) for this train trip, which doesn't include food or bedding. When the porter walks through the cars with a chime, ringing out the dinner tune, we ignore it.

The train stops regularly to pick up passengers and cargo, which is why it takes 14 hours to get to Mombasa by train and only eight hours by bus. This is my first overnight train trip, and I'm enchanted with the side-to-side swaying. It's a wonderful sensation, lulling to the beat of the clanks all night long.

I awake in the night and am compelled to look out of the window, as though there's something fantastical waiting. I very quietly lift the leather screen and see mountains lit by the moon. No towns, no houses—just land and mountains. I go to the restroom and practice my balancing skills before stepping into the dining car. Someone left a window open, so the cool air flows in along with night sounds and the rolling of the wheels. I sit in a diner booth and look to the south for a while, then to the north. A porter comes through the car and, although he is startled to see me, is very courteous.

"Ni saa ngapi?" I ask him.

"4:30."

Not much later, we pull into a station where civilian men gather in a circle with uniformed trainmen, their heads close together. There is only minimal light, but I see several women walking across the platform with packages on their heads and babies tied to their backs, taking their goods to market. We pull away from the station and I stand to leave the dining car. The cool air moving through the open windows captures me. It feels fresh and significant, bringing Africa's precious aspects to me in these early morning hours when all but the crew are sleeping. The rocking bunk calls, however, and I return to slumber, waking each time the train brakes into a new station.

When morning arrives, we're still an hour outside of Mombasa. The scenery is similar to other parts of Kenya, especially the mud and cardboard houses built close together and the children running along the track, waving and asking for money. Nearing Mombasa, the industrial buildings increase; although it's an ugly part of capitalism, the huge buildings and earth-moving equipment speak to me. We don't see many of these things back in Kisumu. Rain drizzles as we glide into the station. Then it pours.

Tom, a fellow VSO volunteer, meets us. We wait under a shelter until the rain eases before taking a matatu to a nearby store owned by Tom's friend. The owner graciously allows us to store our luggage in the back while we explore Mombasa. When we drink Arabian coffee and eat bahjia (Indian fried potatoes), Tom tells us about a ship docked in the harbor, something of a traveling bookstore, selling new books at greatly reduced prices.

"Books?!" I exclaim.

Yes, I'm assured. Books.

We head to the harbor before we go to Fort Jesus, Mombasa's most famous landmark.

Doulos, which means "servant" in Greek, is an old passenger ship sponsored by a German organization. Built in 1914, the Doulos is now the oldest active ocean-going passenger ship in the world (she's even in the Guinness Book of Records). What makes her story even more remarkable is her benevolent mission. Run by a Christian organization, the Doulos travels the world, docking in port cities for two or three weeks and inviting the populace aboard. The store is manned by 300 volunteers from all over the world who sign on for two-year missions.

The ship carries discounted books on history, philosophy, art, architecture, gardening, hobbies and cooking. And lots of music. The floors are dark wood, and fans keep us cool as we browse. I look at tables laden with journals, pens, note cards and games. I am in heaven. In Kenya, books are printed on low-grade paper and cost far too much. To stand before shelves of gorgeous books—printed in full color and on quality paper—moves me immensely. I buy three books on different subjects: architecture, Impressionism and modern art.

We exit the ship and head to Fort Jesus, a fortification built by the Portuguese between 1593 and 1596. Nearly a hundred years before the fort was built, Vasco da Gama sailed to Malindi, north of Mombasa, where he received a warm reception. There he set up a base. From this base, the Portuguese attacked and burned Mombasa four times before the town finally gave in. After a hundred years of occupation, Mombasa was overtaken by the Arabs of Oman; Mombasa's Arab influence is still quite evident. The Imperial British East Africa Company took over administration of Mombasa in the late 1800s. They abolished the slave trade, which reversed Mombasa's steady growth and ended a period of great prosperity.

Although early history of the East African coast is centered around trading towns that date back to the second century AD, records do not mention Mombasa by name until 1154, when Al Idrisi, the Arab geographer at the court of Roger II of Sicily, notes the city's existence. Early settlers along the coast were controlled by the Swahili, or "Moors," as they were then called. As Mombasa became more prosperous, inhabitants traded spices, gold, ivory and iron for cotton cloth and jute from India as well as ceramics from Persia and China.

Fort Jesus is remarkable. It sits on Mombasa Island by Old Harbor, overlooking the entrance to the old port. The buildings are a mosaic of walkways and steep steps made of aged stone, its walls often covered with a reddish compound that spreads light and dark over their surfaces. Cannons sit throughout and porticos allow a view of the Indian Ocean.

Old Town Mombasa, next to Fort Jesus, offers sights influenced by Arabia, India and Britain. Arabian and African ways mesh in the Swahili-style houses found along the coast. They have flat roofs topped with thatch or tin, long, narrow rooms and beautifully carved wooden doors. The doors are my favorite. They're found in Mombasa, Lamu (up the Kenyan coast) and Zanzibar in Tanzania, dating back to Arabic coastal settlements of the early middle ages. In the late nineteenth century, teak imported from India and Burma was the popular choice for carving doors; the buildings of that period frequently have a round-headed door with spokes, much like a fanlight.

The Swahili culture is also evident in the baraza, which are couch-like stone seats built just outside the front door. They are built to allow the man of the house to accept visitors without the women being seen. In some areas, a man will knock at the top of the door and a woman at the bottom, allowing the inhabitants to always know which sex is calling. Women inside can remove themselves if a man is knocking.

Mombasa is also home to people from the Indian subcontinent, who contributed to the architecture. Kiswahili and English are the official languages, but we also hear Arabic and many Indian dialects. In fact, at its root, Kiswahili is a mixture of Arabic and Bantu languages spoken by indigenous peoples of East Africa.

After exploring the fort and Old Town, we visit Tom's workplace; Bombolulu Workshop employs physically challenged people who make jewelry, clothing, shoes and bags. Most of the 100 people living and working at the workshop have disabilities from polio or malaria. Tom's job is to help Bombolulu Workshop market its goods, which are sold wholesale to companies worldwide. One fair trade retailer, Ten Thousand Villages (www.tenthousandvillages.com), sells Bombolulu goods in their stores and online. Tom has also made arrangements with local hotels encouraging them to bring their clients to Bombolulu for a tour. When we arrive, three white people are in the cultural center dancing to drum beats with Africans in traditional dress. We soon learn the guests are from Asheville, North Carolina. The couple is visiting their daughter, Susan, a doctor who is conducting AIDS and tuberculosis research in Mombasa.

Ed and I take the official tour of Bombolulu Workshop, guided by Chris, who's from Kisumu. We are greatly impressed with the grounds, workshop, artisans and gift shop. We're amazed to find they've created life-sized replica homes from seven Kenyan tribes. Each home is made from mud, thatch, stone or coral rag. In addition to a Swahili house, they've constructed homes in the Luo and Luhya style, which dot the area where we live. Touring Bombolulu Workshop is worth the trip to the coast.

In the evening, Tom, Ed and I meet Wendy, another VSO volunteer from the UK, at Bob's, a local restaurant. After we eat, we head to Il Covo, a club on the beach. An Indian family has rented the bar for the night, so we sink into Swahili couches (giant chairs with huge, soft cushions) on a terrace overlooking the beach, drinking wine. The moon skates across the water toward us. We laugh about the cheesy dance music coming from the party and talk about life as volunteers in Kenya. Tom and Wendy are leaving in September when their terms end. Both are going back to the UK.

It's late and I'm tired, but Wendy insists on stopping by the Causarina bar on the way home. Ed is crashing at Tom's, so it's just me and Wendy in the matatu. She promises we'll only stay five minutes and we won't get beers—she just wants me to see the place. It's an open air bar sitting only a few yards off the two-lane highway, enclosed in woven walls with a thatched roof and a wooden dance floor. In the center of the floor is a pole, and from the pole are suspended six young men who are part of an acrobatic team performing for the crowd. The music is pumping and they do amazing things: hard-to-watch things. Wendy orders a beer, a 500 ml, and I calculate how long it will take her to finish.

Wendy seems energized by the scene, but as I look around the crowd, I notice a number of old white men talking with young black girls. Sometimes they're seated together, and sometimes the old white man is on a bar stool taking liberties with a series of young women as they pass by.

To kill time, I go the bathroom, but I can't find Wendy afterward. The crowd is young, except for the old, weathered white people. A tall man steps behind me and slowly runs his fingers down my bare arm. His friend looks on as the guy says, "Are you having a good time?"

"No," I say like an unhappy child and walk away, looking for Wendy. She eventually appears with a Maasai friend. As they talk, I scan the crowd and find an older white couple sitting with a young black couple. The woman, bottle-blond with too much sun on her skin, is leaning into the young, black man, their shoulders resting against each other. Across from her sits the white man, who's nestled into the young black woman. I've heard about the tourism sex trade on the coast, but to see it is disgusting. I simply cannot understand the mindset of someone from a "rich" country coming to a developing country and preying on the vulnerable.

The evening finally draws to a close. We walk to Wendy's apartment two blocks behind the Causarina. The rains have flooded the street and created giant puddles the width of the road. It's nearly 1:00am and not at all a good idea to walk, though Wendy seems to feel safe in her neighborhood. A car rolls slowly by us and the passenger calls out to us. We ignore him as we dodge water puddles and hope they'll keep rolling away. I'm relieved when they leave us alone. I cannot breathe deeply until we're within the guarded gates of her compound. When we get there, the guard is sleeping. Wendy admonishes him for falling asleep, but it still takes a few minutes for us to get in and up the five floors to her door, which is covered with a metal grill. When we're inside and the grill is once again bolted, I finally relax. Somewhat.

Ed and I leave Mombasa and take a matatu to Watamu, a tiny hamlet on the coast. Known for its three lagoons, Watamu is far from the maddening crowd and is casual (except for a very nice resort, Turtle Bay, which is out of our price range). Since it is low season, few tourists are about; men selling their fish, handmade sandals, boat rides or guide services have an extremely limited audience. Upon arrival, Ed and I hop out of the matatu and decide the first thing to do is check out hotels to see what rate we can get. The first place we visit, Marijani, agrees to the price we offer: 800 shillings per night, including breakfast. We settle in. After three days of travel and sightseeing in Mombasa, I'm ready to kick back on the overstuffed Swahili sofa and simply read. It's wonderful.

Later in the day, Ed and I walk over to the lagoons, followed by herds of goats that ramble about the village by day and return to their masters in the evening. The lagoons are gorgeous. They have coral islets mushrooming from the surf, and when the tide goes out, we walk right up to one of the massive coral "islands" and examine its miniature wildlife.

Our next stop is Malindi. With its tall buildings, loud calls to prayer, men pushing their services (of all kind) and constant matatu traffic, Malindi is a typical coastal town. Paul, a fellow VSO volunteer who lives in Malindi, is back in his native New Zealand for a short while. Fortunately for us, Paul's wife, Nina, graciously allows Ed and me to stay with her. Nina and Paul's apartment has three bedrooms and a guest bath.

The muezzin begins the day's first call to prayer at 4:30am. It's very loud, because the mosque is on the next block. Although it's our first day in Malindi, Jan, Nina's best friend, calls to tell us they're cooking dinner for us at the African Pearl.

"Who's Jan?" I ask.

Nina is originally from Canada, and Jan was her best friend back home. Jan came to visit Nina and Paul last February. While visiting, Jan met Jeff, the owner of the African Pearl. (Jeff is the only Kenyan who owns and operates a hotel on the coast.) Jan met Jeff on the fifth day of her three week vacation. When she left Kenya, Jan shut down her Canadian life and returned to Jeff and the African Pearl.

Malindi has very few boda bodas. Instead, most people get around in tuk-tuks, which are motorized, three-wheeled cars built to hold three passengers comfortably. Slightly more expensive than boda bodas, but still less than taxis, tuk-tuks are seen all over town. They appear to be safe. We take a tuk-tuk to the African Pearl, a neat and active hotel near the beach. Next to the pool is a huge thatched pavilion with a bar, an L-shaped pool table and lots of comfy Swahili-style seating for socializing. Tonight, Jeff is cooking stewed chicken with chappatti. We sit under the pavilion, listening to easy rock music, drinking cold beer and discussing Kenyan politics. The stewed chicken doesn't last long. Even though it's sprinkling, we decide to walk back to Nina's. Tomorrow is Madaraka Day; a national holiday celebrating the 1960 granting of self-government. People are out partying on a weeknight and we figure there is safety in numbers.

On Kenya's Madaraka Day, we go to the beach. A tuk-tuk drops us on a white sand beach sprinkled with a few Europeans and locals who offer to take us snorkeling in the coral reefs. We decline, opting instead to walk a mile down the beach, seeking shade. I spend my afternoon in the surf and on the sand, reading Dervla Murphy's *Full Tilt: Dunkirk to Delhi by Bicycle*. With an occasional look out over the Indian Ocean, I absorb Dervla's travel tales. She rode her bicycle from Ireland to Delhi in the winter of 1963. Alone. At the age of 31.

Here I am on the coast of Africa, having traveled safely by bus and train and matatu, reading about a woman who braved extreme cold and heat to peddle across Europe, into Persia and Afghanistan and Pakistan. She saw the giant Buddha statues in Afghanistan, which were later destroyed by the Taliban. Statues that no one will ever get to see again, except in photos. Dervla writes that on her 10th birthday, she received a bicycle and a map. Dreaming over the map, she had the idea to take the tremendous trip to India. Throughout her life, Dervla never told anyone, afraid that sharing her vision might diminish its power. Twenty-one years later, she made the trip on a bicycle named "Roz" with a .25 caliber gun in her hip pocket. It didn't take long on her trip before she had to use the gun!

On our way to Lamu, Ed and I take a detour to the Gedi ruins. Hopping from the matatu, we walk down a dirt road and pass wooden stalls where women sell fruits and haircuts. In the middle of the road, a dirty young man, obviously mentally imbalanced, seems to sing while crying and shuffling his feet. The ladies working the stalls on either side ignore him. As we near the gate to the Gedi ruins, a white vehicle pulls in front of us. Inside it, three Italians look up one road and down the other, informing us they're searching for mushrooms that have blossomed with the recent rains. They laugh good-naturedly when we pass them again near the ruins.

I opt for a guide to show us around the ruins of this Swahili town. Without him, we're simply looking at crumbling walls. Founded sometime in the late 13th or early 14th century and occupied until the 17th century, Gedi has been well-excavated and preserved. The site was undisturbed until the 1920s, when it was overtaken by the surrounding forests. It was named a national monument in the late 1940s. James Kirkman excavated the site over a 10-year period in the mid-1900s. Historians speculate about the reasons for the city's abandonment; theories range from invasions by inland cannibalistic tribes to the influx of Somalians or even Portuguese.

It's also possible the water supply simply gave out. Kalama, our guide and a student on a two-month attachment from Tsavo University, has conducted a study on the well system at Gedi. He's determined the settlers built too many wells, draining the water table and driving the people away. Gedi residents did use a lot of water; because cleanliness is an essential element of Muslim culture, they dug huge wells outside each mosque and smaller wells at most of the homes.

Kalama tells us about an archaeologist who is currently unearthing the Mosque of the Outer Wall, even though it appears very little excavation has been completed. Leaves cover the site and everything is still at ground level. Overall, very little digging and documentation have been done along the coast, making this area ripe for exploration. Although establishing digging sites will help preserve the coast's history, preservation efforts seem to be too few and haphazardly undertaken: another victim of Kenya's poverty.

Built of rocks and stones, Gedi buildings often show remains of porcelain shards, inset into walls and wells in the traditional Swahili fashion, but also from use in everyday life. Porcelain from China is used to date the city. Gedi, sometimes called Gede, is a Galla word meaning "precious." (The Galla were nomadic people from Somalia; they are thought to have advanced south and overtaken Gedi and other coastal towns.) All the buildings in Gedi are one story, distinguishing it as a country town when compared to Lamu, Malindi and Mombasa. Originally, the roofs were made of lime concrete, as were the floors, which were also sometimes ballasted with coral chips. As a decorative touch, cut coral blocks, sometimes cut from the fine-grained live sea coral, were used to edge doorways and steps.

If anyone has an inclination to study archeology, he or she should hasten to the coast of Kenya to study the cultures buried around Watamu, Gedi, the Tana River and the Lamu archipelago. The Lamu archipelago boasts another 16th century Swahili town that was mysteriously abandoned, the Takwa ruins on Manda Island (just across from Lamu).

Gedi's main mosque has a large holding container near its entrance. Muslims must clean their faces, hands and feet before entering any mosque, and this one was no exception.

Inside the mosque, the mihrab is built into the north wall. We can tell it was once decorated with inlaid porcelain bowls. The mihrab has built-in acoustic qualities allowing ceremonial words projected into this niche to bounce back into the mosque. Men kneeling in the back could hear clearly. To the right of the mihrab is a minbar, or pulpit, composed of three steps. Kalama stands on the top step to demonstrate how the service was offici-ated. Women have their own section of the temple, a narrow room just outside the main gallery.

The palace, the supposed home of the ruler of Gedi, also served as the municipal center of town. Measuring more than 45 acres in all, the entire town was at one time enclosed in a nine-foot wall. The currently excavated portion of Gedi, including the palace and 14 large homes, makes up the more prosperous area; it was enclosed in an inner wall. This prosperous part of town faces north, toward Mecca. The poorer houses, usually built of mug and wattle, were located outside the inner wall on the south side of town.

Archaeologists named the houses for the items found in them while dig-ging: there is the House of the Scissors, House of the Porcelain Bowl, House of the Cistern, House of the Venetian Bead and House of the Iron Lamp. These finds, especially the porcelain bowls, indicate residents traded with people coming from Arabia, India and China. Luckily, many of the items are preserved in Gedi's on-site museum and in the museum at Fort Jesus in Mombasa. Despite Gedi's evidence of trade with other seafaring cultures, there is no written record—in either Arabic or Swahili—mentioning the town. Some feel it was hidden so deeply in the forest and away from the coast that even the Portuguese, who ruled for more than a hundred years, never knew of Gedi's existence.

Walking through the excavated town is extremely peaceful. Massive Baobab trees provide shade in the coastal heat and humidity. (Spongy pulp from the giant Baobab fruit is mixed with sugar and red food coloring to make "African Candy.") A tomb at the northern entrance of town is inscribed with the Arabic date of AH 802, which corresponds to 1399 AD on the Christian calendar. Several tombs on site have been excavated, revealing corpses, but Muslim law prohibits carbon dating tests. Luckily, this dated tomb helps fix the time of Gedi without going against anyone's wishes.

Our bus leaves for Lamu from Malindi at 9:00am. Ed and I take Takwala, a bus line owned by Muslims, because they are the least molested by bandits. About 45 minutes into our trip, the bus stops and takes on a soldier, complete with camouflage outfit, army boots and a rifle. VSO, taking a cue from the British High Commission's safety reports, has declared the Malindi to Lamu overland route a "no-go zone" for volunteers. The latest VSO newsletter says:

> For security reasons, and also because of the condition of the roads, visitors to Lamu Island are strongly advised to travel by air. Buses and other vehicles on the road to Lamu have been attacked by armed robbers and must travel in convoy on the Malindi-Garsen-Lamu section. Cattle rustling and banditry can affect rural areas, especially the more remote parts not normally frequented by tourists.

I rationalize the trip. Air travel is costly, and people travel this route all the time. I can't help but feel the chances the bandits will choose our bus to rob are fairly slim. Ed has taken this trip before, so maybe his confidence makes me feel it is a safe decision. Once the guard comes aboard, we drive another 15 minutes before turning off the paved highway onto a dirt road. We remain on dirt all the way to the island, but the driver doesn't let up. He keeps rolling over the rutted road at 80 kilometers per hour, probably to discourage any bandits from stopping us. Every 40 minutes or so, we pull into a hamlet and take on a new soldier, the old one alighting. We pass several police checkpoints, where they inspect our baggage holds and let us move on.

The scenery is absolutely amazing. It seems deserted, though there are numerous tribes living out in the bush. Between the incredibly tall pines that divide and branch out at great heights, and the low grassy swamp, it reminds me of the Florida Everglades, only prettier. The sun kisses occasional water surfaces amongst the grasses and trees and winks at us from the roadside. No wonder this route is susceptible to bandits. It's totally isolated.

At a clearing near a bridge, a group of men stand under a tree. This isn't a town or a hamlet, but we stop anyway. The men move toward the bus. One young man rides a wheelchair with three wheels; it is self-propelled using hand pedals. When the man looks up, I say "Jambo," and he replies in kind. The soldier alights and stands next to the bus, beside the wheelchair. He places his rifle on its butt and I worry that the barrel is pointed under his chin. He's rather stocky and kind looking. I sit sideways to see everything that is going on. I especially want to make sure they don't take my luggage off the bus. Our conductor jumps off and climbs to the bus roof, where he tosses down a foam mattress.

Back on the ground, the conductor opens the luggage compartment and pulls out a box tied with string as well as two big bags. He also pulls out my red backpack and a suitcase. He replaces the suitcase but not my backpack. The soldier follows the conductor back onto the bus. The engine revs and we start to move. I feel a rising surge of panic, as my backpack is still on the ground at the feet of the men. When we've picked up speed and it's clear we are moving out, I shout out to the conductor, not caring that I'm disturbing everyone, "There's luggage back there!"

"Where?" he asks.

"Back there where you dropped the stuff off!"

The driver slows, and the conductor jumps off and trots back. I check to see if Ed is okay because I don't want to embarrass him with my loud voice. He's turned and peering through the window at the conductor, as are most other passengers.

"That red backpack is mine," I call to the conductor through the window.

By now, we've traveled about 200 feet, so it takes a little time for him to get back to the clearing. One of the men picks up the backpack and hands it to the conductor. I watch as he replaces it under the bus and secures the door.

My camera and money are in that backpack. I make a mental note to never put anything but clothes into the cargo hold of a bus from now on. Ed and I look at each other without saying anything, but it's clear we're both relieved, but cautious.

After three and a half hours, we pull up to a docking area where the ferry to Lamu is moored. It's hectic and crazy as various men lunge for luggage, hoping to snag a tip. We crowd onto a motorized wooden dhow and cruise for 25 minutes to the Lamu dock. Rounding the bend, Lamu rises up at the water's edge, which is framed with old, white buildings. Above them are layers of buildings with thatched roofs and flat roofs and some roofs made of tin. The land rises away from the water and the town, making Lamu look like an ancient and dilapidated Monaco. There's something beautiful about layers of white ancient buildings.

Julia and Joseph wait for us on the pier. They immediately take us to Hapa Hapa, a restaurant on the waterfront where Joseph works. Julia is a VSO volunteer working on water and waste management for the town of Lamu. With all the old houses and buildings constructed so closely together, the "roads" are three to six feet wide, and water is carried away from the homes in narrow drains. Mingled with donkey droppings, the water becomes a health issue. Julia has been here nearly two years and has extended her work with VSO and Lamu for another year. Joseph grew up in Lamu; he and Julia plan to marry.

After settling in at our hotel, the Yumbe House, Ed and I meet Julia at Hapa Hapa for dinner. We're talking about VSO when a voice asks us, "Would you like to take a dhow ride tomorrow to see the Twapa ruins?"

The voice belongs to Baba J. A participant in the local tourist business, he walks the small town of Lamu offering visitors dhow rides and tours of local sights. So far, he has booked a single female client for tomorrow's tour and would like to increase the party.

"Yes," we say, and agree to meet him at Hapa Hapa at 9:00am.

We meet Baba J. and follow him to a medium-sized dhow manned by Hasan and Jamal, two slim 23 year olds. They will be our captains for the tour while Baba J. goes back to stir up more tourists for tomorrow's excursion. I hear a female voice and turn to see a large and beautiful smile. I know immediately she's American. Her name is Anita, and she is our boatmate for the day. Anita lives in Washington, D.C., but she's taking a vacation from work to travel through Africa for two months. Lamu is her first stop. After this, she's going to climb Kilimanjaro.

Anita is energetic and funny and extremely warm. Her family is originally from India, though her father now lives in Cairo and her mother lives in Philadelphia. We have a great time talking together, even with Hasan and Jamal periodically telling us to move to the opposite side of the boat. When they do, we climb under the sail, avoiding aged ropes and swinging boards. As Anita talks about her travels, I tell her about the woman who rode her bicycle from Ireland to India.

"Dervla Murphy!" Anita yells before I can complete the sentence.

"Yes," I laugh, pleased she knows the author.

"My father would marry Dervla Murphy if he knew where to find her. He's read all her books," Anita says.

"She must be 73 years old now," I say, "if she's still living."

"Oh, I think she's still living," Anita reassures me. Anita has read several of her books. I carefully climb over the boat boards to pull the book out of my bag and Anita yells with delight. She says most of Dervla's books are out of print and hard to find. I tuck the book back into the bag to keep it safe from sand and moisture. I've been reading it slowly, even re-reading some sections, to keep myself from finishing the book before the end of this trip.

Hasan and Jamal serpentine the boat across the channel, directing us on the way toward the Indian Ocean. But we're not going into the ocean; we'll cross the channel and sail up a narrow passage, lined with mangroves, to reach the Twapa ruins.

The sail is full and we're clipping along at a breeze-stirred pace. It's very relaxing. Jamal is seated at the back, his right arm casually resting on the rudder. He holds up a fat joint and asks if we mind if he smokes a little weed. We laugh and say no. Marijuana, or bangi, is illegal in Kenya, though it is legal in Tanzania. Just when he has a great mellow buzz going, our dhow collides with some mangroves, which become tangled in the back poles holding up our canvas cover. We all grab mangrove branches, pushing and pulling, trying to get away from their grip. After quite a struggle, we're free, and there is no lasting damage to the dhow.

Hasan announces it's time to fish for lunch. They pull out blocks of wood with fishing line attached. A weight is wrapped about 12 inches from the hook. They thread tiny prawn on our hooks and show us how to toss the lines. I was expecting a rod and reel. Or perhaps a cane pole like my Granny used.

We float and snag seaweed while the fish eat the bait off our hooks. Hasan pulls in three fish. Jamal pulls in two. The idea is to jerk the string when the fish tugs at the bait. So I wait, holding the line ever-so-lightly between my thumb and forefinger. When that tug finally comes, I pull back, jerking my wrist. The tension holds. I'm really excited at the thought of catching this fish. As I roll the line onto the wooden block, I see the form of the fish surfacing. It's a white snapper, about ten inches long. Anita pulls one in, too, so we tighten down the boat to move up the stream toward the ruins.

Ed, Anita and I tour the ruins with our guide, Mohammad, who works for the national park service. Meanwhile, Jamal and Hasan build a fire on the beach and cook our fish. They also toast bread and make a wonderful salad from shredded cabbage, tomatoes and onions.

We walk around the old Twapa houses, examine the city wall and listen to the surf of the Indian Ocean. When we walk to the beach, we see a goat herder and his goats on the white sand. My mind immediately envisions him as a Robinson Crusoe on an untouched and unspoiled beach (except, of course, for goat droppings). We look at a tomb and, because she knows a little Arabic, Anita reads the date. Mohammad tells us people still travel to Twapa to worship at this tomb.

Speculation about its abandonment says Twapa was invaded by a tribe from Pate Island, which is nearby and part of the archipelagos. When the people fled Twapa, they went over to Lamu Island, which is only a 30-minute sail away, and started the Shela village. Shela, the most developed part of this area, shares the island with Lamu town. Shela hosts the homes of several famous Europeans, including Princess Caroline of Monaco. Vidal Sassoon's house is currently under construction. Shela is extremely remote and makes the perfect getaway for celebrities who want to avoid the media.

Shela also has the only beach on Lamu Island; its sand dunes are gorgeous and high, protected from development by the ministry. (Although the minister is building a home for himself on the dunes. His house is going up next to the strangest sight in Shela, a "castle" built by an Italian. It's rather ugly and makes no sense with its tiny windows facing such a fantastic view of the Indian Ocean.)

After Anita plays Mohammad in a game of checkers, using metal bottle caps as game pieces, we climb aboard our trusty dhow and eat our freshly grilled fish. We're headed to Manda Island, across from Lamu, where the Manda Beach Resort draws in Europeans tourists. As we approach, I can see three white men on the beach, one who appears to be in his 40s, completely unselfconscious in his Speedos.

We pull up in our unpainted dhow and climb out, wading toward the beach we will soon have to ourselves. If it were high season, the place would be packed and we'd be prohibited from setting foot on this exclusive property. As it is, we're practically the only people around. While Anita takes two shots of sugar cane liquor at the bar, I drink a Coke and Jamal joins a group of men who puff bangi from a pipe.

We walk into the blue waters of the channel and race, swimming against the tide carrying us down the beach. Hasan, Jamal and their friend are on the shore doing push-ups, after which they practice a stylized form of karate. The next time I look, they're performing acrobatics on the beach: handsprings and back flips. Then they're in the water, racing each other. Ed, Anita and I can only laugh. We cannot fathom where they get the energy after manning a sailboat and smoking weed.

We board the boat and head toward Lamu. It's nearing 5:30pm. Jamal and Hasan begin singing, "Take me home, country road, to the place I belong." When they get to the part where they're supposed to sing, "West Virginia, Mountain Mama," they switch the lyrics to, "West Lamu, Ocean Mama." We laugh out loud. They want me to sing it, the original way; and I do, loudly. We sing a little Beatles and the men sing songs in Italian that they learned from tourists, playing water jugs as drums all the while.

We disembark and give hard-earned tips to Jamal and Hasan, saying goodbye.

"Do you think Ali Hippy has room for us at dinner tonight?" I ask Anita.

"Let's go find out," she says and we walk toward the Sun Sail Hotel.

Anita, Ed and I run into Ali Hippy on the steps of the bus station. He's about five foot-two inches with a belly rounder than Santa's. He wears a kukoi wrap around his waist and a Western-style dress shirt. Ali has a funny accent—slightly British—even though he's local. He's rather famous and is mentioned in all the guide books. Ali Hippy walks around town inviting tourists to his house for dinner. He usually charges 500 shillings.

Ali is rather distracted as we try to talk to him.

"Do you have room for us this evening?" Anita asks.

"Yes," he says.

"How much?" Anita asks.

Ali Hippy and Anita get into some real down-and-dirty negotiations. I'm impressed with Anita's skills, learned from shopping in the Cairo bazaars. She gets Ali down to 400 shillings for each of us. However, he tells us another guy is joining us for dinner; since he's paying 500, it would be best if we don't mention our good deal.

As pre-arranged, we meet Ali at the bus station at 7:00pm. The other guest does not show. Ali is constantly looking down the waterfront, hoping to spot him.

"We'll give him 15 minutes," Ali says. We're fine with that, even though everyone in town knows where Ali lives, so someone can simply escort the man if he does show up. He still doesn't appear, so we walk along a dark, narrow street, past a video store and a general store. Ali stops in the latter to buy throat syrup.

"I want my voice to be golden for you tonight," he explains.

We walk on and on through the narrow streets, turning this corner then that, until Ali steps into a courtyard and introduces his wife, his sons-in-law and several grandchildren bouncing around us.

Inside the house, there is no electricity. The only visible light is from a kerosene lantern on the floor. Linoleum covers the cement floor and there is no furniture; all we see is an electronic keyboard and a flute recorder. He tells us to sit next to the wall facing him. Ali removes his shirt (after asking our permission), plays the keyboard and yells to his wife in Kiswahili. He slides the keyboard across the linoleum and asks Anita to play something. She and I play chopsticks.

Ali yells again until his wife enters with plates and mandazi. I LOVE Mandazi. It's like a doughnut without the hole or the sweetness. This mandazi is different in a totally delightful way. Ali's wife has filled it with crab and fish seasoned with garlic. It is absolutely the best thing I've eaten in the last year. After we devour them, she brings in fish and rice, which we eat with our hands in the traditional Swahili way. Once we are done with dinner, Ali serves Swahili cake for dessert. It's a lovely candy made from sugar, milk and a touch of cardamom. It's almost caramelized. As we nibble the "cake," Ali's extended family comes in, including his four grandchildren aged between three and seven years.

His daughters and sons-in-law play drums on empty canisters while Ali plays the keyboard. His throat is irritated but he insists on singing. The children are superb dancers and keep us laughing with their antics and suggestive moves. Ali and his family sing "Lala Salama," which means "sleep peacefully," so I figure it's time to go.

I've brought a bag of bubble gum balls for the children and leave them with Ali, who is is still worried about the guy who didn't show.

"If he turns up tomorrow," Ali says, "and says he was sick, he can come to dinner tomorrow night." That sounds reasonable to me.

"Hakuna matata," I tell Ali. It means "no worries," but I can tell that Ali is worried. He'll be worried until the guy comes for dinner or leaves the island.

Lamu looks like it is out of an Arabian Nights story. Time has left it behind, except for the telephone lines and television satellites. One bar shows movies every night on an honest-to-god big screen. "Collateral" with Tom Cruise is showing, but we don't go to see it. Another theater in town has "Ladies Only" nights for the Muslim women.

Practically everyone in Lamu owns a donkey. Care must be taken when walking the narrow streets because donkeys will come from any direction, usually quickly, carrying large loads or men riding sidesaddle. When I'm walking through town on Saturday morning, a man comes through with a loud speaker. I hear him say "punda," which means "donkey." When I ask a local what he said, I'm told the man is announcing anyone caught riding a donkey on the main road through town will be jailed and fined. They're cracking down on young men who race donkeys through the streets.

On Lamu's waterfront sits an organization devoted to donkeys: the Donkey Sanctuary. It provides free veterinary care for all donkeys, and they also take in old donkeys too frail to work.

These numerous donkeys—young and old, infirm and in the strength of youth—bray loudly at all hours. Sometimes it sounds just like a screaming woman. Added to the braying are 20 or so muezzins calling Muslims to pray throughout the day. Lamu can get quite noisy at times.

The coasts of Kenya and Tanzania seem like different countries from the inland areas, and for good reason. Throughout the 16th, 17th and 18th centuries, the British, Portuguese and Arabs were fighting to control the coast. From Zanzibar to Lamu, they took turns dominating the region. Even when an Arab Sultantate in Zanzibar ruled the coasts of present day Tanzania and Kenya, the British still handled administration of the coastal towns. It wasn't until 1963, when Kenya gained independence from the British, that the coast became an official part of Kenya. These numerous, competing influences have created a laid-back and tantalizing atmosphere.

Younger women wear the buibui—usually black—which flows from their heads to the ground. Full purdah covers everything but the eyes; it is becoming increasingly common. We see a lot of it, especially in Lamu. Older women wear wraps around their waists called kangas. Women from Uganda to Kenya to Tanzania wear them. They are brightly colored pieces of cloth with bold patterns and a Kiswahili proverb printed on the lower edge. The proverbs say things like, "Blood is thicker than water."

In East Africa, Muslim women keep their heads covered. These days, the trend is for women of status to remain sequestered. The more elevated the women's status in society, the less she does. For instance, a woman of affluence will never leave the house to go to the market. Instead, servants do the marketing, the cooking and the cleaning. As long as staying out of the public eye is considered "fashionable," coastal women are a rarity in the streets. They will continue to be kept in the home or covered, purdah-style, when they go out.

The men of Lamu wear the traditional full-length white robes known as khanzus as well as kofia caps, which fit snugly. Most kofia are white and embroidered with silver and gold thread. Although we see women in purdah and men in the long robes and caps in Kisumu, it's not nearly as common as it is in Lamu and Mombasa.

Mosques are everywhere; they are in rural communities, tucked into tiny town squares, and in the cities on nearly every street corner. Lamu alone has 26 mosques in a total land area of less than two square miles. Women are not allowed into most of the mosques of Lamu. One mosque does permit women, but their quarters are on the second floor and have a separate entrance. Even then, only Muslim women can enter. Non-Muslim women like me are not allowed. A male non-Muslim tourist is allowed to enter a mosque, but he must wear a long white robe like the khanzus. (The mosques in Shela, the community next to Lamu, will allow non-Muslim women to enter.)

Mombasa and Lamu are conservative cities. Guide books and local postings remind female tourists to keep their bodies covered. A guide book to Mombasa reminds visitors, "as you explore the Old Town, PLEASE: keep an eye on your belongings; do not photograph people unless you ask them first; avoid entering mosques unless you are invited to do so; wear clothing that covers you decently."

Fresh fruit is abundant and squeezed on site for the most deliciously refreshing drinks, especially when the juices are slightly frozen and served with ice slivers. Mango, papaya, pineapple, lime, orange, passion fruit—they fill handcarts on sidewalks, fruit stands throughout the cities and along the coastal highway. Coconuts and seafood are plentiful. In addition to Swahili-style food, coastal dishes have a distinctly Indian taste. Colorfully packaged spices from the Middle East, Asia and Zanzibar are available everywhere. Homemade sweets are sold on the street, by the pinch or in paper or plastic bags.

Julia and Joseph invite Ed and me to their place for dinner. They put on quite a spread, serving up prawn sauce over rice and grilled crab legs. Joseph is an expert at making fresh fruit juice. We sit on a mattress on the floor and eat, surrounded by maps and books. It all feels rather bohemian.

Their apartment is on the second floor of an older building, a block or two from the waterfront. It consists of an open courtyard area, bedroom, bath, office space and kitchen. Joseph likes Neil Diamond, so he puts on a CD until Julia can't stand it any more. Julia and Ed, both from the UK, have a long conversation about music and the bands they have in their collections.

Julia has a friend from the States who lives nearby. Her name is Heidi, although she Islamicized her name to Heidija when she married a Muslim man in 2001. After dinner and washing dishes, the four of us walk over to Heidjia's house. She has just returned from Mombasa on a shopping excursion for the store she and her husband operate in Lamu. A new freezer, complete with packing bands, stands in the middle of the kitchen area. They are putting produce away, so they tell us to go to the second floor, have a seat and relax.

The house is typical of Swahili homes. It is walled in from the street and has a central area open to the sky. Around this central space are a number of rooms, which are usually long and narrow. The kitchen is on the bottom floor, and when we reach the second floor, we see children sleeping on mattresses at the far end. We sit on the floor on mattresses and watch as Heidija gives medicine to a child who has malaria. The children are her husband's from a previous marriage.

Heidija is originally from Washington, D.C., although she lived in Atlanta while working on her master's degree at Emory. We talk about Atlanta for a while before her husband joins us. As we talk, the locals chew miraa and smoke cigarettes. Miraa is a stimulant grown near Mt. Kenya and shipped immediately after harvesting. Chewing miraa is extremely popular, especially with men, even though it's illegal in Tanzania and it is usually chewed with gum to cut the bitterness. It's also called "khat" or something similar in other areas of Africa.

Although we planned to stay for only a few minutes, since it's late and they're tending to a sick child, we end up staying for two hours, sitting on the floor and discussing tribal customs. There are 42 tribes in Kenya, each with its own language and customs, so we chat about their different traditions and rituals. Heidija studied African history and knows a great deal about the Luo, who populate Lake Victoria's shores. She also lived in the Mt. Kenya area for 12 years.

Heidija and Julia exchange news of Lamu. It's one of those places where everyone knows everyone else as well as what they're all up to. Heidija says a man came to their shop last night, dressed in a red buibui with his face covered. She laughs, recalling the sight of his beard peeking through. He was on his way to crash the Ladies Only Night at the movie theater. Heidija told him he needed to add breasts to his costume or he'd never make it in. He tried, he said, but they simply fell out. Although there is an enclave of young men who dabble in homosexuality and hang around Shela beach, Lamu will not tolerate such activity. One gay couple who tried to marry in Lamu were attacked and had to be escorted out of town under police protection.

It's nearly midnight, so we finally leave Heidija's home. We pass through the dark, narrow streets, unable to see the "road" but trusting Julia when she says there are no drain breaks until the next block. She knows these streets by heart. We part at an intersection—Julia and Joseph going home, and Ed and I turning toward the Yumbe House. We leave early tomorrow and won't see them again. Goodbyes are hard, especially in darkened, tiny intersections.

Just as I consider the area a hotbed for anyone interested in archaeology, I can't help but encourage those interested in the art of woodworking to move to the Kenyan coast to learn how to carve doors and keep their traditions alive. Woodworking enthusiasts will find plenty to do here; they can also build dhows, which are constructed manually in Lamu and a nearby village called Mantidoni. Dhow building, is, like door carving, a skill that's fading. In many respects, these are not just artistic but practical skills; Dhows take on water, a perfectly natural occurrence considering their design, and water must be bailed daily to avoid sinking. Old dhows are found resting in peace all along the coast. New ones are constantly needed, but it takes about two years to build a dhow.

We look keenly at a boat-making shack on our walk to Shela, curious to see the boat being built. We walk past the shop, eagerly turning back when the owner's son follows and invites us to have a closer look. He takes us into the building and allows us to crawl into the belly of the boat. Its ribs make me think of Jonah in the whale's belly.

One of the most interesting things he shows us is the device he uses to drill a hole. They don't use nails; only wooden dowels are used to fasten the boat together. To drill, the young man presses the bit tip to the wood and wraps a piece of rope around a molded track built into the bit. The bit is a foot long. The rope has a wooden handle that is pulled perpendicular to the bit, left to right and back again, creating tension and turning the bit. No electricity or batteries required. It is manual, intricate labor.

When I visited San Miguel de Allende in Central Mexico in 2000, the beautiful, old, massive wooden doors thoughout the city captivated me. As we walked through the streets of San Miguel (the entire city is a historical monument), I photographed doors, their casements and their brass adornments.

The East African coast is just such a door lover's paradise. In fact, Mombasa, Lamu and Zanzibar are known for their carved doors: national treasures carried off as booty by invaders. Not only was I in ecstasy over seeing these lovely works of art up close, but I also crossed paths with Sir Captain

Richard Burton. He came through East Africa in the mid-1800s and actually spent time in Mombasa and Lamu. "Mountains of the Moon," the movie about Burton and Speke's journey to find the source of the Nile, was partially filmed in Lamu. Baba J. was able to show me the alleys and the fort where some of the scenes were filmed.

In a booklet about Old Town Mombasa, Burton is quoted regarding the carved doors of the coast. In addition to being prized possessions, Burton notes, "the higher the tenement, the bigger the gateway, the heavier the padlock and the huger the iron studs which nail the door of heavy timber, the greater is the owner's dignity."

Many doors in Lamu, Mombasa and Zanzibar have eroded, while others have been broken up and sold as souvenirs. Still others were looted. Demand for restored and new doors continues. An estimated 500 doors remain in Zanzibar and around 200 in Lamu. The total number of doors in Old Town Mombasa is unclear; maybe 100 are still in their frames and in use.

Door carving is an Arab art, but it has many Indian influences via Zanzibar. The Indian style of carving sports coffered panels, elaborately carved lintels of leaves and flowers and protruding corbels (normally two), which are similarly carved. The Lamu and Zanzibar style of carved doors typically has rows of studs, a carved frame of stylized leaves and flowers, a "chain" pattern and extra lintels on the sides. Arabic sayings are carved into semicircular, or round-headed, doors. Older Arabic doors favor a more linear and abstract design, complete with stylized rosettes and hooks on the lintel, along with the chain and rope designs typical of the style. I want to capture all the doors with my camera before we depart.

Ed and I leave Lamu on a dhow with a motor, packed with people sitting wherever they might fit. We exit the dhow and climb onto the dock to find our buses waiting. Once our gear is stored underneath (only clothes under there for me), we pull away from the coast, listening to rocking Arabic tunes. Our bus ride is non-stop to Mombasa.

From Mombasa, we take a bus straight through to Kisumu—a 14 hour trip. Coach Line, which is run by Muslims, has a 6:00pm overnight bus. We'll reach home at 8:00am tomorrow.

Once we're underway and the sun is setting, Ed mentions this overnight bus trip from Mombasa is frowned upon by the VSO. I can tell why; there are bad roads peopled with erratic drivers forced to navigate pot holes and washed-out portions in the dark. It will be dangerous.

We pass an accident involving six trucks. Traffic on the two-lane highway is piling up. Our industrious driver backs up about 100 yards and turns onto a parallel dirt path running behind roadside shrubs. We crawl past and see the trucks crammed into each other, their headlights still on. Traffic moving in the opposite direction sits motionless, a string of cars already in line. We're fortunate to be moving, even if we inch along the dirt path, rocking crazily in the ruts.

Despite the shaky movements of the bus, Ed and I drop off to sleep. The bus stops regularly at little stores and rest stops, picking up or dropping off packages and passengers. Africa, at night and along the highway, is serene. Our crowd is quiet, milling around, stretching their legs, getting a bite to eat. Sometimes we stop in the middle of nowhere for the driver to urinate. Then other men will climb out and they all line up shoulder to shoulder, backs to the bus, facing the bush. The women step into the black shadow of the bus for privacy. I sleep some more, until about 2:00am, when we pull into Nairobi to take on more passengers. It's chilly in Nairobi and chilly on the road to Nakuru.

When we pull into the Mobil station in Nakuru, passengers file on board. I hear a man saying, "Hey, there. Hey, there," with his hand reaching toward me. I look up to see Tonny Bolo, my coworker from TICH, smiling down at me and Ed. My sleep-fuzzy mind registers his presence but not much more. After two hours, we reach Kisumu; by now Tonny and I are awake and able to talk. He's headed to TICH after spending the weekend in Nakuru. I'm going home to rest.

As I walk home, a bicycle pulls up beside me and Walter Odede says, "Hello, there." He straps one of my bags to the back of the bike, greatly reducing my burden. We walk along, talking about everything that's happened in the last 11 days since we've seen each other. He took medicine for malaria, went to his home place for four days, and is now better. I give him a paper bag of Swahili cake bought from a young woman at one of the bus stops. At my gate, Walter understands my intense desire to get inside and shower, for I'm filthy and tired. It was lovely to end my vacation by running into Tonny and Walter upon arriving home. Of all the people in town to see, I was fortunate to bump into my two favorites.

Chapter Ten

Russia

*P*arham and Karen, medical students from the University of Ottawa, are on attachment to TICH for six weeks. During this period, they will both work at the Provincial Hospital—Parham in the surgical ward and Karen in pediatrics. One morning, I am allowed to make a visit with them to Nyanza General Hospital, a government-run medical center servicing Nyanza Province.

The cost for a bed in the hospital is 100 shillings per day for adults (about US $1.30) and 50 shillings for children (about US $0.70). Although being seen by the doctor and receiving a diagnosis is free, any treatments or medication will cost the patient.

Our group separates as Parham goes on morning rounds with the head surgeon and Karen and I tour pediatrics with two Kenyan student nurses. In pediatrics, each room holds four or five beds. It is not uncommon for two or three children to occupy each bed. As we walk through room after room, we see countless mothers who hold their babies and look up without smiling. Several of the mothers are breastfeeding; others are lying or sleeping next to their dozing babies. In truth, most of the mothers have little to smile about; many of the children have malaria, while others are dehydrated from diarrhea. Some have AIDS.

Many of these children also have Burkitt's lymphoma. The first sign of the disease is usually a tumor growing along the child's jaw line. The disease then manifests a second tumor on the opposite jaw and, in later stages, causes tumors in the abdomen. It can also cause tumors on other parts of the head and face. Many of the children we see lined up for treatments have enlarged jaws, bulging necks and distended bellies.

Young children sit next to each other on beds and on the floor. They are all plugged into IV bags that hang in a row above their heads. If the disease is caught early enough, their chances of survival are actually fairly good. However, although few children die from the cancer, the treatment can be incredibly uncomfortable.

Four treatments are administered while the children are in-patients; these children, aged three to 10 years old, take the medicine through needles in their hands. The chemical burns as it enters the veins. The usual procedure is done by inserting the syringe into the container and allowing the medicine to drip slowly, mixing with saline solution as it flows into the child's hand. Not today. The nurse squeezes the entire syringe into the container and moves efficiently to the next child. Some of the children cry openly, some sit silently with tears streaming down their faces and others just sit quietly, staring straight ahead.

The Kenyan nursing students tell us that Burkitt's is generally believed to be a result of malarial infection combined with a strain of the Epstein-Barr virus. Other theories advocate that Burkitt's is a malarial virus morphed into EBV. Without a medical background, these terms mean little to me; it also doesn't seem clear to Karen exactly how malaria leads to Burkitt's. I trust the nursing students, however, because it certainly explains why this rare disease is so common in Kenya. Malaria is a tricky illness. Its symptoms are quite varied; it can take on the appearance of other sicknesses such as pneumonia, arthritis and flu. In this area, people running fevers or experiencing pain of any kind automatically assume it's malaria.

Before we came to the hospital, Parham and Karen told me about some of the cases in the surgical ward (such as a gunshot victim and burn patients), so I prepare mentally as I leave pediatrics with Parham and climb the stairs. I'm expecting to see some really bad stuff.

Parham stands in the hallway and looks toward the first room.

"Would you like to see a horrible wound?" he asks. Wanting to decline, I instead accept with optimism. As we step into the room, we see a woman sitting on the bed next to the door. She's 50 years old and her right foot sits flat on the bed. Parham explains that she is diabetic and due to of lack of circulation, a sore in her foot became a deep tissue infection. Praham believes she is also HIV positive, so her body was unable to fight the infection effectively.

Many of the patients have diseases and infections complicated by HIV. However, when they come in for treatment, they refuse to be tested. They would rather not know their status. A stigma around HIV/AIDS still exists in Kenya, even though education campaigns have been launched by the government and NGOs.

Many patients feel that if they know for sure they are infected, they will be ostracized by their family and friends. People with HIV/AIDS are often alienated from entire communities or treated as though they are cursed. For the hospital staff's safety, it should be clear whether or not they are working on a patient who is HIV positive so they can take precautions and treat the patient effectively. Unfortunately, the hospital often does not test the patient because the patient simply cannot pay for the test.

Recent research shows an interaction between HIV and malaria that increases the chances of contracting both. There's a myth that HIV/AIDS is rampant in Africa because the people are overly sexual or amoral. Although cultural practices do play a part in the disease's prevalence (including wife inheritance, men being uncircumcized and the stigma associated with discussing the disease even for educational purposes), scientific evidence suggests that the HIV viral load of someone infected with the disease actually becomes elevated during a malarial episode. If someone's level of viral load is raised, the disease is easier and more likely to be transmitted to others.

Additionally, because HIV impacts the immune system, people with HIV/AIDS have an increased risk of contracting malaria. Research conducted by Abu-Raddad, et al., involved a study of the adult population of Kisumu, which is comprised of approximately 200,000 people. Using a mathematical model of dual infection, the study estimates that disease interaction may have caused 8,500 excess HIV infections and 980,000 excess malaria espisodes in Kisumu's population of adults.

Nine hundred and eighty thousand excess malaria episodes. That's an incredible number of cases, even when you consider it outside the ramifications to the medical community. When someone is down with malaria, they miss work, they cannot farm and they cannot buy or sell at the market. Multiply that by 980,000 and the resulting losses are staggering.

HIV also complicates other illnesses. This is evident in the woman with the foot sore. After Parham and I talk, he points to her foot and she lifts the piece of gauze covering it. I expect to see redness from exposed veins and capillaries, but instead, her open wound is entirely white with pus. The wound covers the top of her toes and foot and travels to her ankle, skirting around her ankle bone to the back. Her tendons are exposed. Instead of being horrified, I'm curious and lean in to get a better look.

"Don't get too close," Parham warns.

He's right. When we entered the room, a stench like rotting flesh greeted us. I can't imagine the pain of this huge, open sore, but the woman sits placidly on the bed next to the open door as people file by, curiously looking in.

This lack of privacy astonishes me. We walk anywhere we want and enter any room, even as patients lay fully exposed. Because I am with Parham, who wears a white coat and a stethoscope, most people think I'm a doctor too. I am amazed at the patients' openness and stoicism.

In this same room is a mental health patient. She sits on a mattress on the floor, naked underneath her dress, which is pulled up and gathered around her waist. The top of her feet have wounds caused by a car running over them. A stranger brought her to the hospital. We notice she has defecated on the floor next to her mattress and we leave the room, walking past the woman with the rotting sore on her foot, which she has since recovered with the gauze.

"Asante, Mama," I say to her. Her face lights up with a huge smile. Parham tells me her foot requires a skin graft that will cost about 3,000 shillings (US $35). If she doesn't have the money, they'll send her home until she can pay. An orderly passes us, entering the room to clean up the feces.

Hospital mattresses are about three inches thick and covered with green vinyl. The hospital does not provide linens, so patients must bring their own (if they can't afford linens, they just lie on the hard, cold vinyl). Their medical chart is a piece of beige paper taped to the wall, much like the beige construction paper we drew on and displayed as children. X-rays are kept between the mattress and bed springs.

The next room, neatly labeled "Septic," contains patients with infections. We enter and a stench—a new and different stench—slows us down. Four beds are filled and each patient has a family member (or two) standing by his side. Parham brings me to the third bed, where a man of 50 or so reclines with his wife nearby. The man has a scrotum infection but didn't seek treatment until he could no longer walk. On the rounds earlier, the head surgeon decided to release the patient.

"How are you feeling?" Parham asks.

"My stomach is hurting a great deal," he tells Parham.

"It's possible the infection has spread to the lining of his stomach," Parham tells me in a whisper. He presses on the man's abdomen, eliciting a grimace.

"I think I'll say something to the doctor on duty," Parham says, "if his stomach is infected, he shouldn't go home yet."

Parham indicates for the man to lift his sheet, which he does without hesitation. The patient's legs are spread, to keep them from touching his testicles, and his scrotum looks just like the woman's foot wound, skinless and white with a thick layer of pus. The infection hasn't spread to his penis, but his testicles are slightly enlarged and stand out in their stark whiteness against his dark buttocks. I have to remind myself not to make faces, instead just nodding my head knowingly as Parham talks to me about the patient's prognosis. As with the woman in the other room, this man may be HIV positive, which would account for the extent of the deep tissue infection and the excessive recovery period.

In the next bed is a man, weighing about 65 pounds, who is dying from cancer. His ribs show plainly through his skin and his face is taut over sharp bones. He looks as though he is in the last stages of full-blown AIDS. A large tumor was removed from his abdomen a few days ago and he lies on his side, the sheet falling away as a woman replaces it over his jutting hip. Parham knows very little about this patient, so we don't stop, but I make eye contact with him and the woman, hoping to convey sympathy. In this case, speaking just doesn't seem appropriate or effective.

By comparison, another patient in this room has a very good prognosis. He was hit and run over by a bus, losing his left ear and gaining a huge gash down to the skull on the right side of his head. The gash is bandaged but his left shoulder has an open wound smeared with antibacterial cream. He is ambulatory and should recover nicely.

The next room also contains four beds and four men. Parham begins by telling me about the young man in the bed nearest the door. His spinal column was injured, leaving him paralyzed from the knees down. He looks to be in his early 20s and is lying on his left side, with his legs slightly bent toward the wall.

"I'm going to try to straighten out your legs, okay?" Parham says. The young man looks frightened at these words but agrees. He holds a bar over his bed while Parham grips his right ankle and presses down above his knee. The leg trembles, the young man's eyes glass over and the knee barely gives.

"You must straighten your legs out every day," Parham coaches, "even if you have to ask someone to do it for you. Every day, okay?"

"Okay," he says. His left leg extends much more easily with Parham's manipulation. He's a student from the University of Nairobi who came to Kisumu on an attachment to Standard Charter Bank. He tells us he went to the ATM to withdraw funds for his bus ticket back to Nairobi. He then took a boda boda. The driver had seen him getting the money from the bank and tried to rob him. When the young man fought back, he was hit across the back with a large stick, causing the spinal cord damage.

"When did it happen?" I ask.

"March 28," he says, "and if I only had a wheelchair I could go back to Nairobi and finish my studies. If I had a wheelchair I could get out of here and get on with my life and graduate."

Parham and I walk down the hallway and he says, "I think he wants you to buy him a wheelchair."

"Yes," I agree, "that's what he was asking. How much are they?"

"The government has made arrangements with a supplier who sells the chairs for about 3,000 shillings," Parham answers. Three thousand shillings is not a lot of money (US $35), especially considering it will get him out of the hospital and back to his studies so he can graduate. At this point, only the wheelchair seems to be his worry; he accepts the loss of his legs without complaint. Otherwise, he is young and healthy, nice-looking and strong. Not to mention stoic.

The next room also has four beds with four patients. The woman nearest the window, who looks to be about 60 years old, is in her fifth day of a diabetic coma. Several family members stand by her bed, one young woman holding her hand while an orderly empties the catheter bag. Next to the coma patient is a boy who looks to be about 19 years old. He's from a rural community, where he burned his hands while tending a fire. The burns were third degree, damaging the nerves and resulting in virtually no pain. Because he didn't feel pain, he didn't seek treatment. The four fingers on his right hand decayed and fell off. The doctors are trying to save his left hand.

The next patient is a 28-year-old gold miner. Standing by the bed is his elder brother, who tells me what happened. The gold miner went 70 feet down into the mining shaft. Apparently a gasoline-powered pump was leaking, so when the gold miner went to light his kerosene lamp, the match ignited the spilled fuel and engulfed him in flames. Third degree burns cover 80 percent of his body. Without his skin, the young man's face, torso, arms and legs are white. Only the dark skin under his underwear remains intact. A semi-circular iron frame covers the length of his body. A sheet covers the frame, but a doctor is inserting an IV into his ankle (they can't find any veins in his arms), so the sheet is pulled back, revealing the length of his white and brown body. He is so young. When I look at the young man's face, he looks away. I take his brother's hand and say, "Pole sana." He bows toward me, and it's hard to let go of his hand.

Before our visit, Parham told Karen and me about a young male patient who was shot while trying to rob someone. Because he's a criminal, the medical staff is not completely thorough in their care. People here think criminals deserve such punishment, and mob justice is common. If a man robs someone on the street and the vicitim yells, "He's robbing me," people will gather immediately. They may beat the thief or even stone him, sometimes until he dies. Jackie, the young Canadian student nurse, told me about another man who was caught stealing. He came into the district hospital yesterday. The crowd had stoned him and then set fire to his foot. Unlike the gunshot victim, at least this man will probably survive.

"This guy is nice-looking," Parham says of the gunshot victim, "he has a nice build but he's probably going to die. And he just looks at you with these pleading eyes."

We enter the room where the gunshot victim is naked and lying on his right side. He's in respiratory distress, his chest rising and falling rapidly as he tries to breathe. The area below his heart is slightly sunken, showing us where the bullet destroyed his ribs. He has a six-inch incision with massive black stitches running parallel to his ribs, and a tube is going into his skin beside the incision. He also has an eight-inch incision running from his lower abdomen straight up to his chest. This is where they went in to check for damage to his internal organs. Above that incision is a pink spot. Parham and I can only surmise this is where the bullet entered. It is in the exact middle of his chest at the base of his breast bone. He was supposedly shot point blank.

A doctor clumsily covers one incision with a folded piece of gauze while the young man breathes rapidly, his eyes moving from face to face. He's dying and his eyes are pleading, just as Parham described. When his eyes move to mine, I say very quietly, "Pole sana." My words register slightly on his face, even amongst his distress.

When we go through the door marked, "ENT," I'm relieved. My only thought is that nothing terribly serious can come of ear, nose or throat infections.

I'm wrong.

A boy named Michael is sleeping in the fetal position. He has chronic ear infections. In the West, a child with Michael's persistent ear infections would have tubes placed in his ears to allow the fluid to drain and keep infection at bay. But not here and not for Michael. The largely untreated ear infection took hold and moved into his skull, right next to his ear. The infection entered the lining of his brain, then the brain itself, which I'm told is extremely painful.

"He should not be here," Parham says, "he should have tubes in his ears, not be lying unconscious in a hospital."

The remedy is to operate, removing the infected portion of the skull.

"Michael," Parham says loudly, "Michael." His eyes open ever-so-slightly. They're reddened and he can't open them all the way. Then he's gone again. Michael is 14 years old.

Next to Michael, sitting erect against the wall is a man in his early 20s. The left side of his face is swollen about three inches above and below his jaw line. His eye is swollen and the lower lid is pulled open by the pressure.

"He came here two weeks ago with a tooth infection and received antibiotics," Parham says, "but he wasn't given enough antibiotics. The infection flared back up. He really shouldn't be here. What he needed was a dentist."

The last room we visit contains patients with broken bones. One young woman, about 15 years old, sits on her bed as a companion braids extensions into her hair. She has a lovely woven blanket fitted over her mattress. She is in traction for two breaks—one below and one above the knee. Behind this girl, next to the window, is Parham's special patient. He brings her milk every time he comes to the hospital. Mentally and physically challenged, she cannot talk and Parham does not know her name. No chart is taped above her bed and no family members sit nearby to care for her or to offer her comfort. Her left leg is broken, which is actually the least of her problems. The doctors think she was hit by a car. A stranger found her and brought her to the hospital. She is malnourished, weighing maybe 50 pounds. She is naked beneath a filthy, gray tattered sheet. She lies facing the wall on the green vinyl mattress. When we enter, Parham speaks to her, and she turns her face toward us. We open the milk and pour it into Parham's empty Dasani water bottle. He tries to hold it to her mouth, but milk pours onto her face and neck.

"I don't want to move her and risk moving her leg," Parham says, "because she'll cry." I move behind her head and lift the mattress, elevating her head so Parham can put the bottle to her mouth.

"Be careful of your hands under there," Parham warns. When the bottle is on the young woman's mouth, she begins to suck the milk like a baby. The bottle sides are pulled inward as she drinks.

"How old do you think she is?" Parham asks. I look down at her bony arms, her ribs, her undeveloped breasts. From my position behind the mattress, I can see a thick scab on her head, probably an injury from being hit by the car.

"I don't know," I say, "maybe late teens." Since she's extremely malnourished, she has no typical markings of age. Her hands seem tiny as she holds the bottle. There is no air left, so milk does not flow. Parham is afraid to reach for the bottle because she might think he's taking it away. We wait until her lips tire and weaken their hold. I hear air rush into the bottle, and the remaining milk goes into her mouth. I lower the mattress and she lies flat once again. Parham pulls a piece of cotton from a dirty wad and wipes the milk from her mouth and from the depression at the base of her throat. She drank 250 ml of milk very quickly and appears to want more. Parham worries about over-feeding and vomiting, so he asks the young women in the next bed if they'll make sure she gets the other two containers of milk later. They say yes.

When I step to the side of her bed and look at her face, she is beautiful and I picture her with more flesh, a full face. She lifts her hand, open palm towards me, spreading her fingers. I swear she's waving goodbye. I lift my hand next to hers, imitating the open palm and spread fingers. I wonder if she isn't waving after all, since her eyes simply stare. But, then again, maybe she is. I smile and say, "goodbye," softly, then "kwaheri," softly, hoping she understands. Parham says she will die. His milk is the only thing prolonging her life. I think he wonders if he should continue to bring her milk.

Outside, bed sheets hang from lines strung across grassy courtyards as the staff cleans hospital laundry. Family members also camp out on the grassy lawns, some washing and hanging their own laundry, others lounging through the mid-day, sleeping on pieces of cloth spread over the grass. We pass through to the front yard of the hospital, a dirt and rock expanse. We move toward the guarded gate, toward the busy, noisy highway just beyond the fence. Because Russians paid to have the hospital built, locals say they're going to Russia when they go to the hospital.

We're leaving Russia. Parham and I part downtown and say goodbye. Suddenly, Parham turns back toward me and says, "Go wash your clothes."

A group of us head to Chiga Community near Kisumu to meet with 30 widows. Our team consists of the Canadian medical students (Karen and Parham) and nursing students (Jackie and Angela). And me. Our mission today is to begin medical files on all the widows, young and old. Our work will include recording their medical histories, hearing about their current ailments and performing complete physicals.

Aga Khan Hospital has promised to loan us the necessary equipment, so we stop by to pick up the blood pressure machine, weight scales and scopes for checking ears, eyes, noses and throats. We purchase a thermometer and tongue depressors at the hospital pharmacy.

To get our work done efficiently, we have developed a system: I'll begin by taking and recording blood pressure, temperature, and heart and breathing rates. We'll also measure height and weight. I'll ask the women questions about their occupations, incomes, possessions, number of pregnancies and deliveries and basic hygiene practices. Karen will continue the medical history interview by asking about past illnesses, surgeries and current maladies. Once the chart is complete, each woman will visit Parham to have a complete physical, including eye chart exam, hearing test and pelvic exam. The larger group will congregate under trees as Jackie and Angela educate them about diet and health (particularly diet and nutrition related to HIV/AIDS, since all the younger widows in our group are HIV positive).

When we pull up in two cars, the ladies are waiting. They give us a traditional welcome, standing, clapping and singing as we climb out of the cars. Our "office" for today is a compound of five houses. Two houses have been set up for the exams: one belongs to an older widow, the other belongs to a younger widow. The older widows cannot enter the bedroom of the younger widows; it would be too much like lying on the beds where their sons slept. We decide to begin with the older women, since they've been waiting and are tired. They range in age from 60 to 85.

The houses are very neat. Linens are draped over the backs of seats and couches. The walls and floors are made of mud and cow dung; this type of house is considered a semi-permanent dwelling. Although some houses have layers of cement spread over the floors and walls, making them permanent dwellings, the homes in this compound are not.

It takes me a couple tries before I get into the swing of taking blood pressure with the borrowed machine. The older women speak Dholuo—not Kiswahili or English—so we all need translators. The most challenging aspect for me is getting the ladies to put the thermometers under their tongues. Although they are all so obedient and earnest, many don't want to shut their mouths. One woman keeps her head tilted back the entire time, as though the thermometer might slip. I realize we should have learned the very basic Dholuo words for "sit," "stand," "close," "open" and "please."

One of the most important things we want to know is how many times they have been pregnant and how many of those pregnancies were full-term. We really want to capture whether they experienced miscarriages or abortions, but this topic seems too private for the women to discuss. When I do ask (through an interpreter who is 15 years old) how many pregnancies and how many deliveries each woman has had, it is always the same number. I attempt to explain that it's possible to be pregnant but not to have a baby as a result. This concept just doesn't get through to the interpreter or the women; that part of our record-keeping may be skewed.

These women have given birth 13 times, 10 times, eight times. Only one woman had no children of her own. At 66 years of age, she's now the guardian of two children, aged four and six years old, the offspring produced by her husband's second wife. Her husband and his second wife both died from AIDS. Many of these women have outlived all their children. Some only have one or two adult children still living. All of them are responsible for young grandchildren living in their homes.

I love sitting with each older woman and talking to her through the interpreter, finding out about her house, toilet and bathing facilities. Some have pit latrines in their yards, but a handful do not. They simply use the fields near their homes. None of them have piped water, most using rain water and river water in its place. Some purify their water with WaterGuard or by boiling it. Several women simply drink and cook with the water as it comes out of the river or rolls off their rooftops.

Of the 14 older women I interview, only one reports having an income. All the others tell me they are too old to work or they can no longer see well enough to work. Those who are able typically keep a home garden. The one woman with an income makes it by weaving and selling baskets for 50 shillings each at the weekly market. All the women own their homes and a few have cows, goats, sheep and chickens. Some women have nothing but their homes. Not one woman owns a car or bicycle. They all tell me they have pain in their feet, lower leg, knees and hips. Some have pain in their shoulders. It's a common complaint (and an understandable one), since their old bodies have worked hard for decades, plowing and tending crops by hand, taking care of livestock and birthing many babies. They all suffer from arthritis; though they often think it is malaria. Many of them have cataracts. One woman has a protruding throat that Parham later confirms to be an enlarged thyroid.

The ladies have arranged lunch for us, which is totally unexpected. At 3:30pm, they insist we stop working and go to an adjacent house. They've prepared stewed beef with potatoes, rice and ugali. We eat gratefully. After lunch, we must rush through the remaining interviews to get the equipment back to Aga Khan Hospital by 5:00pm.

Dropping the equipment at the hospital, I watch with amusement as Parham walks the halls. He is astounded at Aga Khan's shiny floors, uniformed doctors, chairs at desks and no blood on the walls (this is a private hospital). We go to Mon Ami for refreshments. As we sip our drinks, we all agree it's been a great day. We didn't accomplish as much as we had hoped (naïvely, we thought we could examine all 30 women in one day) and it was hard work, but we agree it was a great day nonetheless.

After our drinks, Karen, Parham and I walk to the bank so Karen can use the ATM. It is almost dark and the street boys are out in full force. They all wear shorts and shirts so old they've turned into a sort of dark gray uniform. The boys are dirty and often barefoot. When they see white people, they latch on and ask for money. As Walter and Tonny showed me, I usually stop and buy bananas for them, which gets them very excited; however, even buying bananas is tricky because when two or three boys are around a white person, all the other boys coming running.

Walter comes up behind us. We were probably pretty easy to spot; aside from our white skin, Karen, Parham and I were also collecting boys as we walked. I introduce Walter to Karen and Parham over the heads of the boys. As we chat, Walter naturally puts his arms around the boys. He's on the street this evening to counsel them. Walter tells me he recently had a long talk with the owner who donated the land for the Pambazuko building. Everything is in place for progress. We agree to meet the following week to discuss the next construction phase for putting on the roof.

The street boys are really collecting around and letting off some energy, making it hard to hold a conversation. One boy, about 12 years of age, is walking behind with a friend. He is crying. Tears roll and his breath comes in jags. We pull him into our circle, and Walter learns someone hit the boy on the head, resulting in a severe headache. Walter rubs the boy's head and Karen holds my backpack so I can dig out Panadol, the local pain reliever. Parham pulls his flashlight from his backpack and looks into the boy's eyes for a long time.

"Everything looks okay," Parham assures us, "hopefully the pain relievers will work on his headache."

It's rather hectic with the 20 or so boys hovering around, some still asking Parham and Karen for money. I smell glue and find two boys in front of me holding their glue bottles to their noses. I point them out to Walter, and the boys hide the bottles under their shirts. Having three white people on the street is creating too much confusion, so Walter tells us we can go. Later, we pass on the opposite side of the street and see Walter talking with the boys. We're all impressed with his compassion.

Karen and Parham have adapted quickly. They've worked at the hospital, visited orphanages, built medical records for HIV positive widows and now want to meet with Walter to learn more about Pambazuko. Parham runs nearly every morning and Karen takes Kiswahili lessons. On top of all that, they're constantly looking for ways to help the local people, using funds donated by their generous friends in Canada. Their energy is constant and stupefying. I feel the same for Angela and Jackie. Meeting these four bright, caring and energetic young people has been a treasure.

I ask Parham about the patients we visited last week at the hospital.

"How is the girl with the broken leg and no family?" I wonder. He informs me she's doing well and is being fed.

"I bought some things for her and would like to take her some sheets and a blanket and pillow," I tell Parham. I also plan to give her a t-shirt, underwear and socks.

"Okay," Parham says, "I'm going tomorrow if you would like to come along."

While we're talking, Parham tells me about how he was looking for the gunshot victim in the surgical ward earlier but couldn't find him. It wasn't until later, when he was in the morgue, that he saw the guy. When Parham tells me this, he is laughing and says, "I couldn't find him, then I see him in the morgue." He must laugh to keep from going mad.

"What's the procedure for getting a wheelchair," I ask Parham. "I'm thinking about getting a chair for the university student who is paralyzed from the knees down."

"I'll ask the physiotherapist," Parham says, "he procures the chairs." I'm not alone in this plan; Parham is also thinking about getting a wheelchair for another patient, a young boy.

The following morning, we take boda bodas and then a matatu to Russia—the Provincial hospital. Karen goes straight to the maternity ward to see her first Kenyan baby being born. Parham and I go to the surgical ward. As we approach, we meet Margaret, the head nurse. When she hears I work at TICH, she says, "I'll be a student there soon. I want to work in community health in the rural areas." With her experience from the hospital combined with a degree in Community Health and Development, Margaret will be invaluable to rural communities. Most of the rural patients in the hospital are here because they didn't have the money to go to the doctor in the first place. Many worsen until they may never recover. By working at the community level, Margaret knows she will be able to treat these people before their wounds and illnesses progress to such severe stages.

There's a new patient in the bed next to the woman with the diabetic foot. He is a very skinny man, his wound covering the top of his foot, the entire front of his shin and up to just above his knee; it is a huge, skinless wound exposing his muscle and bone. On May 28, he was using a panga (machete) to clear his field, accidentally cutting his leg mid-shin. When asked his HIV status, he says he doesn't know, but Parham and Eric, a Kenyan medical student on rounds with us, believe he is HIV positive. This would explain why his cut became infected and spread so quickly in only three weeks. He'll require a skin graft and may need to have his leg amputated if it doesn't heal properly.

The man with the scrotum infection is gone. Although Parham told the head surgeon the patient's stomach lining is infected, the head surgeon released the man anyway. Eric and Parham say, in all likelihood, the man will die. His scrotum is gangrenous and should be removed. His infections will only worsen because he is probably HIV positive.

"So he came to the hospital," I say, "to be treated, and now he's being sent home where he'll die."

"People don't come to this hospital to be treated," Parham says, "they come here to die."

Austine, the physiotherapist, greets us in the hall. Parham asks about the process of getting a wheelchair. We learn the chairs are made by APDK, the organization in Nairobi where Heidi and Tom, two of my fellow VSO volunteers, work. (They are the pair from the Netherlands who planned to work together, Heidi as a speech therapist and Tom as an engineer.) Tom is currently helping to improve the wheelchair design as well as increase production from 80 to 200 wheelchairs per month. Through donors, APDK provides the wheelchairs for free, but patients must pay 2,500 shillings to cover the cost of transporting the chair from Nairobi, a membership to APDK and other incidentals. Although the total cost to the paitent is approximately US $32, the wheelchair actually costs about 30,000 shillings, or nearly US $400.

I ask Austine to order one for the young man I met earlier. Parham orders one as well.

"The boys can have their wheelchairs tomorrow," Austine says.

We visit Vincent, the young boy for whom Parham is ordering the wheelchair. He is 12 years of age and paralyzed from the waist down. He has scoliosis (curvature of the spine), an illness that may have impacted his spinal cord, although his doctor thinks he might have had a bone infection in the past which could also be responsible for his paralysis. Vincent is not a big boy. He sits on the bed on his elbows. Because he is incontinent, Vincent has a blue plastic water bottle resting between his legs, holding his penis. Bed sores are beginning to form on his knees. This concerns Parham, Karen and me because we've seen how horribly extensive bed sores can become.

With a wheelchair, Vincent will be able to get out of bed and go home. Although he'll still come to the hospital each day for physiotherapy, the only reason he's been in the hospital for so many months is because he didn't have a wheelchair. As it is, his mother carries him on her back to school and returns him to the hospital each day. When we stop by to tell Vincent and his mother he'll have a wheelchair tomorrow, he smiles more broadly than usual. His mother shakes our hands, endlessly saying, "Thank you, thank you, God bless you." We tell them the money is not coming from us but from our friends in the United States and Canada.

We then visit the university student. Parham and the physiotherapist straighten his legs. He tells us once again he could leave the hospital if he had a wheelchair. His mood is optimistic and he smiles a lot. On his bedside table (really just a plywood box nailed together) is a book called *Practicing Godliness*. When we tell him his wheelchair will be arriving tomorrow, not only does he beam, but I look at the three older men in the room, who are all in traction, and they're smiling, too, nodding their heads up and down. Now he can leave the hospital, concentrate on his studies and graduate as soon as his research is complete.

In the hall, we pass the man with the tooth infection. His face looks much better—the swelling has reduced a great deal. I smile and give him a thumbs-up, and he returns the gesture. The guy who had been run over by the matatu, the one who lost his left ear, is not doing very well. Last week, he had the best prognosis of all the patients. This week they dress his head wound and the bandages are bloody; a pool of blood is at his feet. He seems depressed and when Parham and Eric speak to him, he complains of having mental problems.

"You mean with your memory?" Parham asks.

"Yes, my memory," he says quietly, looking at the blood on the floor.

"I'm going to give you three words and I want you to repeat them back to me, okay?" Parham says.

"Okay."

"Car, apple, banana."

The young man replies, "Car, apple, banana."

"Good," Parham says, "now remember those three words and I'll be back in five minutes to ask you again."

We go into the next room to visit a new male patient suffering from spontaneous paralysis. Parham and Eric talk to his wife, who looks to be about 20.

"Did he have a fever or night sweats before the paralysis?"

"No."

"Did he experience any physical trauma?"

"No."

It's unusual for people to become paralyzed overnight. Tuberculosis can seed in the spine (or any organ) instead of seeding in the lungs, its usual rooting spot. That's why the two men ask about fevers or night sweats; both of these would indicate a TB infection. But the wife can't remember her husband complaining about fevers. His biggest problem now is bed sores. He stayed in one place too long and has developed giant, open wounds. One wound covers his entire lower back and upper buttock area. There are two openings on his right thigh. These wounds look as though someone performed a dissection. His muscles, tendons and bone are visible.

A nurse is cleaning and dressing his wounds, cutting away gray, dead tissue with a razor blade. Parham said this is not her job; a surgeon should be "debriding" the wound (cutting away dead tissue). Two young nurses look on as the older nurse presses moistened gauze into the wound, between the muscle and bone. Tragically, while the young man can't move his muscles from the waist down, he still has sensation. He feels everything the nurse is doing. It takes her quite awhile to dress his wounds. Meanwhile, he frequently closes his eyes, and I expect him to pass out.

TB can be nasty. It's not just the lungs that worry doctors, it is the way it shows up in other organs. Another patient, a woman in her early twenties, is lying on her side, face down, writhing in pain. Austine holds up her x-ray.

"Oh, my God," Parham says.

TB lodged in this woman's vertebrae, about mid-way down her spine. She has been in pain for four months but this is the first time she has come to the doctor. The x-ray shows a destroyed vertebra. She leans forward to relieve the pressure, causing her spine to bend inward. There is a jutting point on her back where her spine climbs up and turns in sharply. She requires traction, which will relieve the pressure and stop the progression of spinal erosion. If she is left like this, the spinal cord will be damaged, leading to paralysis.

Traction costs 1,000 shillings. The hospital will not put her in traction until she pays.

"I don't understand why this hospital, established by the government to keep its citizenry healthy, doesn't go ahead and start traction," I say. I don't understand why she will be forced to writhe in pain and become paralyzed because she doesn't have about US $12.

We visit Parham's favorite patient, the mentally challenged young woman. As we put sheets and a blanket on her bed, the movements make her cry. Her cast comes up around her waist, and the hospital doesn't put diapers on her; they simply allow her to defecate in the bed. At least she has a catheter to catch urine. It would be useless to put underwear or pants on her. We learn from her roommate that she tries to pull her clothes off anyway, so we simply leave her naked.

I give the clothes to the head nurse and ask her to dress the young woman when her cast is removed and she's able to leave the hospital. Before we leave, the roommate also tells us our favorite patient chews on everything, including clothes, the back of her hand and even her urine collection bag if it's left on her bed.

We go back to the memory patient. Parham asks him to repeat the three words. The patient's face is concerned as he searches his memory for them. He is obviously experiencing distress over losing his memory loss. He has certainly worsened since last week, when we had so much hope for his recovery. His deterioration appears to be caused by his worsening mental and emotional states, not just his physical wounds.

Parham leans in and asks the patient to repeat the words.

"I cannot remember them," he says.

Ever so quietly, flat on his back, eyes downcast, he repeats, "I cannot remember the words."

As I lay waiting for sleep's happy attendance, I hear the sounds of Raju's television floating across the yard from his bedroom. I can make out American accents, though I can't quite make out the words. Intermittently, a laugh track flares. Like a crashing wave, the laughter rolls for two seconds, crescendoes, then fades, only to begin again. Wondering what show uses a laugh track every five seconds, I can suddenly hear singing, "I'll be there for you, you'll be there for me, too." Friends!

I drift away with Phoebe, Joey, Monica, Ross, Chandler and Rachel talking between waves of laugh tracks. I picture the Central Perk coffee house and the girls' apartment. I'm in Africa, with giant, exotic plants growing in the yard just beyond my window. Africa, with people living in mud houses two blocks away. Africa, with cows and sheep tucked safely in their pins next door and rooster crows mingling with the canned Hollywood laughter.

Yesterday, as I put clean sheets on the bed, I heard the kids from next door playing and shouting. Their father recently chopped down the corn plants and tilled the yard in preparation for the next crop. Through the hedge of lantana outside my living room window, I could see chickens pecking the dark, newly-turned soil. A child's voice sang out, "Who let the dogs out?! Homf, homf, homf, homf, who let the dogs out?"

On our way to Chiga the other day, our taxi driver pushed a cassette into the tape player. Traditional country music rushed out of the speakers and soothed my heart. There was a slide guitar and lots of minor chords, words about love being hard, so hard it turns into a diamond. We rolled over dirt roads, passing weathered, shrunken men swatting cow butts with sticks, cautious girls with bundles of tree branches balanced on their heads, slender lads pulling hand carts of potatoes and beans. Country music, the traditional soundtrack of the American blue collar worker, reached out of our windows to serenade the crowd.

Jackie and Angela take me on a tour of the district hospital, which looks like an army barracks; it's a small compound across the busy road from Kisumu's central park. Because nurses recently went on strike in Kenya, many people took their relatives out of the hospital and returned to their village homes. Now, slowly, the beds are beginning to fill up again. Still, Jackie is amazed by how few patients there are, since most beds only hold one person, instead of the usual two or three. Every building is a ward (e.g., women's, men's, gynecological, pediatrics, surgery, psychiatric, etc.), and each ward has two wings, which are large rooms with about 20 beds lining the walls. One wing of each ward holds infectious patients.

Jackie and Angela show me the theatre—the hospital's surgical ward. The hospital has one operating room. Surgeries are performed Tuesday and Thursday mornings only. This morning, staff is cleaning the ante-room, the surgical room and the post-surgical room. They mop buckets of soapy water across the cement floors as they stand in gum boots. The windows are left open, even during surgeries.

Jackie and Angela have worked at this hospital, in different wards, over the last few weeks. They mention seeing staff neglect criminal patients and patients who speak only Dholuo. The staff also neglects patients who do not have family members to care for them. One older man, who suffered a stroke, was in the hospital for two weeks without a bath. Angela suggested they bathe him and wash his bed linens. No one wanted to do it. It took Angela 30 minutes to convince them it wasn't THAT much trouble to carry water to the man's bed to bathe and dress him.

Two male prisoners in their vertically striped suits are handcuffed to a bed at the end of the men's ward. We walk past the prisoners to find a boy of about 13 years making noise. He is rising up after being replaced on his bed by two male orderlies. The boy is obviously mentally challenged and has difficulty extending his right arm.

After rising from the bed, he walks to me (he's about my height) and says, "Give me 100 shillings."

I laugh and say, "Pole sana."

"I'm a clever boy," he says with an ever-so-slight slur. He stands erect, looking me in the eyes.

"Yes, you are," I agree with gusto.

"See my clothes?" he asks.

"Yes," I say, "you're in a school uniform and you are a clever boy."

"Give me 1,000 shillings," he then says.

Again, I laugh. "You've gone from 100 to 1,000 shillings! You are smart."

The orderlies come and direct the boy away, telling him we'll visit him another day. I like this boy. Very much. I like looking into his open face, his bright eyes, and hearing him assert he's a clever boy. I want to protect this boy—this boy who will not sit still and continues to rise from his bed despite the obvious resistance. Unstoppable, indefatigable, this big boy with the straight back and loads of dignity. You can tell by his clothes, he's a clever boy.

We return to the Chiga community to continue building medical histories and to give physical exams to the younger widows. These women, between 22 and 45 years of age, are all HIV positive.

A cat walks the ceiling beam overhead as I talk with the young women through a translator. The translator is a mother of five. She holds her one-month-old baby girl, and continues to translate while pulling her breasts in and out of her shirtwaist dress. Widowed seven months ago, she already has a new husband because she was inherited by her late husband's brother. She reports not having had sex with her new husband yet. We learn couples celebrate a child's birth by having sex soon after the child is born—sometimes within three days of delivery. Couples are being educated about the dangers to the mother of sexual intercourse, and they are encouraged to wait at least four weeks. In this culture, however, men make decisions about when and how often they'll have sex, if they'll use birth control and, often, if additional wives will be taken; even though the custom is to have the first's wife approval of subsequent wives.

Men and women do not hold hands or show other signs of affection in public. It's extremely common to see two men walking through town holding hands or having an entire conversation with their four hands clasped together. But men and women simply do not touch in public.

In Chiga, I record vital signs and medical histories on eight young women. Parham manages to examine seven of the women. The last widow I interview, a woman named Rose, tells me about her complaints. They are fairly common: headaches, pain in her shoulder (which Parham thinks is bursitis and may require surgery) and sores on her feet.

The ladies have brought us cold sodas and cookies. Rose and I complete her history and relax on the couch, eating cookies, until Parham is ready to examine her. I ask her about being hospitalized last August with typhoid. She said they wanted to test her for HIV while she was in the hospital and she agreed. Her husband died in 1999 from AIDS; up until her own hospitalization, she had avoided being tested. Rose leans forward, her elbows on her knees as she looks intently at her cuticles. In a soft voice, she says, "I waited for the results and when the doctor came into the room, he told me I was positive." Her eyes moisten.

Rose is the first woman to describe to me how she learned of her status. She's the first one to show emotional pain and fear. Most Kenyans are stoic and seemingly numb about life's hardships. It's difficult to see this woman of 35, who has five children, grapple with the fact she is HIV positive. I listen to what little she wants to share and simply nod.

Rose wants to take the blood count test so she can qualify for Antiretroviral Therapy. The drugs are given free by the Kenyan government, but only to people with blood counts of 200 or below. Only people in later stages of the disease have counts that are less than 200, so even if Rose can come up with the 1,000 shillings (US $12) for the test, she won't get the free drugs if the count isn't low enough. It would be like giving up 1,000 very valuable shillings for nothing. Most people in Chiga live on less than 100 shillings per day (less than US $1), so 1,000 shillings is a great deal of money. This woman has five children to care for. Five children she would like to see grow up.

Free drugs, but only for the really sick.

When we leave, the women are sitting outside the mud house. They all stand, shake our hands and thank us in Dholuo. Rose asks when I'll be back, and I tell her in the next week or two.

"Good," she says, "you look beautiful to me."

"You look beautiful to me, too," I say as I turn my back on her.

I glance around, just a quick peek, to see Rose and the other ladies smiling and waving, looking healthy for now.

And beautiful.

Chapter Eleven

Celebration

Walter gives Karen, Parham and me a tour of Nyalenda slums to see the second site for our water collection project. Because Parham and Karen have also decided to sponsor school fees and uniforms for a few of the children in Nyalenda, Walter invites selected widows and their children to the building site. Karen quickly becomes the proud "mother" of Akinyi, a nine-year-old girl with seven siblings. Parham takes on three other kids. After inspecting the building's progress, we spend the next two hours looking at water sources and millet drying in the sun (which will later be fermented into the local brew) while collecting a vast group of curious children.

Walter shows us a local well surrounded by three mud houses. At first, clothes hanging out to dry shield our vision. When we step through them, all we can see is a large hole in the ground. It's dangerous, especially to children. Parham decides he'll provide funding to have the well cleaned, covered, water-shocked and installed with a manual pump.

At one house, a woman is drying coal balls outside her front door. Walter demonstrates how coal balls are made from smaller coal fragments left in the fire's ashes. The coal chips are mixed with moist ashes and rolled into tennis ball-sized chunks, which then sit in the sun to harden. It takes six or so to fuel cooking fires.

Walking through Nyalenda with Steve, a Pambazuko member who looks like a bodybuilder, we see hogs and cows and goats and ducklings. We also see two sweet, nude babies—twins—playing in the doorway of their home while their mother washes dishes outside.

"The next time you have visitors," Steve tells me, "I'll give you a goat to feed your guests."

"Wow, Steve," I say, "that's terribly generous. The next time I have visitors, we'll take your goat!"

As we're headed toward Ring Road and out of Nyalenda, Parham tells us he's thinking about foregoing his trip to Mt. Kenya next week and, instead, spending his time in Nyalenda working on the well and other water projects.

"Man," Parham says, "I can't believe I've wasted a month in Kenya."

While I'm thrilled Parham thinks there are many worthwhile things to be accomplished in Nyalenda, he's certainly wrong in thinking he's wasted his time in Kisumu. He and Karen have done so much while working at the hospital, visiting orphanages and examining widows in Chiga. And now he and Karen are sponsoring children through Pambazuko, planning to take the children shopping for uniforms, shoes and school supplies. Wasted a month in Kenya?! Far from it. Impacted destinies is more like it.

As if to provide further evidence, a very small boy walks up and takes Parham's hand. He is silent, his little legs pumping hard to keep up.

"Please leave the children in Nyalenda," Walter teases us.

We turn the small crowd of children toward their homes. A funeral is going; people are eulogizing the deceased woman. An elderly woman, who's obviously been enjoying the local brew, begins talking very loudly to us. Walter calms her down. Another young man, also quite drunk, tries to shake our hands, but Walter tells him he's not sober and is, therefore, wasting our time. Parham walks quietly, contemplating the well and the children's needs, taking little notice of the drunks. We leave the slums, the funeral songs and the little nude babies behind.

"The next time you have visitors," Steve reminds me, "I'll give you a goat!"

Me, Parham and Karen leave Nyalenda and the children and go to Kiboko Bay to see the hippos. In a wooden boat manned by hired guides Kennedy, Paul and Charles, we skirt the shore of Lake Victoria searching for submerged hippos. Our journey is accompanied by a loud rap, rap, rap.

Charles is beating his wooden oar on the boat to disturb the hippos, calling them to us. "It's okay," Karen and I laugh nervously, "we don't need to see the hippos that badly."

Hippos stay out of the water during the night and return to the lake each morning. We slip past women washing clothes on the lake's edge and men bathing naked and drying in the sun, sitting on rocks the exact color of their skin. Most of the hippos gather about 100 yards offshore and submerge as we approach, with the exception of the biggest one, who keeps his ears and eyes above water to monitor our approach. We glide past, enjoying the feeling of floating.

As the men cut their oars in and out of the silvery water, we see the lake's fishing industry up close. The men do the fishing and the women do the trading. Typically, guys with boats, like the one we're in, will go out at night, net the fish and fill their boat full of tilapia and Nile perch. The men who fish during the day do so while standing on rocks or floating on traditional crafts. Each fisherman will have about four poles (experts can handle up to six poles), which are baited and cast. They usually have their worms or other bait in a plastic Kimbo container hanging around their necks. We pass two men in a boat. They have their net in a large circle. One of the guys jumps in the water and continually dives to the bottom of the lake, placing the net firmly against the floor, trapping fish in the circle. They then gather the net and dump the catch into their boat.

The Kenyan media is using the words "Killer Brew" to sensationalize 51 recent deaths. Of 250 people who drank from a batch of illicit brew last weekend, 51 have died, 10 have gone blind and the death toll is expected to rise. It is not clear if the woman who made the brew will be punished.

This is not an isolated incident; the government is currently proposing a way to supply the population with safe, cheap beer. The government is also paying the burial costs for the 51 victims, including providing coffins.

Deaths and casualties from illegal beer, while tragic on their own, are made more so because of the horrifically graphic descriptions of the dying people and their grieving family members. News stories—both broadcast and printed—appeal unashamedly to emotions.

We'll soon address this in communication class at TICH.

Mitch Odera, a longtime friend of TICH, was editor-in-chief of the Standard, one of Kenya's two national newspapers, for many years throughout President Moi's tyrannical rule. Now serving as chairman of the Kenya Media Council, Mitch also runs a media consultancy service and teaches part-time at TICH. I'm thrilled to co-teach with Mitch on Communication and Advocacy for the next week. Mitch and I are tasked with instructing students on how best to work with the media when promoting causes and community work. In addition, we'll expose the students to persuasive theory and public speaking practices to ensure their messages are constructed properly for their audiences.

Mitch lives in Nairobi but travels to Kisumu to teach an occasional class. We have tea at St. Anne's Guest House to discuss content for the course. Mitch and I are the only people in the dining room. The windows behind Mitch are open, allowing a cool breeze to toss the lacy white curtains throughout our conversation. No lights are on in the room; filtered illumination comes through the windows casting everything in a perfect tea-time glow.

Mitch, only slightly taller than me, is solidly built, with a strong face and kind eyes. His hair, I notice, is going gray around the edges. I guess Mitch to be in his early 50s. Our tea consists of traditional East African tea (tea, milk and water boiled together and then strained) along with sugar. The waiter brings out four pieces of bread, untoasted, with softened butter.

I butter my bread and prepare my tea while Mitch tells me about his background as editor of the Standard as well as his current trials with Lucy Kibaki, President Kibaki's wife. During Moi's years as president, he ruled Kenya by intimidation. It's hard to believe his reign of terror ended only three years ago with the election of President Kibaki. Stories abound of people being pulled from offices, homes or the streets by Moi's police to be taken in for interrogation. These "interrogations" often included torture until the abductee signed some sort of confession, landing him or her in jail for years. Mitch himself was taken from his press room and planted in a chair in an interrogation room. They placed a written confession in front of him and insisted he sign. If he signed, Mitch would be confessing to working in collusion with rebel forces who were using his newspaper to overthrow Moi's government. He refused to sign, even when they used persuasive tactics too gruesome to mention. Lots of people "disappeared" in the Moi years.

Today, Mitch's biggest concern is how to handle Lucy Kibaki, Kenya's First Lady. She recently hit a photojournalist, who immediately brought assault charges against her (the charges were later dropped). When her neighbor, a minister of some governmental department, threw a party, Lucy tramped across the lawn in the wee hours, clad in only her nightgown to break up the party. The press was there, naturally filming the first lady in her gown, ranting at the noisemakers.

Fed up with the press' portrayal of her, Lucy went to the Nation's news center, and berated the journalists for five full hours on what she perceived as their unfair coverage of her. Five hours. Some people say Lucy is not quite right in the head. Mitch thinks the Kenyan public should be compassionate toward Lucy, recognizing she has a slight mental imbalance. Others speculate Lucy is under pressure because President Kibaki has a girlfriend the press calls his "second wife." Whatever the source of Lucy's angst, she feels the press has no right to portray her as someone who hits journalists and traipses about in the middle of the night breaking up parties and holding the press hostage, even though that's exactly what she's been doing.

After Lucy chastised the press at the Nation for five hours, Mitch phoned her assistant and reminded Lucy she can bring her complaints to the Media Council of Kenya, which will act as mediator between her and the press. Within a few days, Lucy delivers to Mitch an 11-page complaint detailing every incidence of her perceived mistreatment by the press. Mitch then shares the complaint with the media houses (newspapers, television and radio) and asks for their responses.

While we're teaching, Mitch tells the class about the media issues with Lucy. We discuss how public figures are not protected. In Kenya—just as in the United States—anyone who places him or herself in the public arena is forced to accept unflattering things will be written. They have very little recourse apart from suing for libel, which is a long shot if they fit the definition of a public figure. This week, as Mitch and I are in front of the class, he takes a phone call, pacing up and down the hallway while I talk to the students about persuasive theories in the field of social psychology. Mitch returns and tells us he's just received word that all the media houses have submitted their responses to Lucy's accusations. Mitch and the Media Council will now set a date for a hearing.

The next morning, Mitch brings the Nation and the Standard to class. On page two of the Nation, an article quotes Mitch as saying the media houses have responded and a date for the hearing will be set. The article represents correctly the information Mitch expressed when on the phone. I read the article to the students. They've heard Mitch tell his views of the "Lucy" tale and how he has communicated with the media. Now they get to see the results on the printed page, including quotes from their esteemed instructor.

Together, Mitch and I share information about the academic field of communication, the media, public speaking, persuasive techniques and ways of overcoming cultural and language barriers. It's a full week and Mitch's knowledge areas dovetail ever-so-well with mine.

Co-facilitating with Mitch has been uplifting and eye-opening. At times, when I'd be talking about the roots of rhetoric from Aristotle to the present, I'd notice the slightest nod of encouragement from his open face. He would interject tidbits and facts to my presentations, and I'd do the same when he was speaking. Even though he normally teaches this section of the course alone, he completely opened up the curriculum and included information I wanted to impart.

Hopefully our students will take what they've learned and apply it to their work of changing people's lives for the better. This class has only reinforced how honored I am to get to know our TICH students better. They are a varied and interesting group. Many of them are in their 30s and already hold nursing degrees. Others currently work with NGOs in Kenya and other African countries. One student owns a pharmacy in town. They are intent on helping their respective countries develop by sharing what they've learned at TICH to improve the lives of their fellow countrymen and women. They exhibit earnestness and selflessness daily.

While the students prepare presentations for class, Mitch and I suggest they use topics that arise naturally during class discussions. For example, when the topic of wife inheritance comes up, we decide to use it. Wife inheritance is practiced by the Luo and other West African communities. The students divide themselves into three groups according to ethnicity. The group representing the Luo community develops a persuasive speech on the merits of wife inheritance, and the other two groups create persuasive speeches on the dangers of wife inheritance.

Wife inheritance is considered one of the cultural practices that con-tributes to the high rate of HIV/AIDS in West Kenya. When looking at a map of Kenya depicting the disease's incidence, the wide bands surround-ing Lake Victoria have the highest rates of infection. While the national average of HIV infection is 6.7 percent, it rises to 15 percent in our part of Kenya, with Kisumu acting as the hub of the high percentage area. Many pockets around the lake—including slum areas—have rates as high as 38 percent.

At its roots, wife inheritance is fairly simple, as we learn from the stu-dents. If a woman is widowed, her husband's family attaches her to an-other man within the family right away. Usually, this man is the deceased's brother. He takes the widow as his wife, even if he already has one. The Luos believe the practice provides care for the widow and her dependent children. According to tradition, the woman is to have sex with her new husband before her deceased husband is buried. If it doesn't happen be-fore the funeral, it must happen within four days after the burial. They also want her to become pregnant within three months of her husband's death. When the child is born, it is given the name of the deceased and treated as his physical embodiment. According to the students, Luos be-lieve deceased relatives oversee their welfare and act as intermediaries with the spirit world.

If the man is thought to have died from a curse (which is often what AIDS is called), the woman must be cleansed before having sex with her new husband (the same holds true for men who lose their wives to curses and/or AIDS). This means a man, acting as a "cleanser" from outside the family, will have sex with the widow. If she is HIV positive, she may infect the male outsider, who then goes on to have sex with other widows who may or may not be infected. Most likely, the "cleanser" is already HIV posi-tive and therefore has a high likelihood of infecting widows who were not infected by their husbands.

Opponents of wife inheritance say the primary reason people want the wife attached to a new husband is so their family will retain rights to the man's property. If the woman is left to her own devices, argues one Luo student, there will be a line of men at her gate, and she may let them all in, one at a time. Others argue that a woman should not be required to have a man. They say when a woman is widowed, she should get to choose if, when, and whom she remarries. If she is okay living on her own and taking care of her children, she should be able to live as she chooses.

When one anti-wife inheritance group speaks too harshly against women who are inherited, a female who identifies herself as Luo speaks up. Her name is Elizabeth. She participates fully and strongly in all discussions, her words always come across as confident and sharp. Elizabeth's comment to the anti-wife inheritance group is that their attitude during the delivery of their speech put her off, because as a Luo woman, she wants to be inherited should her husband die. She tells them that their closed viewpoint caused her to shut down to their message. I take this as my opportunity to jump in and reiterate what we had already discussed about knowing one's audience. Only when a speaker knows the attitudes and beliefs held by his or her audience can he or she construct an argument to meet that belief and then work to change it. Attitudes must be changed before behavior will change.

Wife inheritance is a fascinating, heart-breaking topic; the students are fully engaged for the two hours of presentations. Because the topic of wife inheritance is important and deeply felt by everyone in the room, I struggle to view it purely as a topic for communication instruction. This continual stepping back to examine delivery was a good way to get the students to take a meta-approach to this and other topics.

Orphans also come up during our discussions. One student says he read a news article about street boys in Nairobi being taken to the Congo and trained in military tactics by rebels. Mitch Odera immediately turns to him and says, "I wrote that article." Mitch proceeds to tell us that soon peace will arrive in the Congo—and perhaps even Sudan—where many boys are taken and trained as soldiers.

"They're taught to torture and kill without remorse," Mitch says, "when fighting stops in these countries, the militant boys will return to Kenya and Nairobi. I have pled with the government to prepare for their return, because Kenya has never dealt with street boys trained to kill."

An orphan is defined as a child who has lost one or both parents. Vera, a research intern at TICH who's originally from the Congo, says her father was killed in their civil war in the early 60s. Because of the stigma of being an orphan, her father's family and her mother's family ostracized them. She says her mother had a bitter time taking care of her family without a husband and without the assistance of extended family.

This stigma holds true for the nearly one million orphans in Kenya. If the parent(s) die from AIDS, they are even more likely to be shunned out of fear the children themselves might be infected. There are an estimated one million orphans in Kenya, and the government cannot afford to build orphanages. In most cases, grandparents care for orphaned grandchildren.

Sue, a student nurse from the UK, has traveled to Kisumu for three weeks to learn about health issues and health care practices in Kenya. She's traveling with her friend, Anna, who works at a UK college, assisting adults with disabilities.

When I mention the Provincial Hospital to them, they're both keen to visit and ask if I can arrange it. With Parham and Karen now in Nairobi, I've lost my connection for access to the various wards. We decide to go to the hospital anyway, to possibly see Margaret, the head nurse of surgery. I figure she might be able to arrange a tour appointment, or, if we're lucky, she might take us on rounds with her. When we arrive and make our way to the top ward, we learn Margaret isn't working this afternoon. I see no problem in our walking the halls and, instead of going into the rooms, simply standing outside. I should be able to update Sue and Anna on the patients I recognize. It's the best we can do, so we walk slowly. Our white skin gives us uninterrupted access.

The first door we pass is the room of the young university student who is paralyzed from the knees down. He was supposed to get his wheelchair and leave. I'm dismayed to see his face through the door. Despite my plan to stay in the halls, we go into the room and I introduce everyone, telling them about his case—how he was mugged and beaten, damaging his spinal cord.

"Why are you still here?" I ask, "You were supposed to get your wheelchair and go back to school."

He points behind us, to his wheelchair.

"They want me to get around on crutches before using the wheelchair."

That sounds reasonable to me. But before they can get him on crutches, they must straighten his legs. And to straighten his legs, they need a splint and crepe bandages. The hospital has the splints but not the bandages. Our friend, Austine, the physiotherapist, told this young man there are no bandages.

I'm irritated and ask Sue how much bandages cost.

"One pound," she says.

For less than two dollars, this young man can have his legs straightened. So he can use crutches. So he can get in his wheelchair. So he can go home. Less. Than. Two. Dollars.

I figure they probably sell the damn crepe bandages in the hospital pharmacy, so I tell the young patient we're going to look for Austine. In the stairwell, two men follow us and introduce themselves.

"What are you doing at this hospital?" I ask the more outgoing of the two. He tells me his father is in traction with a broken leg. His father's cow knocked him over and stepped on him.

"Can we meet your father?" I ask. Sue and Anna understand this is a way for us to visit patients and get their stories without requiring permission from the hospital's personnel. The man and his friend are more than happy for us to meet his father, so we all turn and walk back up the stairs to enter the same room where the paralyzed university student resides. Big laughs all around as we re-enter the room.

The man's father is a long, skinny old man who fought in the Second World War in Kenya. He must be 85 years old and doesn't understand a word of English, but we can tell he is strong. He happily shows us his leg and we ask to see the x-rays stored between his mattresses. The break is in his shinbone, and the fracture is so severe the bone pieces are parallel.

"A cow did this," Sue says, not really asking.

"He loves his cows," the son says, and we all agree cows are mighty fine things, as long as they're not stepping on you.

We leave and pass the burn room. I point out Janet's bed. Janet is a 23-year-old woman who had an epileptic seizure and fell into the fire, burning her face, head and shoulders. She has the requisite iron half-hoop frame over her bed. At the foot of the bed is a much smaller hoop frame— a child-sized one. When we visited last week, Karen and I stopped to talk to Janet and to see the baby girl sharing her bed. (The little girl had been burned on her arm and leg; supposedly, she pulled hot water onto herself, though she seemed to be just an infant.) At the time of our visit, Janet's head was bare and her face and shoulders were white with red splotches. She didn't wear clothes under her hoop. Although her mouth was disfigured from the skin tightening as it healed, she could still speak. Janet's eyes were burned in the fire and she cannot see. Doctors aren't sure she'll regain her sight. We don't bother her today.

Downstairs, we pass a room where a teenage girl sits nude, covered to her waist by a sheet. I think she's the 16 year old we visited last week. We pause in our trip through the hospital so I can tell Anna and Sue the story.

When Parham, Eric and I were touring last week, Karen joined us after her rounds in maternity.

"You guys want to see a membrane coming out of a vagina?" Karen asked. We all looked at each other and said "yes." As we walked, Karen explained how the girl had just arrived after having a Caesarian (the hospital was not sure where the operation took place or who performed it).

"The surgeon must have perforated her bowel," Karen said, "because feces were coming out of her Caesarian incision. The baby didn't live. Now there's something that looks like a membrane coming from her vagina."

After we talked to the girl, with Eric, the medical student, acting as our interpreter, Karen lifted the sheets. There was a string of dark gray, moist tissue extending about eight inches from her body.

"Is it her fallopian tube and ovary?" Parham asked. No one knew. They had only seen healthy ones.

"Is it fixed?" Parham continued.

"Yes," responded Karen.

The medical experts of the group decided to test it. Parham put on his gloves and tugged gently. Fixed.

I'm still asking myself how I was able to stand there while this poor girl, who lost a baby and survived a perforated bowel, had to just wait while doctors debated about this strange anatomical displacement. I wonder how I am able to continue seeing such things without running and screaming from the building.

We were told even the tiniest of cuts on the bowel can cause great damage, and ultimately death, if not corrected. Because she was nude, I gave the young woman a small t-shirt that said "Canada" across the front. She smiled gratefully. A woman sat next to her bed, caring for her. We learned later it wasn't her mother, but the mother of another patient.

After telling Sue and Anna the girl's story, I tell them about going to Dr. Okeyo's office at Aga Khan last Friday. He's an Obstetrician/Gynecologist and head of TICH's Health Sciences Department. His office has a poster of the female reproductive system on the wall. When I was there, I studied that poster. The fallopian tube and ovary were EXACTLY what we had seen lying on that girl's bed. I told Dr. Okeyo and Dr. Michael Clarke the details of the perforated bowel and strange "discharge." (Dr. Michael is a microbiologist by training and currently heads the IT department at the University of Ottawa.)

"Was she butchered?" I asked Dr. Okeyo.

"Yes," he said without hesitation.

We continue our hospital tour and pass the ENT room. I tell them about Michael, the boy with the ear infection that advanced into brain infection. As we near the end of the hall, we see our two new Kenyan friends—the ones who introduced us to their cow-injured father—standing outside the room of our favorite patient, the young mentally and physically challenged woman.

The man with the out-going personality is also visiting his sister, who is caring for her daughter; she is the roommate we saw last week while putting sheets on our favorite patient's bed. The man's niece is around 16 years old. He translates for his sister and niece, so we learn the young woman was at a funeral when she was attacked. Called "disco funerals," they have been known to go on for several days and nights with lots of loud music and alcohol. The combination of nighttime, music and alcohol often leads to sex, further spreading HIV. Many communities have banned these disco funerals.

This girl was walking home from the party when a thug attacked her with a machete. She put her hands up to protect her face, and both wrists were hit and broken. He also cut off her right index finger, and her right thumb was left dangling (it, at least, has been re-attached). Flies crawl on the big, black stitches around her thumb and on the knuckle where her index finger was. She has a machete wound in her left thigh. It is healing nicely, though. Her leg was broken just below the knee, so she's in traction. They tell us the man who attacked her was caught and is in jail.

Our favorite patient lies once again on a bare mattress. The only item left from our visit last week is the pillow (but without the new pillowcase). I ask the girl in the next bed if they've been keeping our favorite patient's sheets clean. She says the sheets and blanket are out being washed. She also says they've been feeding her. Right now, she is wide awake and taking Anna's finger in her palm and squeezing, trying to put it into her mouth.

"She needs a toy to chew on," Anna says, "she needs something that's her own, that's comforting. Everything goes straight to her mouth." Anna promises to get her a toy. The nice man who's visiting his niece says he'll make sure the pink sheets and the gray blanket are returned to the girl's bed. We leave strangely at peace.

Anna and Sue later tell me they returned to the hospital. They gave the young university student crepe bandages. They also took our favorite patient a soft toy, which she liked to lay her face on, as well as a teething-type toy with spinners and other movable, shiny parts. Anna gave the girl the toy, which went straight into her mouth. She then removed the toy and gave it back to Anna, who placed it on the side of the bed. The girl reached for Anna's hand, guiding her to the toy. Anna gave the toy to our girl again, and she once more put the toy to her mouth, watching Anna's hand and the toy the whole time.

"It was a little thing," Anna tells me, "her taking my hand. But it meant so much to me."

Crepe bandages and shiny toys. In Kenya, little things are often mighty powerful.

On most days when I return home from the hospital, I pass a corner house with a huge wall and Maasai men at the gate. In the morning, there are usually five or six men sitting on stones outside the compound wall. They are all slim and tall, with their bright red robes wrapped about their shoulders. It has been cold these last few weeks, and the only thing they wear are pieces of cloth, draped and flowing.

Maasai warriors grow their hair long and braid it, doing the most interesting things with the braids, like upsweeping or looping them around their ears. Ma is their first language, but these particular guys know a little Kiswahili. We nod, wave or speak each day and for some reason, they almost always end up laughing at me. The men have their spears, and when they walk down the street—usually in pairs or larger groups—they balance the spears across their shoulders and rest their wrists on either end. This is how they walk and stand about while tending their cattle in the open areas of Africa. Employed as escaries (watchmen), they have no cattle to tend in the city.

Today, I come to the gate and find one lone warrior. He is sitting on a stone in Rodin's "The Thinker" position. At first I don't recognize him, until I look into his face. He is wearing a crisply ironed, long-sleeve dress shirt and navy dress slacks. He seems taller than normal, but large holes in his earlobes and his familiar face give him away. I can't take my eyes off him. I yell out when I recognize him, and laugh. Two Kenyans on the opposite corner start laughing, too, saying he is dressed differently today. I say, "Nzuri sana," meaning "very good," and that he looks nice.

It really messes with my mind, to see this man in Western clothes. It is almost as mind-twisting as seeing a real Maasai warrior for the first time.

Maasai warriors stare at me as much as I want to stare at them. I'd love to take their photos, but feel it would be exploitative. I'm left with only the pictures captured in my memory. Even today, this young man's image stays in my mind, him leaning forward, his chin on his hand, his long, lean body covered in a dress shirt and slacks instead of the usual bright red plaid folds. His face turns toward me, looking at though he might, suddenly, understand English.

Chapter Twelve

R e n o v a t i o n

I'm a fool.

I'm constantly touching my hair, catching it up at the roots to test its thickness. It doesn't feel as full as when I first got here. I know hair loss is a side effect of Lariam, the anti-malarial drug, so I make plans to talk to Dr. Sokwala about changing to a different prescription.

During lunch I go to town and run into Walter Odede. He asks if he can walk with me to the doctor's office. He wants to talk. I'm ashamed to tell Walter why I want to see the doctor—because I think I'm losing my hair—but I do. When Walter is sick, he can't afford to visit the doctor. Not many people in Kisumu can.

"I want to tell you about a boy. A street boy," Walter says.

Walter is around street boys all the time, so for him to mention one particular boy means something. I listen carefully as we dodge pedestrians on the narrow city sidewalks. The boy's name is Vincent. He's from Kisii, which is about 75 kilometers from Kisumu. He's an orphan with six children in the family. His older sister, aged 15, disappeared, and Vincent thinks she may be married now. Vincent somehow made his way to Kisumu and is living on the street, even though he doesn't speak Kiswahili or Dholuo. He speaks Kisii. Through an interpreter, Walter has been learning more about Vincent; although he hangs out with many street boys, Walter is certain he is not sniffing glue. Walter is taken with this boy and wants to sponsor him in school.

"If someone can give the boy a place to live," Walter says, "then Pambazuko can send him to school."

"If you feel he should be sponsored before the other children, I trust your assessment," I say to Walter. He's happy.

We've reached Dr. Sokwala's office, and a note on the door says she's away until next Monday.

"Would you like to walk to the tailor's shop?" I ask Walter.

We turn the corner to find two men standing outside a hardware store, next to a pump. This is not just any pump—it is the very pump we want to buy for the well in Nyalenda. It costs 6,999 shillings (about US $90). Made of steel and painted turquoise, the pump is manual and looks like a stair-stepper, an analogy that means nothing here, because few Kenyans would understand the concept of someone stepping on a machine to exercise.

The pump is a great piece of engineering. Two pistons must be primed by adding water before beginning. These pistons are lifted up and down by stepping on the foot pedals. The water is forced into a tube or hose (the advertising poster shows a man in his garden, irrigating his crop with a long hose). This pump is large enough to force water 200 meters. It looks durable. The well is now covered and we'll be ready to set the pump next week.

Once we're in the tailor's shop, I try on the top to my custom-made Punjabi suit and show Hitesh, the tailor's son, how I want it to be shortened. I also show him how much to take it in on the sides. His father sits behind a sewing machine, eye-level to my navel, telling Hitesh to measure my hips. When we're through, I ask Walter if he knows where Cut Above is. He does. We walk back through town, talking about Pambazuko business.

Cut Above is across from the Imperial Hotel, which is unarguably the nicest place in Kisumu. We stop to talk outside the Imperial, where doormen stand nearby in full-length uniforms. They soon ask us to either enter or leave. Walter goes to work and I notice the sign outside the salon. It says "Specialized in Asian and European Hair." Here, beauty shops or stylist shops are called "salons" and pronounced "saloons." Indians are referred to as "Asians."

A cut is 500 shillings (about US $6). The shop is empty of clients. A middle-aged Indian woman sits behind the desk. She rips through my wet hair with a comb, but I have to admit she does a very lovely job cutting it. Suddenly, without the 2.5 inches of dead, thin ends, my hair feels abundant once again. I am overjoyed to think that perhaps it's not falling out! I walk back to work heartened and somewhat glad Dr. Sokwala wasn't in to hear my paranoid suspicions of losing my hair.

Later, Tonny comes into my office. His mind is working something over. He's just returned from town—from seeing Walter—where he met Vincent, the street boy from Kisii.

"I was so moved," Tonny says, rubbing his forehead with his hands. Hard. Twice.

Tonny grew up in Nyalenda. He's seen everything. Every kind of cruelty and injustice people can inflict. For him to be moved is something. He echoes Walter's impressions of Vincent: he's a good kid, a kind kid, one who appreciates any kind of help.

What Walter didn't tell me was Vincent has a large, infected sore on the back of his head. Together, Walter and Tonny took Vincent to a doctor in town. He saw them on the side and said Vincent will need six injections, which he'll gladly give free of charge if Walter can buy the drugs and bring them in. The six doses cost about 300 shillings, so Walter and Tonny rush to get it right away.

Tonny leans on my desk, rubbing his forehead. His mind is working something over. And I know what it is.

"Think about it, Tonny," I say, "think about it at least two days."

He's grinning, knowing he won't think about it for even half as long.

"I'm going to do it," he says, taking up a piece of paper and writing "bed, table, mosquito net." He wants to put the boy up in his house, temporarily. I tell him temporary may not be in Vincent's best interest. I want us to think about how we can create a permanent solution before rushing into any decisions. A house is for rent next to Pambazuko's building site for US $10 a month. If we have two rooms, we can have boys in one and girls in the other. Tonny says we can have bunk beds built, stacked three beds high. Two beds will fit in each room, which means we can handle six boys and six girls. Tonny decides he wants to pay the rent. With a bed and roof, Vincent can go to school. Tonny is no longer rubbing his forehead. He is grinning.

Tonny has seen everything. He has seen all kinds of cruelty and injustice; yet his heart still swells and he still gets excited, thinking about helping Vincent and other children.

"Walter didn't tell me about Vincent's sore," I tell Tonny. Walter didn't tell Tonny, either. Tonny saw it himself. And he was repulsed. He couldn't look at Vincent's head. (Tonny was accepted to study medicine, but in Kenya, students first learn to dissect corpses, to weed out the intolerant. Tonny was weeded out fairly quickly.) The doctor said Vincent's sore needs to be cleaned with an antiseptic, which Walter will do. Which Walter had in mind to do all day today and all day yesterday and all day the day before, ever since he met Vincent and learned the boy's story through an interpreter.

Walter walked with me to the doctor because I was worried my hair is falling out. He watched as I acted silly in the tailor's shop. He directed me to the place where I got my hair cut—a place specializing in "soft" hair. All the while, Walter didn't tell me that Vincent has a gaping hole in his head and is in real need. Walter and Tonny are doing everything they can to take care of the boy. Don't I feel like a fool with my hair and clothes concerns?

Yep. Yes-sir-ee.

I'm a fool.

Early morning and a bird sits outside the living room window, yelling, clearly. I tiptoe over and peek, not wanting to scare him away. Searching the branches of the lantana fence, I finally spot the noisemaker, a fantastically brilliant bird. He has a glossy black back like a tuxedo with elegantly long tails, and a red, red, densely red chest as his captivating cummerbund. He tweets and twills and looks about, hopping amongst the spade-shaped leaves.

A glimpse of divinity.

He follows the turn of the fence and is soon out of sight. But he's still there, still twilling and tweeting. With the sounds of his song come twills from other birds and flutters in nearby trees. The rooster in the corn patch next door crows, causing roosters in other yards to crow, causing a dog to bark, causing dogs up and down our street to bark. I can hear the echo being mimicked by dogs all over Kisumu, like the wave baseball fans make in a stadium, eventually returning and seemingly never-ending.

A cow moos—deep, loud and harmless. Cow feet shuffle in the dirt and clop on the pavement, passing just outside our gate, headed, herded on their daily round of grass seeking. I can see them in my mind's eye, usually tended by an old Mama in her scarf-wrapped head or young boys with sticks, walking barefoot, trying to keep the spring calf from leaping playfully into a car's grill.

Thin music comes on the wind, sometimes, from a nearby house or passing car. Dishes settle musically into their rightful places on shelves, glasses clink into rows in neighboring cupboards. Tiny claps sound as beads tied to cloth—makeshift curtains—billow in the slow breeze and fall back against the window frame.

But there is more to this soundtrack. Screaming and shouting comes loud and harsh from a nearby bandstand, where preachers use amplifiers to reach large audiences. A man and a woman sing, then scream at each other with the spiritual music in the background, tension building and building until I begin to look for earplugs. Children sing spirituals in imitation and run in the red soil, pounding the earth into wisps of dustlets, laughing up at the palest of moons. Darkness arrives, slowly, and the loudspeakers are turned off. Night birds get busy with their twattering. Boda boda bells on handlebars send their tinny twirps as warnings to walkers in the lowing light.

Voices glide gently from other places, other spaces, other tongues. Female on female, male on male and then a glorious mix of the two, melodic. Comforting. Steady. Sounds.

Songs.

Of man and beast, fauna and fowl. Birds become frisky in late hours, increasing their volume, their pitch, their frequency. But the steadiest background noise, both day and night, is the call of the cockerel. He's in every yard, on every block, and he loves to sing his might.

A grounded bird, but singing nonetheless.

Dr. Michael Clarke, the head of the University of Ottawa's IT department, is in Kisumu. He's here to help TICH write a proposal for funding for a new internet access system. Michael wants to visit the Center for Disease Control (CDC) in Kisumu to see what system they use so we might potentially mimic theirs.

Michael, Tonny and I ride with Dr. Stephen Okeyo, the head of TICH's Health Sciences department. It takes us awhile to get to the CDC, not because it's far away, but because Stephen wants to go by his OB/GYN office at Aga Khan (the very nice, private hospital). Once we're there, he has a patient waiting. He finishes his work in good time, so we drive to the CDC and pull up to the gate. Stephen's car seems to be overheating. We can smell the heat as the engine chokes and sputters.

The guard is too slow opening the gate and the car dies. It won't start, so Tonny, Michael and I climb out, pushing the car backward until Stephen pops the clutch and it cranks. We all yell at him to keep his foot on the gas while we climb through the one door that opens. We're feeling very accomplished until we come to a second gate. Even though we have a piece of official paper, they're not going to let us enter and the car dies. We get out and push backward again. And again. Stephen is finally able to drive the car and park it.

The CDC has security. Even though every home, office and building in Kenya and most of Africa has security—guards at the gate or entrance or door, dogs, high fences with broken glass set in cement, padlocks and mazes of barbed wire under walls to discourage climbing—the CDC has electric door releases activated with security badges, just like offices in the United States. They also have air-conditioning, not just for the computer center but for everywhere. Their lobby has black leather chairs and huge colorful posters. People wear business clothes. It is quite a treat to enter this well-organized and carefully maintained place.

Erik, the manager of the CDC's computer center, is from Holland. He shows us their servers and their firewalls. We're all a bit envious but try not to show it. He's extremely helpful and provides quite a bit of good technical info. Once our tour is complete, we return our visitors' badges and leave, hoping Stephen's car will crank now that it's cooled down. It does.

A couple of days ago, a coworker, Lynette, told me about how she was called to her friend's house early Sunday morning. Her friend was pregnant, but like many women in Kenya, she couldn't afford to go to a doctor to monitor the pregnancy. Her friend was in severe pain and Lynette could see she was going into shock (Lynette is a nurse by training), so they took her to Aga Khan. An examination revealed the pregnancy to be ectopic and the fallopian tube ruptured. An operation was needed right away. Lynette called Dr. Stephen Okeyo, who was on a plane just touching down at the Kisumu airport. He rushed to the hospital, examined the patient and arranged to have her moved to a hospital that wouldn't charge a great deal for the operation. Within an hour, he had operated and the woman is now on the road to recovery.

When I see Dr. Okeyo after hearing Lynette's story, I shake his hand hard and long. I go on and on about how wonderful he is, saving this woman's life and charging the most minimal of fees because the family is struggling. He says it was nothing, that ectopic pregnancies are the easiest of operations. (Turns out ectopic pregnancies are common in Kenya because of the prevalence of Sexually Transmitted Infections.) But I know better, because here's a man driving a car that overheats and must be pushed backward to start. Yet he's saving lives without worrying about what's in it for him.

Dr. Okeyo shuffles his feet and looks at the ground when I commend him.

He's my hero.

TICH will have an exhibit for the first time at the annual Regional Agricultural Show in Kisumu the first week in August. We're renting an existing building from a cookie company, but must make cosmetic repairs on the walls, ceilings, floors and windows to make it gleaming and appealing once more. As marketing manager, I've taken on the task of getting the building ready for the show. This means hiring carpenters, painters, masons, electricians and a multitude of others to complete the repairs in time.

At TICH, we have two vehicles with drivers who are available to take folks on work-related business when needed. To get a vehicle, I have to fill out a vehicle requisition form, have it signed by the department head and then turn it into George, head of security. But just because I fill out a form and request to leave at 4:00pm doesn't mean we'll leave at 4:00pm. Sometimes we'll sit and wait for others, combining trips and sharing resources.

Anyone specializing in a skill—such as painting, carpentry or repairing boda bodas—is called a "fundi," or expert. No fundi in Kisumu has his own transportation. Few have their own tools. When we hire someone to paint or landscape, we usually have to transport them to the show grounds. We also have to buy all the supplies. I've spent many a morning and afternoon running from the accounts office with a purchase requisition form in hand, carrying it to be signed by the department head, followed by the Reverend, head of HR. If I'm lucky, I'll run into Director Dan Keseje. He has power to authorize anything TICH-related, and if he signs, no other signature is needed.

Most days, I'm running around to get money for turpentine or paint or sand paper or ballast so our fundis can do their work, while at the same time running around getting signatures for the vehicle so we can get the fundi to the site. Even if our fundi shows up promptly at 8:00am, it may be 10:00am before we reach the show grounds; we are often detained by last minute notices about supplies or transportation. This is Kenya. Things take time. One must take lots of deep breaths.

Every day, without fail, when we pull up to our building on the show grounds, people flock to us. We drive through the gates and through acres of roads leading to our exhibit. The groups of men and women lounging under trees rise, as though we're dispensing money, and follow. They come into our yard and into our building, uninvited, making it incredibly difficult to hold private conversations with our hired help.

"Excuse me, Madam, I'm a graphic artist."

"Madam, may I speak to you? I'm a carpenter."

"A mason."

"An electrician."

Sometimes it's so overwhelming I could scream. And I do, ashamedly.

We arrive one morning to hire two ladies to clean the floor, to prep it for painting. When we invite them in to discuss their tasks and payment, some people just walk in, while others block the doorway. Frustrated, I turn to ask them to step outside, so we can talk privately. Instead of saying anything, I lift my left hand and wave it toward them, in a shooing motion. I am instantly ashamed. I'm also instantly surprised to see their eyes widen as they jump with the movement of my hand. They jump back and spin and almost run away.

I feel like the white colonialist commanding people. It's a horrible feeling. Never do I want to treat them as a group, as a lump. I always want to relate to Kenyans individually, as the valued humans they are. And here they are, en masse, appealing to me for jobs, for work, just so they can prepare dinner for their families. Sometimes the weight of this is too much, especially when I'm feeling the pressure to the get the work done on time; especially when I'm feeling the pressure to hire someone who is reliable and skilled. How can I tell who's reliable and qualified when there are fifty men and women standing and staring, waiting to be chosen?

After I lift my hand to shoo them, after they turn and scatter back behind the ragged picket fence at our property edge, I feel like less of a person inside. Still, I close the door and turn to Ruth and Esther, the two women we want to hire, and find ten faces peering into the window. Ten other faces peer into the next window. There is no such thing as privacy in Kenya.

We hire a man to cut (slash) the grass. Dr. Lucas Ngode, head of TICH administration, speaks to him in Dholuo and Kiswahili. I've turned the negotiations over to Lucas since the grass-cutter doesn't seem to understand me, even though he shakes his head as if he does. There are very few lawn-mowers in Kenya. People here use a machete, called a slasher, which they swipe over the grass. We explain to our grass-cutter that we want the grass shortened and any dirt or grass on the paved walkways removed.

When I arrive the next morning without Lucas, I'm dismayed to see the entire yard plowed. Not one blade of grass remains, and there is only dark, loosened soil across the grounds. Walkway pads made of 2 x 2-foot cement slabs have been uprooted; many of them are broken.

Vitalis, our driver, tells me he was given a tip by one of the other workers that this young man, our grass-cutter, is not quite right in the head. Vitalis was given this tip the day before, but didn't tell me or Lucas. He told his boss, George, who manages our guards and janitors and drivers. But even George didn't pass the information on. Now we have a freshly plowed yard where we wanted a nicely manicured lawn.

The show is one and a half weeks away. Our reliable painter, Peter, has shown up every day on time. He's worked hard to paint all the interior walls, the floor and the trim on the outside. Today he's starting on the exterior walls. It's an extremely rough surface and will require quite a bit of paint. I go to town and buy two 20-liter containers of third-quality white paint. Peter doesn't own a sprayer so he uses a six-inch brush. He also uses TICH's ladder. He's by far the hardest working man I've seen in Kenya.

I take quotes from three artists to paint our name across the front eave and to paint our logo on the building. Their charges are wildly disparate. Although it's a joy to tell men and women when they have the job, I find it difficult to tell the ones who are not selected that we've chosen someone else. The ones we do hire often smile big, wide smiles. Some even jump up and down while shaking my hand and sealing the deal. Kenyans do not show this kind of joy often.

I like it when they smile and jump.

Every day I make two or three trips to the show grounds, dropping off fundis, hiring others, checking on the work completed. Every time our truck pulls up, there are more and more people asking for jobs. If I don't mentally prepare myself and tell the driver how we're going to handle certain tasks before we get there, it's very easy to be swamped and swayed and irritated by so many pleading, serious faces. The drivers are wonderful and understanding. They help me communicate with compassion. When I worry about our fundis not eating, they figure out how to get food to them. Every day I'm reminded how caring Kenyans are: the ones with money as well as the ones without. Even though there's competition for jobs, they're all very respectful to each other, because they're all in the same boat.

I wish we could hire them all. I wish I could go to the show grounds and be open-hearted and never irritated. I don't want to shame them or myself.

Around noon, we head back to the office from the show grounds. I ask Vitalis to drop me in town so I can buy a radio to hear the BBC world news. I look for Walter at his spot on the sidewalk, where he hawks his handmade goods when he's not tending to Pambazuko business. Walter is there and we walk down the street for a short while, looking for a private place for me to pass shillings to him, shillings to purchase materials for the roof of Pambazuko's building.

Walter walks out of town with me, and we discuss Vincent. He is doing well and his sores are healing. At a small shack on the side of the road, we run into Phoebe, a woman who works with Pambazuko. She is 22 years old and has four children. Phoebe is a widow, her husband having died from AIDS. Her youngest child, only a year old, is not well. The baby, who actually looks like she's half that age, is sleeping soundly on Phoebe's shoulder. Very soundly. Too soundly. It turns out they've just come from the district hospital, where they were told the baby has pneumonia and malaria. In the baby's medical book, the doctor has written a list of seven prescribed medicines. Phoebe could afford the malaria medicine, but not the fever reducer and the pneumonia drug and all the others listed.

I place my hand on the baby's head. She is burning—the hottest I've ever felt a child. The baby doesn't stir the slightest when I touch her and I find myself putting my hand to her head repeatedly. The fever should be reduced at once.

"Will you take some of the money I just gave you for the roof materials," I ask Walter, "and buy the medicines?"

About 400 shillings (US $5) will buy the pain reliever and pneumonia drug. Walter readily agrees. I ask him if he'll go to town right this minute and buy the medicines, so Phoebe doesn't worry, so she doesn't have to carry her sick, sleeping baby all over town, so she can simply go home and wait for Walter to bring the drugs.

It's a lot to ask of Walter, to trek back into town and then back to the slums. But he truly doesn't mind. I touch the baby's head again. Phoebe has a slight smile on her face—a morsel of joy seeping through. I know how she must feel with three other little ones at home and this very still, too still, baby lying against her breast.

Walter waves a boda boda driver down and is on the bike before we can blink. As Walter and the bike are cycling toward town, and we watch them fly away, Walter looks very much like an angel of mercy. A large, loving Angel of Mercy on the back of a boda boda.

It's Friday and I'm home by 6:00pm, grateful to settle into a quiet, relaxing evening. It's been a hectic, exhausting week with numerous trips to the show grounds. As I sit in the living room with my feet up, enjoying sliced tomatoes, a voice calls out "Hello" through the front window. It's Priya, a young Sikh Indian friend.

"Are you ready to go out?" she says.

"Go where?" I ask, looking down at my grungy t-shirt and feeling my hair pinned up in the most unattractive way.

"Come on," she says, "change your top, leave on your jeans. Let's go!"

Priya became engaged six weeks ago. Her fiancé lives in Arusha, Tanzania, and she's only been alone with him for 15 minutes since they became engaged. It's an arranged marriage. Tonight, the Sikh Temple committee (all male) will be visiting Priya's father, to congratulate him on the engagement of his daughter. She wants me there for company and moral support.

It's hard to resist a party, especially when the guest of honor is requesting my presence. So I put on a long-sleeve top, let my hair down and put on shoes.

"Lipstick?" Priya asks. Yes, lipstick.

Her driver awaits us. Priya's family lives on the block behind ours, so we're there in a flash. The Ruprahs are sitting in the living room along with other guests. Priya shows me her bedroom. She opens two narrow doors and we step out onto her balcony, where the moon is full and glowing through clouds. It's enchanting. She tells me about the text messages going back and forth between her and her intended. Priya is falling in love with him and is simply bursting with joy. Guests arrive and we wave to them from above.

Temple committee members show up and fill the living room, which has been cleaned and arranged in a large circle for the men. Huge posters of Sikh gurus look down from the walls. All of the ladies—myself included—scurry to the kitchen. Priya's older brother acts as server. He keeps the Tusker and White Cap beers moving from the back room to the men's glasses. Priya's father pulls out a liter of Famous Goose whiskey and teases all the ladies, pretending to pour it into their glasses. Priya leans toward me and whispers, "It's the fifth one today. The fifth liter."

A friend of the family has cooked mutton, very spicy. Priya's mom has set up a gas cooker in the center of the kitchen and is heating oil to fry samosas. I help Priya bring in the samosas she and her mother prepared the night before: more than 200 of them! Mrs. Ruprah slides the samosas into the hot oil while a young woman stirs to keep them from burning. They've also prepared fried peanuts, lots of Indian sauces and dips, salad and several types of chappatti and naan.

Priya pulls me outside, onto the back patio, to tell me about a poem she wrote for her fiancé. Her father calls her from the kitchen so she runs in, refills the peanut bowl, and returns. When she comes back, she tells me about the poem. When she shared it with him, he was impressed. I'm not surprised; Priya is pretty, slim, intelligent, loving, mature and a wonderful catch. I'd be more surprised if he hadn't been impressed. Her father calls again, so we stop whispering and rejoin the others. There are about 18 men in the living room, making speeches and throwing back beers and whiskey. The ladies are in the kitchen or on the back stairs, where we eat. The mutton is so hot I begin to sweat.

Priya's phone rings from her bedroom upstairs. Technically, it's really her father's mobile phone. She's using it because her phone is filled up with text messages between the two lovebirds, and she can't bring herself to delete any of them. She rushes up the stairs and soon returns, a crooked grin on her face. It's a text from him.

"He wants to know how the evening is going," Priya grins at me, "and he says 'good luck with hosting.'"

"Very thoughtful," I respond.

"I'll answer him later," She says, "when things are quiet and I can't sleep."

Apparently Priya is losing considerable sleep due to daydreams about her future husband. But she doesn't mind. When the house is quiet and everyone is asleep, when duty isn't demanding she take sewing lessons or cook dinner or complete her father's business books, she has a few uninterrupted hours to re-read her fiancé's text messages and blush and dream of their future together.

In the quiet night hours, Priya is daydreaming.

We're in a staff meeting at TICH, with about 40 people in attendance. Director Dan Keseje informs us a group will be going to Goma, in the Democratic Republic of the Congo (DRC). Because TICH does not yet have university status, we're providing a master's program through the Great Lakes University in Goma. Students educated at TICH will graduate from the Great Lakes University of Goma in the Congo next week. The concern is how they'll get there. The option of air travel is eliminated immediately because of the cost. They talk about taking matatus to the border of Uganda and chartered buses from there.

The director says they discussed hiring a private vehicle, but don't have anyone who can drive on the "wrong" side of the road. Since the "wrong" side here is the "right" side as far as I'm concerned, I raise my hand without thinking and say, "I've been dying to get behind the wheel again. I can drive on the wrong side of the road."

Everyone laughs. Dan admits they never considered me.

When I speak to Dan later about show ground matters, I reiterate going on the trip. Not only can I drive, but I'd like to take photos and write about the trip for our newsletter and website. Dan agrees I should go.

The plan is for the hired driver to take us through Kenya to the Uganda border, through Uganda and into Rwanda. At the border of Rwanda, where the roads switch to the "wrong" side, I'll take over and drive through Rwanda and into the DRC. Goma is close to the border.

On the morning of our departure for the DRC, Tonny and I head to the agricultural show grounds. Tonny will take over the details of preparing our exhibit. We arrive and hire an electrician. We also ask the landscaper to replace the used fence boards with new ones and put down new gravel instead of the used gravel mixed with bits of soil and hay he delivered yesterday.

Tonny's cell phone rings. It's the school, wanting to let me know our group is leaving for the Congo at 10:00am instead of noon, as planned. We rush back to campus to find a hired matatu waiting. We are to have a devotional before beginning our journey, so we crowd into the chapel and Dan reads from I Timothy, an epistle from Paul. Dan tells us we are like the men in the scriptures: warriors, athletes and farmers. We're pushing forward on our mission to see this batch of students graduate from our affiliate university in the Congo.

For hymns, we sing "Count Your Many Blessings" and "Onward Christian Soldiers." Everyone is praying for our safe passage and return. There are handshakes, hugs and cheek-touching all around. We pile into the matatu (11 of us including the hired driver), and head off, stopping in town to buy snacks for the trip and petrol for the vehicle. We also make a stop at a second petrol station, though no one can tell why. Finally, we're heading out of Kisumu, around Lake Victoria and rolling towards Uganda. The gowns are tucked snugly under the back row of seats.

We eat our snacks and pass them around. Sister Margaret, who works in the partnership department at TICH, is giddy about graduating. The roads aren't bad, which means book reading is possible. We pass a newspaper around, everyone in high spirits. As we near Busia, close to the border, Ogutu's phone rings. He talks for five seconds and is off the phone.

"The graduation has been postponed," he says, "we are to go back."

"Right, Ogutu," Gertrude laughs, "what was the call really about?"

"Turn down the music," someone yells.

"Pull off the road," another says.

"Call the director back."

Lucas dials and puts Director Dan Keseje on speakerphone. We all listen to him telling us the university has postponed the ceremony until next week. We are to go back to TICH. We're all rather stunned, and I feel badly for the students. Melvin came all the way from Malawi to graduate. Richard took a week off work. Others have flights that will need to be rearranged. Maureen, an employee in TICH's Nairobi office, will now have to go back to Nairobi and return again next week.

We turn toward Kisumu. Within five minutes, everyone is laughing again. I'm always impressed with how Kenyans deal with disappointment.

We all decide an excellent reason for the delay will eventually reveal itself. For now, as comfort and consolation, we stop at a restaurant on the lake to eat fish. We roll over a rough dirt road to the water's edge and sit under a thatched shelter, watching cranes and other giant birds preen themselves on rocks in Lake Victoria. Giant fish are brought out on platters and served with sukuma wiki and ugali.

Our bellies are soon full and our feelings are soothed. We can now proceed to TICH and resume work as usual, only minimally inconvenienced by the postponement.

The agricultural show is fast approaching, and our exhibit needs more paint, more custom-made posters, a visitor's book and skirts for the display tables. We must pay the graphic artist for painting our name on the building's eaves and for painting our logo on the front. He also created a "Health Clinic" sign for us, since our health clinic in the student hostel will open a temporary branch in our exhibit to assist show goers. We have a small room where we'll place a table and two chairs, for consultations and dispensing medicine. I'm making curtains for the health clinic, to provide privacy, in TICH green satin to match the TICH blue satin table skirts.

"We need more green paint," our painter, Peter, tells me. His request is followed by another from the graphic artist, who shows up at TICH's gate, burning with malaria, asking for his payment in full so he can buy medicine. We need rugs for the entrance and exit as well as safe drinking water for our staff. I request a hand-painted poster of our partnership sites in Nyanza Province. The director approves one expense after another with a warm smile. Though it seems like we're spending a good bit of money, we are actually getting a great deal done with a relatively small sum. This show provides exposure for TICH, which competes with older, more established institutes. Exhibiting at the show is effective advertising and Director Dan Keseje is supportive of our efforts to dress up our space and really shine.

We plan to move potted plants from our front porch to the event site. We'll also take tables, chairs, and colorful paintings. We're busy printing marketing materials, applications, notices about our upcoming nutrition workshop and color copies of our newsletter—12 pages this edition!

We'll be selling handmade goods provided by community health workers from rural villages. The goods will be delivered on Monday and set up in our "TICH Shop" at the exhibit.

Saturday and Sunday are spent preparing for the show. On Saturday Vitalis, the driver, and I go into town to buy fabrics, curtain hangers and scissors, as well as the guest book and floor mats. Back at school, Director Dan Keseje indicates he's ready to see the exhibit, so we drive out. He immediately disapproves of the dead-gray gravel. The director reminds Simon, our landscaper, that we paid for new gravel; clean gravel will go a long way in inceasing our curb appeal. Simon assures the director it will be done. Other than that, the director is pleased with the progress of the exhibit.

Sunday, I arrive at TICH at 10:00am and begin collecting tables, chairs, charts and potted plants to take to the show. Vitalis and I are moving constantly: carrying and hauling and loading and unloading two trips to the show. After setting everything in its rightful spot, we anticipate arriving Monday morning to put all goods, posters and tablecloths in place.

When we reach the show grounds on Monday morning, all the gates are locked except for one at the back of the arena. Madness prevails. Vehicles of all sizes block the road to the gate, and folks waiting to be hired for odd jobs clutter the road. Two men stand outside the gate, screening entrants. It's pre-show, which means each vehicle must pay 2,000 shillings (US $26), an extremely ridiculous amount, and each person must pay 70 shillings just to get in the gate. Everyone is standing in the way. The man doing the screening is angry and being torn in a thousand directions.

It is total chaos, total disorganization. I'm feeling a little angry myself since the show manager, George, did not communicate today would be a pre-show day where the general public can get onto the grounds and where we have to pay just to get to our booth to complete preparations.

I step out of the van and talk to the larger of the two men at the gate. I'm ranting, "We just want to get to our booth," "We just want to set up," "Blah, blah, blah." There's nothing more disconcerting to Kenyans than to see a white person standing in the middle of a big crowd yelling and pointing and demanding satisfaction. The guy lets our vehicle through to talk to George in the manager's office. We're able to drop the painter, Peter, at the stand so he can begin work, but the manager's office is more chaotic than the gate. We can't get anywhere near George. We retreat from the maddening crowd, returning to TICH. I put in a requisition for the 2,000 shillings to go back to the show and finish our stand.

I hear nothing from accounts. An hour later, nothing. Two hours later, still nothing. I give up and plan the next day's to-do list, telling Vitalis we'll get to the show grounds early because it's our last day to complete the stand.

Today, it's me, Vitalis, Peter the painter and Peter's ladder. Well, TICH's ladder, which we're hauling with us in the van. The ladder is typical of Kenyan ladders, made of long, strong, roughly hewn tree branches. The rungs are nailed and tied on. To fit in the van, the ladder starts at the back window and ends next to my head. We're rolling, approaching the police stop near the show grounds, confident we have plenty of time to complete the stand.

The policeman pulls us over. He's saying something to Vitalis and pointing at our windshield. He looks mean, so I sit quietly.

Vitalis gets out of the vehicle. "He says our vehicle license is missing."

We search for papers in the car but can't find any. Vitalis walks to the back of the van with the officer and calls George, TICH's security manager who handles vehicle registrations. I sit quietly, contemplating how far the walk would be for me and Peter and the ladder. Too far, damn it. In anticipation of reaching the gate, I have a 1,000 shilling note (US $12) in my left hand. I fold it up and hide it in my palm, lest the officer think I'm offering a bribe.

A face fills the open window to my left and another officer, a young, large one, says, "Good Morning, Madam, how are you?" His hand is massive, warm on top of mine, and his smile is cocked, his eyes mischievous. He looks like a chocolate Elvis.

"I could be better," I say, indicating Vitalis standing behind us on the road. Vitalis is pretty far away, so I turn to make sure Peter is still with me. "We're on our way to the show grounds, to work on our booth," I say.

The officer releases my hand and runs his finger up my bare arm while staring at my chest. I'm confused and move away from the window. He pins my arm down.

"I'm looking for an mzungu wife," he says, all smiles. "My sister married an mzungu and is now living in the UK."

"What would you do with an mzungu wife?" I ask.

"We'd move to your country and start a family," he says.

I laugh.

"How old are you?"

"24."

"Ah," I say, "so young."

"How old are you?"

"42!"

"That's okay," he says, still focusing on my chest. Then he sees my 1,000 shilling note and picks it from my hand. It disappears easily in his large grasp.

"Give it back, please," I say, tired of him caressing my arm, massaging my chest with his eyes and leaning so far into my window I have to lean into the driver's side. I look back at Peter, who's a slim, small man. He sits erect, staring straight ahead with an artificial smile on his face. At least he's still there.

"I'll give you 500 shillings, how about that?" Officer Greedy says. I can't tell if he's honestly asking for a bribe or not, so I reach for the money. He pulls back, again with the eyes on my chest and his wily grin. I reach for the money once more, and he allows me to take it back while he laughs. He takes a pen and writes his name and his phone number on a piece of paper. He tells me to call him so we can go on a date. Despite this benign outcome, I'm mad at Vitalis for leaving me exposed. I'm just being silly; he had his hands full dealing with the mean, short, muscular officer by the road.

Vitalis is back in the driver's seat and we're headed toward the gate. I ask him what happened. Why were we allowed to drive on when we didn't have the license?

"George took care of it," he says.

At the grounds, a gate man sees us, flags us down and climbs into the van next to me. He's going to get us into the back gate. We drive around back, fight the crowds, wait for a clear entry. The same man who was here yesterday comes and tells us we'll have to pay. I hand him the 1,000 shillings and he moves inside the gate. Meanwhile, our passenger climbs out, slams the door and puts his face next mine. His expression is mournful as he whispers, "Please, Madam, 100 bob for my troubles." That's a lot of money for doing nothing.

"I just gave all our money to the big guy," I tell him.

He accepts this and moves on to his next mark.

We get through the gate and go straight to George, the manager. He gives me the free passes that come with our stand rental. I stop by the show's accounts office to pay for judging. I give them 1,500 shillings so we can be judged in the category of "Best Institute of Higher Education."

As I pass the 1,500 shillings to the accountant, they tell me the judging will take place this morning. The blue and green satin fabric for decorating is still in the vehicle, not placed in the stand. We don't have our literature printed; Tonny is printing it all today and bringing it tomorrow, the first day of the show. I almost pull the money back, but remember how keen Director Dan Keseje is on being judged.

'Well,' I think, 'we'll enter, but there's no chance we'll be ready when the judges visit.'

Peter is busy. He paints the floor red where we repaired potholes in the cement. He paints the potted plant containers white. He also touches up the well out front and puts a second coat on the exterior. We hire two women to assist. Ruth is slashing the grass in the back, and Grace is mopping the floor and front walkways. She's also cleaning the paint off the window panes with a razorblade. Meanwhile, I begin creating blue satin table skirts: a no-sew version using tacks. A stand across the street has hip-hop music blaring. Outkast and Beyonce mingle with local music. The bass is driving and deep and helps us work more efficiently.

I bought crisp, ultra-white cotton for the tops of the display tables. I spread the white cloth over the entire 16 feet of table when Peter and Michael (who just delivered our partnership map) decide to remove a piece of roofing from the ceiling beams. I recall asking Peter to move the piece two weeks ago. It's very heavy, and the two of them struggle to reach up and support it while they lower it from the ceiling. What no one thinks about is the layer of fine red dust that has been collecting on top of the piece for months. The dirt shifts. It plops down in pyramidal piles onto my immaculate white cloth.

"Crap!" I yell.

Everything is covered in red dirt. Grace stops scraping the windows and immediately begins cleaning the tablecloth and the floor.

The judges arrive.

The head judge is somewhat perturbed when he sees we're not ready. He asks how long it will take. I want to throw caution to the wind and just say, "Who knows?" But I don't.

"Will you be ready by 2:00?" he asks.

"Yes," I say.

When Ruth finishes slashing, she moves inside and helps Vitalis set out TICH's marketing items and books. The two of them hang giant vinyl posters advertising TICH's principles and academic programs. I hang the handmade wooden TICH clock. We hide extraneous stuff under the table skirts. Slowly, things are falling into place.

The judges return at their appointed time. These judges are two women, and they immediately acknowledge our stand is not ready. They'd like to see our literature. (So would I.) I tell them to picture a projector on this satin-covered table. Slides and photos will be flashing onto a nearby wall. Luckily, Michael hung the map of Nyanza Province we'd commissioned, so at least the judges can look at the map to see TICH's partnership sites in five districts. I explain how TICH students and staff conduct primary research in these rural communities. It's a major part of the curriculum, in addition to the rigorous academic schedule student's are put through. Our community work makes TICH unique as an institute. The judges are very interested and ask questions for 30 minutes. After they leave, I look at our TICH mugs on display and exclaim to Vitalis, "Dang! I should have given them a mug, and then maybe we'd have a chance of at least placing!"

My thumbs are incredibly sore from pushing brass tacks into the table skirting. I take pictures, inside and out, for the TICH website. This will be the last time I see the stand, since we leave for the Congo tomorrow. We're all tired after a long day of moving furniture and balancing on the very tips of our toes to hang posters, and from hunching over fabric to iron smooth edges on table skirts. We close the door and I admire the building, proud of the progress we've made. A guard will arrive soon to watch over our work throughout the night.

Chapter Thirteen

Congo

We pile into the matatu once again, the 11 of us. In all, there are seven graduates, three staff members and our driver, Jack. Our students, who are all getting their master's degrees in Community Health and Development, are in their 30s and 40s. Three of these graduates are on staff at TICH: Sister Margaret Nduta, Ogutu Owii and Maureen Kimani. The students are professionals working in development (Kelvin Mindi, for example, works for the Ministry of Health in Malawi).

We leave TICH at 8:30am with as much excitement as the first time. Kenya rolls by in no time, and we soon approach Uganda. At the border, our passports are stamped. We have officially exited Kenya. We then cross over into a "no man's land"—one hundred yards between country gates—before we get stamped into Uganda.

"You know," Julius, a graduate, says, "you can kill someone here in no man's land and there's no law to prosecute you."

Uganda has a new computer system, so they ask us to be patient. Clearing our vehicle for entrance takes longer than stamping all 11 of our passports. We sit in the open matatu, waiting. Two small girls come up, begging. We give the girls potato chips and strawberry hard candies. The older one, probably seven years old, has the sweetest smile and a very gentle way of asking. Both girls have swollen bellies, which my fellow travelers suspect are caused by worms. As we leave, the girls run beside the van, smiling and waving, saying goodbye in English. I wish we could sneak them into our bags.

Through Uganda's gate, we're met by hundreds of boda bodas, each driver wearing a bright pink shirt. For the next several miles, pink shirts dot the roads, everyone riding to the border to buy and sell. Luckily, there's a paved bike lane protecting boda bodas and their passengers from traffic. In fact, the name for hired bikes, boda boda, originated in Uganda and is modified from the words "border to border," which is where you could find them riding. Shops along the border sell goods for very low prices compared to what we pay in Kisumu. We hurry through today but decide we'll stop and browse on our return.

Heading west through Uganda, with Lake Victoria on our left, the scenery becomes more and more beautiful. Men stand by the side of the road with gorgeous lines of fish, holding them up for passersby to see. Throughout Uganda, they grow bananas, rice and sugar cane. Scarecrows dot the rice paddies. Neat little mud huts are surrounded by bare, cleanly swept dirt yards. The huts have markings along their bottoms and tops as well as around doors and windows. Bright flowering plants dress up the yards and lace panels of striking colors billow in most front doors. These homes may be mud with thatch roofs, but they're very neat and well-tended.

The roads through this initial part of Uganda are bad. Washed-out lanes, potholes and eroded edges require us to drive with two wheels off the pavement. It's especially tricky dodging transport trucks hauling sugar cane, petrol and tons of bananas.

A huge, green fruit displayed on most stands catches our attention. At first we think they're watermelons, but closer inspection shows an irregular tubular shape and a dark green, fuzzy covering. Gertrude tells us they're called fenesi. (They're also called jackfruit.) She points to several trees with huge fruit hanging in clumps from tree branches.

This only adds to our already evident hunger. Gertrude says there's a place coming up that sells roasted chicken.

I am reading *Lady Chatterley's Lover*. I am absorbed in the story as Gertrude tells the driver to keep going, the chicken place is around this corner. Lady Chatterley is unhappy. Her husband, injured in the war, is paralyzed.

He's also a superficial aristocratic twit, as are his friends, and Lady Chatterley's only joy these days comes from the chicks being kept by the gamekeeper on their property.

As Uganda's countryside flies by, I read. Lady Chatterley and the gamekeeper are having a really intimate encounter when Gertrude calls out, "Here! Here is it. They have chicken." We pull over and I continue reading. The gamekeeper has spread a blanket on the floor of the cabin so his Lady can relax.

Suddenly, I'm pulled back to Uganda. We're surrounded by men. My window opens and four chicken leg quarters skewered on sticks are in my face. Here comes a basket of roasted bananas and more sticks containing unidentified meat chunks. No other windows are open, so the men have their chicken sticks and faces pressed all around the van. They're four deep, these men, each trying to force out his competitors. Our group decides to climb out and buy the chicken from the cooking pits beneath the pavilion. I'm anxious to get back to that little cabin on the back of the Baron's estate, where the gamekeeper has a fire lit. But the chicken is still in my face, so I can't see the book. I push the man's hand out of the window, followed by the basket of bananas. I try to shut the window, but the basket gets caught. The men try to open the window and I frown at them. They're ruining a very intimate moment.

Even though the group has gone to the pavilion, planning to return with food, the men stay at the windows and watch me read. After a short time, everyone returns, their hands full of meaty sticks and plastic bags of roasted green bananas. We ride on and I am able to return fully to D. H. Lawrence's risqué novel, enjoying the wordlessness between the gamekeeper and his Lady while nibbling on chicken and bananas.

We enter Jinja, where the Nile River exits Lake Victoria, heading north. An impressive hydroelectric plant sits next to the river, fenced in. Police are posted before and after the river. Jack, our driver, flies right through, seeming to forget he had promised to stop for photos. Perhaps all the security caused him to change his mind.

We pass through Kampala, the capital of Uganda, a very modern city with wide, clean sidewalks and buildings one might find in New York. There are Italian restaurants with neon signs. It's clean and big. Jack stops several times for directions to get through the town and toward the Rwandan border.

Somehow, I end up with the Sunday Magazine, an insert in the Sunday Vision newspaper. The cover story is on yoga and its popularity with Britons and American celebrities. For some reason, page 17 comes after page eight, a confusing mix-up. I'm thrown into the middle of a story on the new Sudan, depicting a photo of a woman sitting on the ground next to a wood fire, a child on her left and an AK-47 in her right hand.

Sudan's struggles are covered brilliantly in a well-documented book by Deborah Scroggins. Titled *Emma's War*, it's the story of a British aid worker who became the second wife of a rebel warlord. This book describes in detail the multiple layers of politics, religions and cultures that make up the complex conflicts plaguing Sudan. A Sunday magazine article can't come close to explaining the depth and tragedy of the ongoing conflict in the Sudan.

I'm still reading the Sunday Magazine when we leave Kampala and drive through rural countrysides, where women line up in their fields, hoeing in a row. Mountains become larger and more frequent, their creases crowded with banana groves and tiny huts built on cliffs.

We make it to Mbarara, close to the Rwandan border, at 10:00pm. We check into Canaan Hotel and order dinner in the tiny dining room. It looks like a broken-down diner from the 50s. The front door leads onto a patio sitting pitifully close to a crumbling road. A Coca-Cola cooler stands nearby, chained and padlocked, as usual. As we wait for the food, the World Wrestling Federation is blasting on a television encased in an iron cage. Everyone is watching the big, muscular men acting macho and silly. I'm embarrassed to be an American.

It's nearly midnight before we go to our rooms, but we still plan to meet for breakfast at 6:30am.

Canaan Hotel serves breakfast in the lobby. They bring out pots of tea and distribute cups and sugar and stacks of bread slices to be slathered with soft Blue Band butter. As we're completing the bread, they bring around watermelon slices.

We pack ourselves onto the hard, straight matatu seats and head for the border. We get in line on the Uganda side, where we all wait to be stamped with an exit visa. An hour later, our line eventually reaches the porch of the building, where we wait another 20 minutes. Finally, we're just inside the door, and there is only one person ahead of us. The agent behind the glass turns and plugs in his mobile phone for recharging. Then he unbuckles his belt and unzips his pants, stuffs his shirttail in his pants and re-dresses himself. We're standing, waiting and watching him zip his pants. He turns, walks out of the booth, closes the door and walks between me and Sister Margaret. He offers no word as to where he's going, leaving behind one other agent who is busy stamping entrance visas.

There are about 100 people behind us, and we've been here for one-and-a-half hours. Ten minutes later, there is still no sign of the agent. Twenty minutes later, still no agent. I ask the guy managing the crowd at the door if he will get the agent so we can move things along. He looks shocked and shakes his head no.

Bavon steps up to the other agent.

"Isn't it possible another agent can replace him?" Bavon asks.

Before he can be answered, our agent returns. Still offering no explanation, he goes behind the glass wall, retrieves a piece of paper and passes by us once more. Bavon stops him to ask when he'll return. The man tells us he's helping a "special visitor." Bavon reminds him we have a right to be served promptly, that their signs asking us to be patient only apply to computer problems, not to a lack of agents. His voice gets louder. The agent's does, too.

"We have a right to be served promptly," Bavon asserts.

"And it's good to be delayed, too!" the agent retorts, storming out and slamming the door.

Despite our frustrations, we all laugh—everyone on the porch as well as those lining up in the dirt yard. No one is quite sure what that means: "It's good to be delayed, too!"

The entrance agent steps over and begins stamping our passports. He's not happy about it, but at least we're moving. We're finally through and heading toward Rwanda's immigration stand.

The agents in Rwanda will not let Jack, the driver, pass through. His temporary passport is for East Africa only (Uganda, Kenya and Tanzania). Although I had planned to drive from here, I was comforted to know Jack would be with us, to help out with possible breakdowns and to explain the van's idiosyncrasies.

"Are there are any little tricks or hang-ups about the car?" I ask Jack.

"No," he says and hands me the keys, "goodbye."

He's on his way back to the next town, to wait for our return on Sunday. This is it. It's up to me and this five-speed van to get everyone safely to Goma and back. At least now we're driving on the "right" side of the road.

After 30 minutes, I'm used to the gears and the brakes, to dodging holes in the road, to sitting in a driver's seat on the right side of the van. Rwanda is by far the most beautiful African country I've visited. They call it "The Land of a Thousand Hills," but these hills are more like mountains and they number much more than 1,000. Around each hill are ten more hills; all of them with steep, winding roads. It's impossible to see around each bend, so I maintain a speed that will allow me to brake quickly without harm if a hole awaits us, or if the road is washed out. Sometimes the pavement gives out completely and we must pass over rocky, red dirt roads. Sometimes the holes in the road stretch all the way across, requiring me to leave the road completely. I soon learn how far apart the tires are, the length of the wheel base and how to hit third gear's sweet spot. In one valley, where I slow to a crawl to navigate holes and dips, barefoot boys run alongside yelling, "Rwenzori." They're calling out for empty water bottles (the brand is Rwenzori), and because they speak French in Rwanda, the boys call it out with an interesting accent.

"Toss them on the side of the road," Bavon says, "where the boys will collect them. They'll use them to hold cooking oil, water and many other things." I toss a bottle and hear them shouting their thanks.

Ogutu sings, "Rwenzori," and everyone laughs and sings the word while we frantically look for more bottles to give the boys. The road smoothes out and I pick up speed, a little, climbing onto the next twisting mountain. A big truck flies down off the mountain, and the driver tosses a Rwenzori bottle into the center of the road. It immediately lands under our left front tire. Crunch. "Oh no!" is chorused throughout the van. We all feel horrible when the bottle is destroyed, the boys watching from the roadside.

Back on the narrow twisting roads, we come upon a Land Cruiser. I want to pass it but must wait. I notice a white man is driving.

"What are the chances," I ask Bavon, "that a white woman and a white man would be meeting on a remote mountain road in Rwanda?"

A police stop comes into view. They flag the white man, telling him to pull over, and wave us on. I feel immensely relieved. We round a few more curves, me leaning forward to view every inch of the road, when we come up behind a matatu. This is a real matatu; one that is hauling passengers.

Passing is difficult, so I stay behind at a respectable distance. As we cross a bridge, a shot rings out. Someone screams. I slow down and we realize the matatu has a blown back tire. A blowout is dangerous anytime, but especially on narrow curving roads with a valley dropping down nearly a mile just a few feet away. Still, we're happy to see the matatu passengers will assist with the tire's repair. Rounding a corner, we glimpse Kigali, the capital of Rwanda. It sweeps across several hills, flowing with the waves of mountains. It is built up to the very tops of mountains and to the very bottoms of valleys. It looks like San Francisco.

We need to get fuel and exchange money into Rwandese Francs, so our first stop is the bank. Sidewalk hawkers immediately surround our car. A young girl with a baby tied to her chest stands in the middle of our group. Without saying a word, she simply stands amongst us, looking from face to face, hoping we'll give her money.

We pass through Kigali, through traffic lights that don't work, and pull into a gas station. It's hot, so we drink sodas and wait for the fuel tank to be filled. A cargo truck is behind us and men crawl all over it, unloading various shapes and sizes of packages. I watch the men wrestling with the goods. One man has taken off his shirt and wrapped it around his neck. He and another man lower a wooden crate to the ground. A third guy says something that upsets the shirtless man; the third guy grabs the other man's shirt from his neck and throws it in his face.

The shirtless man goes after his antagonizer. This shirtless man is lean, with a muscular chest and a six-pack. He's also enraged. He punches the guy, which sets them both bouncing and punching the air with their fists. There's so much adrenaline the entire crowd naturally backs away from its force. Bare fists slightly connect with jaws and bounce off collar bones. Their violent dance stretches across the parking lot, and Dr. Ngode takes my arm and moves me out of the way. The shirtless man gets an excellent punch into the other guy, who flies off the ground and twists, unable to catch himself before hitting the pavement. Another guy then attacks the shirtless man, grabbing him from behind and holding him so the other guy, who gets up from the ground, can beat him in the stomach. Finally, a reasonable on-looker enters the dance, to hold off the agitators while another on-looker holds back the shirtless man. They're all spitting words and blood, pure energy.

Some people laugh nervously, but the violence just makes me sad.

I'm reminded of the 35,000 suspects released in Rwanda this week. These 35,000 people are suspected of killing Hutus in the 1994 massacre (when Tutsis killed approximately one million Hutus, mostly with machetes). This is the third wave of suspects being released because Rwanda's prison system can no longer support them. The suspects are not off the hook. They will still stand trial when their time comes. Last week, the BBC World News interviewed a few male suspects being released. They openly admitted to killing people—including women and children. Some showed remorse, some did not. Such an act of hatred and violence is inconceivable and looking at the beautiful mountains, which appear exceedingly peaceful, it's hard to imagine a massacre in this place, even after seeing this fist fight.

Rwanda is overpopulated. In a country of only 10,169 square miles, there are approximately nine million people packed into the nation's various communities. They fan out to tend their plots of land on the mountain slopes. Every inch of the mountains is cultivated. Although I briefly wonder how they manage to farm and irrigate on such steepness, I already know the answer. Everything here is done by hand. By back-breaking hard work.

We leave Kigali, waved on by friendly policemen at each stop. We immediately rise up steep inclines. We climb and climb until the road becomes a ribbon stretching across the tip of a mountaintop. Looking right or left provides a view of a vast, deep valley leading to the next mountain string, and onto the next. Trees have been stripped to form terraced fields. Crops grow on every hill, in every valley.

In places, usually small communities, people use the road as their walking paths. No matter how much I honk the horn, they still swarm toward the center of the road. They are coming from both sides, and it is unnerving, especially because Bavon is encouraging me to "push it." The border closes at 6:00pm. If we don't get through today, we'll have to spend the night in Rwanda.

The lawful speed limit is 80 kph (about 55 mph), and our matatu has a cap installed that will not allow it to go faster than that. Bavon keeps saying, "Just go, just go!" as we sail past people in the roads. I'm trying to use the lower gears to keep our descending speed reasonable, to keep the brakes from melting.

"I don't like speeding through these mountains," I tell Bavon. "This is an unsafe speed. I won't speed when we come back through."

"Just go," Bavon says.

As we're coming out of the mountains, the road is straightening out. I can see a fair distance, but the people are a risk. Somehow, I'm able to keep it at 80 kph by honking people out of the way. Bavon is the only person who knows exactly how far we are from the border. We start moving through a residential area with huge holes in the semi-paved road; when I try to slow down, to keep our passengers from bumping their heads, Bavon continues, "Just go. Just go!" So we fly over bumps and around corners until, up ahead, we see the border gate of the Congo. It is three minutes to 6:00pm. Everyone cheers.

I park the matatu and smell hot brakes, see smoke rising from the front wheels. We have no trouble getting our exit visas from Rwanda, but when we walk into the Congo immigration office, the agent gets short and snappy with Dr. Ngode, who's a very sweet and kind gentleman. Bavon is from Goma, so we ask him to speak with the agent. They begin to argue, in French, their voices getting louder and louder. Some of us step outside to give them room. We made it to the border, but now the agent doesn't want to stamp our passaport because we arrived when the border was closing. Soon, however, the agent cools and he and Bavon become joking pals.

"That's the way we Congolese are," Bavon tells us.

So far on our trip, I have noticed a few white people at every border, including this one. There aren't many, and most look like tourists, but they always stare to see me driving a matatu.

Goma is just inside the Congo border and we're soon there, driving toward the university, to check in. Bavon lived in Goma and went to the university before moving to Kisumu, so he's an expert guide. We pass through downtown, a wide street lined with two-story buildings. Although the buildings are somewhat modern, half of downtown was covered in lava from a volcano eruption in 2002. The lava flowed into town and filled in the first story of some buildings. We see only the second stories as we pass through. The city hasn't paved the streets since the eruption. Hardened lava makes for very nasty and bumpy roads; it is much worse than natural dirt roads. Lava rocks, black and porous, fill empty lots throughout town. Houses stand half covered. New houses and buildings are being constructed on top of the lava. It's getting late and the sun is lowering, causing the devastation from the eruption to look eerie and surreal.

It's been three years since the eruption, and very little clean-up or repair has been done. This doesn't come as a surprise, since the Congo was experiencing civil war from 1997 to 2003. Different factions on either side of the war were supported by other African nations, who were supported with funds and guns from other nations (including the United States). On top of dealing with the war's atrocities, the citizens had to recover from the volcanic eruption. Bavon's house was destroyed by the volcano, and he and his family lived in a refugee camp in Rwanda for one month. He pointed out the camp as we drove through Rwanda. It was a complex of large, green tents, now used for other purposes.

The colonial horrors that occurred in the Congo at the turn of the 20th century, perpetuated by Belgium's King Leopold II, are one factor among many for why the country has been slow to develop. King Leopold deliberately sent his military forces up the Congo River to create a stronghold and find labor to reap rubber from the jungles. If, in the course of forcing men into labor, millions were maimed or killed, King Leopold wrote it off as collateral damage. He hid from other world leaders his true plan to rule the Congolese under the guise of a philanthropic effort.

The Congo's population is believed to have been reduced by half, from 20 million to 10 million people, during King Leopold's reign. Atrocities of this era are covered brilliantly by Adam Hochschild in his book *King Leopold's Ghost: A Story of Greed, Terror, and Heroism in Colonial Africa.* The effects of King Leopold's cruelty continue even today; civil wars in the Congo are estimated to have cost 4 million lives since 1998. Today, 68 million people live in the Congo, and even though peace deals were signed between the government and rebel forces in 2003, casualities of the war still continue; the International Rescue Committee (IRC) estimates 1,250 Congolese die each day from diseases and malnutrition, conditions existing because of the war, itself an aftershock of colonialism.

UN peacekeeping troops are numerous in Goma. We pass truck after truck full of soldiers with guns, heading to their nightly posts. Every other white jeep has a huge "UN" painted on the side. We drive to the house of the university's Head of Academics. As we sit and visit in the living room, people begin to arrive. The public relations guy, who wasn't expecting us until tomorrow, shows up to arrange accomodations for us. Professor Karafuli, head of the Community Health and Development College, and his wife, Head of the Theology College, come in. Kalindi, third in command at the university, arrives with energy and a huge smile, shaking hands all around. We fill the room as our crowd grows.

We are tired after driving all day, so our kind hosts take us to a hotel for dinner. At the hotel, the Ishango, we learn they've booked Dr. Ngode and me into two rooms. Everyone else will go to a nearby guest house. Kalindi says they'll take our group in their vehicle and leave our van at the Ishango. A doorman reaches for my bag and I follow him, in a dreamlike state, to a gorgeous room with a huge tub and king size bed. What an unexpected and greatly appreciated gesture.

Dinner is a buffet, and we sit at a large, round table talking about development. Everyone is giddily excited to be in a different country, confused to hear conversations in French. To me, it's normal to hear foreign languages and to see different scenery. The food is the same. The people look the same and dress the same. They just say bon soir and bonjour (though many Congolese also speak Kiswahili). To my colleagues, this is an exciting international experience.

After Dr. Ngode and I see our colleagues off to their guest house, we retire to our rooms. I fill the tub with hot, hot water and wash my hair in the most relaxing way. What luxury. A Gideon's bible in French, German and English sits on the night table.

Bon soir, Guten nacht, Good night!

Dr. Ngode and I drive from Ishango Hotel to the university to meet our group for breakfast. We pass along the shore of Lake Kivu. There is no water in town this morning, so the lake's beach is packed with people carrying yellow jerricans, waiting patiently to get their water so they can return home to cook and wash. The roads are lined with children and adults, all carrying jerricans on their heads.

We meet our group at the university's cafeteria. The building is made of plywood and is painted white, with open holes covered in lace panels for windows. The ceiling is low and women cook outside in the open air. We breakfast in a back room, set apart from everyone by a thick fabric "door." Breakfast is large slices of bread, butter and tea. Afterward, we take a tour of the campus and meet a law professor, Janine, who's originally from Cameroon. Janine is something of a feminist and I like her immediately.

Our group visits the university rector: the equivalent of a U.S. university president. The rector is a happy, charming man who cannot speak English though he understands us very well. He's incredibly kind. His manner suggests he's someone's secretary rather than the head of the university. We also meet with the chairman of the board (who is four foot tall, looks like a black German officer and speaks only French) and the head of academics, who likes to practice his English with us. Kalindi joins us in this last meeting, which means we've now met with the top four men of the university. They treat our students like royal guests, taking time to chat with us. All this when they have a graduation to prepare!

The rector is printing a copy of the ceremony's agenda when the electricity goes out. The generator will kick on within ten minutes, but we are too excited to wait. Our impatience is misplaced, since the agenda is in French anyway. Everything at the university is in French, all class lectures and marketing materials. Luckily, we have Bavon as our interpreter.

In our spare time before lunch, we want to drive to town, to look around and maybe even shop. Ogutu is marrying soon and wants to buy a diamond ring. I'd like to take photos of the lava flow, the way it divides downtown. The deposit of lava is so distinct that we must drive up the edge of the lava, about eight feet, to reach the higher elevation.

As we're headed to town, Bavon navigates by telling me exactly what to do.

"Stop!"

"Pull up!"

"Go here, go here!"

He points into the windshield, over and over again. Even after I've signaled, even after I've said, "Okay," and "I'm stopping," he's still directing me. Sometimes it gets on my nerves and I must remind him that I know how to drive.

Bavon gives me very detailed instructions, especially when we approach the traffic police. In Rwanda, the policemen on the side of the road would pull us over, walk to my window, and say, "Bonjour!" Then they'd wave us on. Sometimes they'd even call out, "Safe journey!" as we pulled away. Bavon marveled at how they simply looked in the window and waved us on. He attributed this to my white skin and it made him laugh with delight. Today, as we approach the Congolese policemen and women in their bright yellow shirts, Bavon reminds me to slow down in case they flag us to the side of the road. Which they do.

I pull over and wait while Bavon and the officer speak French. The officer is short and has the cruel face of a criminal. He's intense. They talk and talk. Finally, Bavon tells me to show my license. The officer says our insurance sticker on the front window is not valid in the Congo—it's only valid in countries belonging to the African Association of Something or Other. As Bavon and the short man talk sternly to each other, I hear the guys in the back discussing what they'd like to eat for lunch.

Thirty minutes later, Bavon and the policeman are still talking sternly to one another. The officer frequently shoos away peddlers and small children who walk zombie-like toward the van to stare at me. "Bonjour, Mzungu," they all shout.

After awhile I learn the officer is upset my driver's license is not international. He wants to see "internationale" written on it somewhere. Finally, he walks to Bavon's side and climbs in.

"Go," Bavon says and I go, with no clue where we're headed. It's a lot of work for Bavon to have a conversation with the cruel officer and to interpret for the rest of us, so we sit quietly. A matatu passes so closely the officer leaps forward and throws up his arms, as though we're going to crash. I smile, but only inside. We drive for ten minutes before we stop. Bavon, the officer and Dr. Ngode go inside a dirty, crumbling building. We wait for 30 more minutes. Everyone is hot. Everyone is tired. We just want to see the shops downtown and eat lunch.

The road is crowded with walkers and vehicles. A small truck with a butchered cow in the back passes. The bed is full of hindquarters and ribs with the skin intact. The cow's hide is a gorgeous, solid black. On top of everything, held in place by a man riding in the back, is the cow's head. UN soldiers and Congolese soldiers ride by. Men pass us on two-wheeled, handmade wooden bikes. They carry strapped-on vegetables, gas cylinders, bags of potatoes, sugar cane, other riders, long metal poles and firewood. Women carry these same items on their heads, with babies tied to their backs. The women dress in colorful, bold graphics, the fabrics flowing to their ankles and wrapped into elaborate headdresses.

Finally, the men emerge from the building. They are holding a scrap of paper on which the police chief has written a pass, officially stamped with his name and title. This pass tells any officer who stops us to let us go, that it's okay for us to be in town through Saturday. Bavon says he paid a "fine" of US $20.

I wonder out loud if we have to go buy the insurance they were talking about. I'm assured we don't. Now that we have this piece of paper, we can pass through all police checkpoints. I continue to voice my concerns, "What about the insurance, in case we have an accident?" Bavon again assures me that it's not necessary now that we have this piece of paper.

The idea is not clicking with me, so I leave the logistics to Bavon, who is from the Congo. These police officers earn a salary equivalent to US $5 per month—not much at all. It explains why they supplement their incomes by looking for the tiniest offense for which to extract a bribe.

As I pull onto the busy road, everyone wants to go back to the school and park the van to avoid further trouble. Our matatu is dark blue and Congo matatus are white, so we're a sure mark for the Congolese police. We pick up speed and travel for half a mile before the police at the next stand flag us over. They want to see my license. Instead, Bavon shows them our piece of paper. The guy waves us on. Another half of a mile, another police officer waves us over. We show the piece of paper and are released. We get to the border office where Bavon picks up some necessary paperwork for the vehicle before heading back to the university. Of course, a police woman pulls us over on the way. She looks at my license and at our "pass." She confers with a fellow officer. She confers with this fellow officer for ten minutes. Then we go. We're laughing at the ridiculousness of it all.

"Imagine how much money they would make in tourist dollars if they allowed us to freakin' shop in their town," I say. "Instead, they're intent on stopping us and finding some small thing to detain us so they can press for a bribe!"

Another half of a mile, another stop. These officers are friendly and wave us on immediately. We approach a roundabout where we had already been stopped on the other side. A fierce policewoman stops us and wants Bavon to step out of the vehicle. She looks at our pass and questions its validity. In reality, she just wants a little something for herself. "You paid the big boss $20, but what about the little guys?" she's asking Bavon.

I take a photo of the volcano in the distance—the volcano that erupted in 2002—with a lava field in the foreground. The volcano barely shows through the mist and haze of the low-lying clouds. I photograph new houses and buildings being erected on the lava flow. I photograph Bavon and the officers. Fortunately, the police chief who wrote our pass pulls up and assures the female officer he did write it. We're allowed to go.

We're thrilled to be back at the university after being stopped six times in two hours. We're also ready to get the hell out of the Congo.

My luxurious night at the hotel is over, so I'm rooming with Gertrude, one of our graduates and a married woman who has started her own NGO since completing her studies. We're staying in the student hostel, a duplex, and our traveling companions are across campus. We have no way to communicate as a group, so Gertrude and I decide to stay put in case they come for us.

It's an interesting hostel. At first there is no water, and then there is water, but only cold. I give up, spongebathe and dress. Then there is no water again. I take my book of plays written by Oscar Wilde into the living room to read. Night is near. The electricity goes out. Gertrude calls out from her bedroom but remains in the dark behind her locked door. I open the drapes wide to allow in the dying light. It's futile and way too dark to read. Instead, I sit on the sofa facing the windows, wondering how long we'll sit in the dark.

Footsteps crunch the courtyard gravel. I hear a female voice ordering around a man, who appears boy-like in the shadows of our veranda.

"Hello, Cindi!," calls Janine. She lives just next door. I let them in, watching as they bring along heavy bags. Janine pulls out a kerosene lamp, candles and matches. They pour fuel into the lamp, soak the wick, and then light it. The helpful man, who limps slightly from a malformed foot, places candles and matches in the bath and bedrooms. They've even brought soap and toilet paper. He leaves to take these essentials to Lucas' and Julius' room while Janine and I sit in the lamplight and talk.

Janine, from Cameroon, finds Goma a small town with few amusements, but she's here for three more years as a law professor. We also discover we have children the same ages. She wears jeans and sandals, looking very Western.

Janine wants me to meet her students, so we step over to her house and call across the way, where female French accents call back. Two lovely young women, Rose and Leona, come over. Their English is very good, too, though they, like Janine, deny it. They busy themselves making tea. We sit in the dim light and tell our stories. They are like Janine's daughters. Today they finished their exams and feel free so they want to cook. While they pull out the food and heat the oil, I get my camera and a bag of sweets from my room. The electricity returns. The water returns. I wash dishes, to clear the sink for cooking.

A driver arrives from our companions, an envoy to take me and Gertrude to dinner. I decline, pleading exhaustion. They leave without me.

Rose peels green bananas for frying while Leona thaws the fish. More students stop by to say hello. Janine brings her television from the bedroom and puts it on channel five, the French station. She interprets the news for me while the girls cook and chat. Cecilia, a friend of theirs, joins us for dinner, straight from her job at the African Central Bank. She's still wearing her bank uniform with the company's logo repeated throughout her uniform's fabric. Cecilia takes a call while dipping her fried banana into mayonnaise, leaving the table with the phone to her ear.

"Boyfriend?" I ask and they all howl. Janine and Leona insist I eat more and more. It's very delicious. Once the meal is over, as I reach to collect dirty plates, they push me back in the chair.

"Mamas just sit while the daughters clean," they say.

Gertrude returns from dinner so I leave Janine and the girls as they're about to watch a movie made in Uganda. They give me the customary three kisses and I give them a genuine American hug.

Janine calls my name from the courtyard at 7:00am. It's time for our walk to the Karibu Hotel on the lake, one of the nicest hotels and most expensive places to stay in the city. We're also only a five minute walk from Lake Kivu, which looks more like an ocean than a lake. Most people are sleeping as we exit the university's gate and greet Rose as she slips in.

"Where did you sleep last night?" Janine asks. Rose ignores the question and says good morning to me.

"They're young," Janine says when Rose has gone.

The quiet morning is cool and gorgeous; the lake is like a mirror. Occasionally a lone man in a boat casts a line. As we walk the elaborate hotel complex, we see UN vehicles adorning each building.

Today is graduation day. We go to the university, where the ceremony will take place in the school's courtyard. We breakfast. The ceremony starts at 10:00am, but as of 9:00am, the podium floor has not been completed and the sound system gear is lying in a heap on the gravel.

Our graduates are taken away with their gowns to a room to wait. I'm guided to the dignitaries tent and sit next to Vincent, who owns the Karibu Hotel. He's slick and good-looking in a Middle-Eastern kind of way. After a short time, the rector rushes over and signals me, saying, "We together must." I stand and follow him to where the heads of each college have collected. They ask me to wear a gown, so I get one from the van and return. We go to the rector's office and wait to be called out, to enter the procession. The crowd is huge and all the chairs are filled.

Two white women sit under the dignitary tent. The older woman, who looks to be 80 or so, is quite regal; her white hair is caught up in a bun atop her head and she wears a matching four-strand pearl necklace and earrings. She's the benefactress for the university's new Science and Technology wing and looks every bit the part. Next to her is a woman, perhaps her daughter, who is in her 50s with wavy, free hair. Including me, we are the only white people present.

They've placed TICH's group in the front row, right in the center. The Minister of Higher Education is on hand to confer degrees and give a speech. The provincial governor is also present. He is the reason graduation was postponed. He could not make it last week. The governor's speech is about gender equality and he speaks in very plain language (once Bavon has translated it from French, of course) about the dangers of valuing men over women, especially when the entire African continent is working to develop. In fact, the governor says until women are given credit, power and esteem, the country will never develop.

Many people give speeches, including Dr. Ngode, who gives a speech written by Dan Keseje, which Bavon translates into French. Two and a half hours into the ceremony our butts are dead asleep. They finally begin conferring degrees.

Janine sits next to me. On her other side is Professor Karafuli, head of the theology college. Both are women. Of the 121 students who started the law program, only four made it through to their degrees. All four are women. As these women advance to the podium, Janine lets out the African yippee call.

It's hard to describe how women in Africa shout their approval. Something like a high-pitched "Ay-yi-yi-yi-yi-yi-yi" that goes on and on. She does this for every woman. (She also did this throughout the governor's speech on the value of women.) Every time she calls out, videographers spin around and zoom in on her. She is probably the most photographed and filmed woman of the day.

Students go onto the stage, receive their diplomas, accept the mortar-boards on their heads and return to the area in front of the podium. As a group, the rector confers their degrees. While this is going on, security men stand across the aisles holding hands, keeping relatives from rushing toward the graduates before their degrees are conferred. Mostly women, the relatives push and shout and shove and try to bite the security guards.

I am irritated with the photographers, who block picture-taking from the front row. Janine shoos them with her hands while saying, "Si vu plais, Monsieur." Finally, the guards move the photographers, only to have the female relatives rush through the barricades shouting and pushing and falling on us. The crowd is so large and rowdy I begin to fear for our safety. Some people spray cans of a snow-like material on the graduates and guards. Trying not to look how I feel, I sit, watching the crowd and disapproving of their behavior.

Our students are the next group to graduate, and I'm proud when it goes smoothly. I take a number of photos, and when Dr. Ngode returns from the podium, he says, "Let's go." Before the ceremony is even complete. I don't mind. When we reach our van, we rip off our robes and climb in. We want to reach Kigali by nightfall, and it is four hours away.

We must stop for fuel and to check water and oil levels. When we pull into the station, I ask which pump is diesel. Bavon jumps in, telling me to just pull up this way and then back that way. I have no idea where he's sending me. I ask, again, which pump has diesel. Suddenly, everyone in the car and even two ladies under the shelter begin to tell me how to turn the wheel this way and back up that way.

Their instructions are too much.

I've reached my limit with everyone telling me how to get somewhere without telling me my final destination. In a manner I do not like and am not proud of, I throw out my arms and tell everyone to Please. Be. Quiet. I repeat the command to the two women under the shelter who work for the gas station.

I speak to them all, so everyone hears clearly.

"I know how to drive! If you just tell me which pump has diesel, I'll figure out how to get this van next to it."

"Yes, you can drive."

"Yes, Cindi, you're a very good driver."

This type of consoling has a way of making me laugh at my anger and feel ashamed for losing my temper. Bavon ever-so-gently asks the ladies which pump has diesel and they point, not saying a word. I'm able to get the gas tank next to the pump, and everyone is happy.

We munch our packed lunches while the fuel pumps. Lunch is chunks of mystery meat dropped amongst chips and, in a separate pouch of tinfoil, shredded cabbage. I eat hungrily with my fingers as men ride and walk past, staring. Some days I think I'm used to constantly being stared at. Other days I wish for an invisibility cloak.

Skirting the police stops, we hit the border. We are, of course, delayed—this time with a baggage check and a wedding party made up of 30 vehicles honking and shouting across the border. I'm anxious to hit the open road, to be in control again.

We reach Kigali as night calls. When we pull up to the guest house, the brakes smoke so badly Maureen yells out, "Something is wrong with our tires!" I assure them it's just the brakes overheating, but I worry about the black streaks radiating from the hub. I can't decide if it's grease or brake fluid. No matter how much I tried to use low gears coming off the Rwandan mountains, the brakes were still necessary. Toward the end, the brakes felt fluid, which scares me.

The guest house is too expensive for us, and Lucas wants to check out another one. I tell them I do not want to drive the van any more; I don't trust the brakes. As a compromise, they call a former TICH student who lives in Kigali, a man of about 55 years. He assures us he will lead us to another, more affordable, guest house. He climbs in between me and Bavon, and, to my chagrin, begins directing my driving just as Bavon does. He asks Bavon in French if I'm a good driver. I know he doubts my ability and I know what he is asking because I hear him say "madam" and "chauffeur."

"Oui, tre bien," Bavon replies without hesitation.

They direct my driving so closely that as we're riding down the road and it curves to the left, they tell me to go left.

"Are you sure I can't go straight?" I say, just to be a smartass. Clearly there's no road straight ahead, it's just grass and rocks.

"No, no," they answer seriously, "go left, go left."

I take a deep breath and remind myself we're almost there.

The guest house sits on a cliff overlooking Kigali. It looks as though all the stars have fallen into the city, into the crevices and round parts of the hills, smashing into millions of pieces and twinkling brilliantly where they lay. The van is parked on a slope with a 20 foot drop-off behind. I make sure the emergency brake is set and push aside thoughts of the van rolling back. I'm tired. We're all tired. It's been a long, ceremony-filled day.

All I want is to crash on a bed; however, the guest house doesn't have food and everyone is hungry. They want to drive somewhere to get food. In my irritability I tell them I won't drive, someone else can, because I don't trust that 20-foot drop at night, don't trust the brakes and don't trust my judgment under such fatigue.

Julius insists I drink a Coke and sit down.

"If Cindi isn't rested and cared for, then we simply won't get home," Julius says. Someone steps outside the guest house compound and returns with a loaf of bread and drinks. We all stand under the moonlight and chew and drink as our energy slowly returns. They find us rooms and we drop our luggage. Maureen and I are placed in a room with five bunk beds and cold water.

Once revived, I tell Lucas I will drive to get food, but they've already called Bavon's daughter, Lily, who has been waiting for us in Kigali. She's been staying here with her cousin and his wife. These three beautiful souls bring us food. They arrive in an hour's time with three plates, three pieces of fish, rice and ugali. There are 11 of us. We divide the plates and form in groups, picking at the fish and dipping ugali chunks in the fish sauce. Kelvin turns a pot lid upside down and fills it with rice and masala sauce. Amazingly, these few pieces of fish satisfy our appetites.

We all drag to our rooms and wash in cold water by candlelight because the electricity has gone out. It is midnight and we're meeting at 5:00am.

We leave in the early morning darkness and the brakes feel more solid. We're waved through by the police and climb away from Kigali, toward Uganda. The sun rises over Rwanda in a way that makes us glad to be alive. We twist and turn until we find ourselves back at the rutted part of the valley where I must drive two mph to navigate deep potholes and steep road edges. This is where the boys yell, "Rwenzori," and where we all search for empty bottles.

This time we're moving so slowly we can hand the bottles to the boys. Someone also hands out bread. Three young men, aged between seven and 11, run beside us in their bare feet and shabby gray clothes, their eyes shining as they reach for the bottles. They thank us in their native tongue, Kinyarwanda. I remember a bottle in my bag with a little water left, so I dig it out with my left hand while steering clear of holes with my right. I hand the bottle to the smallest boy, who's out in front. He's joyful now, as are the others, as are all of us in the van. When the road clears and I can pick up speed, we all wish we had more bottles and more food to hand over.

The boys are yelling "Thank you" and still running, holding their bottles close to their chests, until we're out of sight. Until they're out of sight.

We get to Uganda in a couple of hours. Bavon leaves the vehicle to call his wife and I'm left to drive the car through the border.

"Here's the paperwork," Bavon says, shoving a file folder at me and slamming the door. I pull up and wait. And wait. Finally, a man looks at my papers and asks for Form 87AC2, an A4 size. I have no idea what he's talking about. He makes me pull to the side, out of the way, and points to a tiny building with an even tinier grilled window. I wait for Bavon, but he doesn't come right away, so I walk over to the window. Before long, Lucas and Bavon show up. They talk to the man behind the grill and figure out we have to fill out another form and pay more money before the car can go through.

The gatekeeper has now poured himself a large cup of coffee and is sitting, relaxing. It's still early morning and a mist hugs the ground and the nearby hills. This border valley is lush with grasses and crops and steer with remarkably huge, slightly curved horns. It's magnificent. A few cows loll on the other side of the fence, where the gatekeeper is facing. I approach and he asks if I'd like a cup of coffee. I know it's very generous of him to offer and that I should say yes. Instead, I ask if I can photograph the fields and cows. I promise not to photograph any immigration buildings. (They're all very touchy about their border security.) He gives me the go-ahead, and goes further to say if anyone questions me, I can send them to him. I photograph the mist and the fence posts made out of tree branches that have taken root and sprouted tiny, leafy appendages.

Once the paperwork is in place, Bavon shoves the file toward me once again and tells me to drive through the next border into Uganda. He promises to be right back. I pass the friendly, coffee-drinking gatekeeper and roll toward the next gate. I'm waved through, but before I can let out my breath, a man runs over and demands a pass of some sort—one that doesn't sound familiar. He tells me to park and go see a policeman sitting up the hill. I start to worry: I've given my passport to Sister Margaret to have it stamped; my friends are all in line with a hundred other people to get their passports stamped; I'm alone with our vehicle, outside the border, facing a mile-long line of double parked transfer trucks. I don't know who will watch our bags if I go speak to the policeman up the hill. I don't know exactly where to park or the protocol for visiting the officer.

I pass into Uganda and move past the trucks, hoping to find a hole to park in. No luck. I drive a mile, turn around and drive a mile back, almost to the front of the truck line. I get out and lock the doors when a man passing by, an aged man with a scowl, tells me to park elsewhere. I curtly tell him, "They told me to park here."

Luckily, Gertrude, Richard and Sister Margaret are headed to the matatu, so I'm free to visit the officer. He sits with both elbows on his desk. Another officer stands behind him, his hands hooked behind his back, staring at me.

"Where have you been?" the first officer asks, as though he's partially interested.

"We brought several students to their graduation ceremony in Goma," I say.

"Where are you going?"

"We're going back home to Kisumu in Kenya," I say, noticing the yellowed, crinkly paper on his desk, feeling bodies lingering in the small room's doorway.

"Where are you from in the U.S.?" he asks flirtatiously.

"I'm from Atlanta, in Georgia. Have you heard of it?"

"No," he says and indicates for me to sign the book.

He hands me a pass the size of a postage stamp.

'That's it?' I think, 'All the questioning for a postage stamp?' I pass through the bodies in the doorway and walk back down the hill. I have a perfect view of the road and the front yard of the border office, which is crowded with people.

We're free to move into Uganda.

Although Jack, our "wrong" side of the road driver, is waiting for us, there is the small matter of picking him up.

"Who's going to drive in Uganda?" I ask Lucas.

"We'll keep the same driver," he says with a grin. I think about it for a moment. Left side of the road. I've been in Kenya riding on the left for six months. Surely it's not that hard.

"Okay," I say and we're off.

"Keep left. Keep left," I say to myself. It's fun being on this side of the road. When someone passes us now, the passengers in the back no longer flip out. In Rwanda, when cars first passed on the left, everyone jumped, thinking we would crash. They are simply not used to driving on the right. I drive on the left for about 50 miles into Uganda, until we reach Mbale, where Jack is waiting. We pass through town, turning here and there, moving through roundabouts and intersections with no confusion. I can't help but think this left side thing isn't so hard after all.

We see Jack sitting on the patio of his hotel. He stands and greets each of us with a smile and handshake. We're early enough for breakfast.

"Jack," I say, "the brakes got really hot, no matter how much I tried to rely on low gears coming off the mountains. They smelled hot, but there's also black grease leaking from the center of the hub." He should know about the brakes, so he can decide if they need be looked at or not. He doesn't seem too concerned, but, after a few minutes, stands and says, "I'm going to take the car in to have it looked at before we proceed."

Now that Lily, Bavon's daughter, is traveling to Kisumu with us, and now that Jack has rejoined us, we number 12. We order breakfast—eggs, toast, fruit, coffee, tea—and keep the staff hopping.

"The mechanic lubed the wheels and we are good to travel," Jack says when he returns. "The black stuff was just grease."

Uganda is huge. Anyone can look at it on a map and marvel at the distance between the Kenyan and Rwandan borders. Jack soon takes the 80 kph cap off the engine, a move that also disables the speedometer and odometer, and we're cruising through the countryside. This time, I'm sitting up front between Jack and Bavon and am surprised to see Bavon micromanaging Jack exactly the way he'd done with me. It's a comfort, knowing the navigation critiques weren't gender-inspired; unfortunately, most of my comfort is reduced by the knowledge that poor Jack has to deal with it as well. By the time we reach Kampala in the evening, he is truly worn out and stressed, though Bavon only means well.

We spend the night in Kampala at the Sports View Hotel overlooking the Mandela Stadium. This is the most expensive place we've stayed during our trip, paying nearly US $20 a room (we stay two to a room). We considered a guest house across the street—one that looks very comfortable—but the toilets are communal and everyone in our group is convinced staying at the Sports View will be better. It isn't.

Even though we run the hot water for 20 minutes in the shower, as the receptionist instructed, it never warms up. We are forced to have another night of sponge bathing. The bathroom tiles are loose, the sink is hanging away from the wall and the toilet has no seat. Our rooms face the highway. Across the highway is a nightclub with pumping music and too many loud young partiers. Below our window is the hotel's own sports bar with its own loud, pumping music. To make matters worse, the window to the balcony has no glass, so when a transfer truck flies past, grinding gears, it sounds like we're on the side of the road. I can feel each truck's breeze.

The nightclub stays open until 4:00am, the music consistently blaring. We also lose an hour by moving into Uganda's time zone, so morning comes quickly. Still, we all agree we were so exhausted we slept well and were only awakened occasionally.

We are all in good spirits, knowing we are headed home. When we reach Kenya's border and have been stamped to return, Ogutu stands amongst the crowd and exults his return to his native country. He puffs up and says, with conviction and volume, "I'm home. I'm a big man here. No one can displace me or shove me. I rule this land and I rule my life and Kenya is MY country." He is certainly feeling patriotic.

"Let's go shopping," I say to Sister Margaret and Maureen. We all turn back to Uganda and walk across the border (people on foot can move easily between countries) on a fabric-buying mission. I tell Sister Margaret that if I see something I want to buy, I'll signal her so she can buy it at the local rate, not the mzungu rate. She says she must ask Maureen to do the same for her because when people see a Sister, they automatically think she is bursting with church money.

Bavon is looking for a computer bag. Lily spots some shoes and a fashionable denim skirt she likes. I buy some gorgeous Royal Wax material, authentic African fabric of the highest quality. Sister tells me the fabric I bought at 450 shillings (about US $5 for five yards) would cost at least 1,300 shillings in Kisumu. We relax and enjoy ourselves, feeling quite luxurious with our time since we're only a two-hour drive from Kisumu.

After shopping, we pass into Kenya, into Busia, a city that straddles the Kenya-Uganda border. Julius directs us to his favorite restaurant. We eat fish or stewed chicken and chug kubwa (large) Cokes in glass bottles. We're nearly home, our bellies are full and we've all bought some goodies we'll treasure and give as gifts.

Later, when we come over a rise and see Kisumu spread out along the lake's shore, everyone gives out a collective, "Ahhhhh."

We arrive at TICH at 5:00pm and are pulled into the director's office, where everyone gathers and welcomes us back with hugs and kisses and a prayer.

"Did you hear about the agricultural show, Cindi?" Dr. Ariga asks.

"No," I say.

"TICH won First Place for our exhibit!" he says.

"What?! You've got to be kidding!"

All of a sudden my exhaustion flees and I'm holding Dr. Ariga's hands and bouncing up and down, grinning like an idiot. He takes me to see the trophy. I photograph the director with the trophy, still not believing our exhibit won when I doubted we'd even place. We beat out several other institutes, including Maseno University, a well-respected school that's been around for nearly 100 years. It is the place where most of Western Kenya's contemporary leaders received their educations. It's just too much to take in: returning home safely, knowing how much everyone prayed for and thought about us and finding out a month of hard work won us the show prize we coveted.

To top it all off, at the end of our trip (the night we stayed in Kampala), we ate dinner together and agreed we had each done things along the way we should apologize for. I thought about my screaming fit at the gas station. Because we each had things we could apologize for—very human things we'd said and done—we decided none us would apologize. Instead, we'd simply forgive each other and move on with our friendships and our work.

After a long and fruitful journey, we simply forgive. And we move on.

Chapter Fourteen

E t h i o p i a

I hear on the radio that Kibaki, the president of Kenya, is in Japan this week accepting donated monies from the Japanese government totaling nearly US $2 million. Another news report said the United States is providing about that much money for water projects in Western Kenya, where I live. I want to shout out to all the governments around the world and say, "Don't send your freakin' money to the Kenyan government!" It'll be spent by politicians to buy houses and cars and travel to Europe and fine dining. It will never reach the poor Mama in the rural community who is suffering from arthritis (from years of back-breaking work) and cataracts, who's raising four orphaned grandchildren and who owns only one goat and a semi-permanent house, whose only water source is rain water collected from the roof or a nearby river, if she's lucky.

Poor Mamas.

Even when the monies go to major projects stipulated by governments donating the funds, corruption causes the projects to stop mid-course. Several incomplete, empty buildings currently stand in Kisumu. Why are they incomplete? Because the builder stole the money throughout the course of the project, and when the money was gone, construction stopped—before windows could be inserted, before electrical wiring and plumbing could be installed. Shells, skeletons of shelters with holes for windows like gaping black eyes. Grotesque monuments to corruption.

Don't get me wrong. Aiding development and increasing the economic prosperity among developing nations are essential and worthy goals. But give the money to the Mamas. When you give money to the Mama, she uses it for household goods. She buys chickens and vaccinates them and sells the eggs, enabling her family to eat. Give money to the Mama and she buys a plow to farm her plot, raising food for her family to eat and sell. The Mama shares her plow with neighboring farmers so they can do the same. Give the money to the Mama and she starts a small business, perhaps raising honey bees or growing soy beans to process soy milk.

Many organizations have already discovered this powerful truth.

Monies do not have to be "given" to the Mamas. Many micro-financiers have had tremendous success loaning money to women, who repay the loans at extraordinarily high rates. Something like 97 percent of all micro-loan payments are made on time. This is quite remarkable in a place where money is scarce. And all we're talking about is original loans of $30 or $50 each.

When the world catches on about the powerful truth of assisting the Mama to assist the family to assist the community to assist the district, province, region, we will see development take off economically and politically. We'll see health for all, not just the few who can afford it. And we'll see clean water sources, free education and all buildings complete—with glass in their windows and electricity in their wiring.

Like the provincial governor of Goma said in his speech at last week's graduation, until developing countries value their women as equals to men, empower their women and elect their women to parliament and other offices, development will never arrive. Director Dan Keseje greatly values women in the rural communities. He has included them in college coursework and international workshops. He rewards them with certificates of accomplishment during the annual graduation ceremony. Dan prizes these women and gives them what they need to lift themselves and their villages out of poverty: knowledge.

Michelle, a VSO volunteer working in Addis Ababa, Ethiopia, has invited me to visit her to learn more about the organization she works with, Rehabilitation and Development Organization (RaDO). RaDO was started to assist people impacted by landmines: more specifically, to provide prosthetics and physical rehabilitation. Most of the victims the organization assists come from conflicts in Sudan or from Ethiopia's war with their northern neighbor, Eritrea. I make plans to visit Michelle in Addis Ababa for one week, after which Michelle and I will fly to Zanzibar for a week's vacation.

The short flight from Kisumu to Nairobi takes 50 minutes. Kisumu looks lovely from the air, and Lake Victoria is massive. When Kisumu ends, green fields lead to the hills of the escarpment.

The international concourse at Nairobi's Jomo Kenyatta International Airport has shops with fancy goods, much like a Western airport. The similarities end when I go to the restroom, where there's no running water. It's a rather large reminder that even though we're surrounded by fancy shops and lots of people waiting to fly to Dubai, Zanzibar, London and Mumbai, we're still in a developing country.

It's been a while since I've been on a big plane with a television. During our flight to Addis Ababa, they show episodes of Home Improvement with Tim Allen. I'm taken aback. America. Americans. I sometimes forget what it's like to be around my fellow countrymen and women.

A piece on Zanzibar is also shown during the flight, increasing my excitement about visiting the island. Ethiopian Airlines' in-flight magazine, printed in both English and Amharic, says the airline gets calls from clients asking if there will be food on the flight. Like most airline magazines, this issue's advertisements feature luxury resorts, expensive jewelry and even a spa; such contradictions to the average citizen's experience.

We arrive in Addis Ababa's lovely new airport at 9:00pm. The Bole International Airport is called "Africa's New Super Hub!" by the airline magazine. The height of a seven-story building, the all-glass structure is well-lit in the night. Addis Ababa, headquarters for the African Union and major UN agencies, has been in need of an airport renovation since the last one in 1971. This new one is spacious and has all the modern conveniences, including state-of-the-art IT.

Getting an entrance visa takes nearly an hour, though. When I'm stamped, official and ready to leave, Michelle is there, accompanied by Yiberta, the director of RaDO. It's a little cold in Addis because the elevation is 8,000 feet. We take a quick tour of Addis, driving through the relatively empty streets and passing the Italian Piazza. Mussolini invaded Ethiopia in 1936 and wasn't driven out until the early 40s. In the interim, he stole many of their cultural artifacts, including the mysterious obelisks constructed centuries ago. With the help of the UN, Ethiopia is regaining those obelisks, which are being shipped from Italy and reassembled in their original locales. Although the Italians left behind excellent coffee, Ethiopia never succumbed to colonization as did all the other African nations.

Yiberta drops us at Michelle's place, a nice two-bedroom, one-bath townhouse with a tiny courtyard and a guard. Yiberta lives four houses down across the lane. On this first night of ours, Michelle and I stay up late talking about our experiences as volunteers. We discuss cultural differences and experiences in getting used to new languages and new foods. In Ethiopia, the official language is Amharic. Some people speak English, but not many. Michelle seems to have caught on to many Amharic words and is able to communicate efficiently.

On Sunday, we walk and talk along a new, wide road into the more prosperous parts of town. We pass a hotel where Michelle says there was a shoot-out in the lobby in May. It happened during the national elections and several people were killed. For a week during the elections, Michelle and other VSO volunteers were told to stay in their houses. Violence of this sort, related to politics and elections, is common in developing countries where political instability is ongoing. It is one of many root-causes for countries having difficulty developing.

We walk for five hours with tiny children who run beside us with their hands out. Ethiopians are small, and years of malnutrition haven't helped them. I'm larger and taller than most of the men. Small children seem even tinier, as do old, old men and women. I am used to people calling out to me because of my white skin, but the young, healthy people do not ask us for money, as they typically do in Kenya and Tanzania.

Michelle and I have collected a three-child entourage before we decide to stop mid-day for a meal. We choose a restaurant called Dashen. When we enter, the children follow. The waitress shoos the children back out the door, where they wait for us. A television in the corner, just over my left shoulder, shows the New Orleans flood damage from Hurricane Katrina. It's the first I've heard of Katrina's devastation. While everyone around us is speaking Amharic and eating injera, the traditional pancake-like Ethiopian food, I'm fascinated by my fellow Americans filling the screen. They seem so foreign to me in this foreign country.

Michelle orders for us. Soon a large, oblong plate arrives. On top of the injera sits a bowl of ground beef in a tomato-based sauce, with a hard boiled egg in the center. Michelle unfolds the injera and pours the contents of the bowl on top. She instructs me to rip off a piece of injera and scoop up the meat sauce. The injera is gray, spongy and tasteless, taking on the flavors of accompanying dishes. I sip orange soda because the sauce is spicy. Michelle orders a second dish, this one with chicken poured over the injera. We complete the meal with strong shots of macchiato. The total is 24 birr, or about US $2.40.

We walk a few blocks to the National Museum where we visit Lucy, the 1.1 meter tall skeleton who is the suspected link between Homo sapiens and Homo erectus. This tiny woman, only three feet tall, is just a replica, the sign tells us, because the real bones of Lucy are locked away in the basement of the museum. Lucy is the most complete early hominid skeleton yet recovered.

On the walk home, I begin sneezing. When I awake the next morning, feeling headachy and stuffy, I know it's a sinus infection. I get them regularly and normally take a 10-day course of amoxicillin to clear it up. I had planned to bring my stash of amoxicillin on the trip, but the bottle of pills is on my kitchen counter in Kisumu.

On Monday, Michelle spends the day at the VSO office facilitating a capacity building workshop with VSO staff. I stay at her place and read and sleep and feel somewhat better. But then I begin to feel worse. 'If I don't get antibiotics,' I think, 'the infection will not get better.'

Over a scrumptious dinner of salmon (from Vancouver), sautéed zucchini, sliced tomatoes and avocados and Stove-Top stuffing (which Michelle has been saving for a special occasion), we decide I'll go to the doctor tomorrow. VSO has great medical coverage for volunteers at St. Gabriel's Hospital in Addis. All I'll need is a letter from the VSO office confirming I'm a volunteer in Kenya.

The next morning, we ride to RaDO's office with Yiberta to meet Michelle's coworkers. They're lovely and kind. The organization was established to provide physical rehabilitation to people with disabilities caused by landmines. They established their rehabilitation facilities in several Ethiopian hospitals, providing both the equipment and trained personnel. RaDO soon expanded into providing prosthetics, eventually creating a landmine education program for people living in or near war zones. Many people do not know landmines and explosive devices aren't always buried. They're sometimes simply lying on the ground, near water sources and in open fields. When both adults and children find landmines, they may not recognize them as explosives. Made inside wooden boxes or metal containers, some appear to be toys. Metal is hard to find in rural areas and many people pick up the devices for their apparent value.

A RaDO driver drops me at the VSO office to get a letter authorizing me to use their medical services. I walk the half of a mile to the hospital and see the doctor. He is about my age and earned his medical degree in Poland. Although his English isn't good and I know no Amharic, we're still able to talk. He asks me about the United States and my volunteer work.

He doesn't look at my sinuses, throat or ears. He simply writes out three prescriptions. I'm disappointed to see antihistamine is one and I feel deflated there are no antibiotics. It's only later I read a medical journal article stating antibiotics do not shorten recovery time of sinus infections, no matter how much sufferers beg for the drugs.

Before going to bed, I take the antihistamine and am reminded why I never use it. The medicine causes my head to stuff up so badly I cannot breathe. Not only am I weak from feeling awful, I can't breathe or sleep. I feel every bit of the cold weather in Addis, so Michelle has given her very comfortable bed to me. She's sleeping on the living room chair cushions and a sleeping bag. She and I argue over the sleeping arrangements (I feel she's being too generous), but I soon become too sick to raise my voice. Tonight I'm grateful for her cozy bed and warm blankets.

The next few days go by in a blur. I just want to curl up and sleep. I have no energy, find it hard to talk and am practically unable to smile. We go to Michelle's office, and she's up and down, in and out of her office. Her coworkers thoughtfully boil water for me so I can breathe in the steam and open up my sinuses. They wonder if it's the altitude, if it's the flu. I tell everyone it's a sinus infection and I just need antibiotics, but they don't really listen because I don't say it with energy. I just want to sit quietly, very still, and let time pass.

Michelle is busy tying up loose ends, since she and I will fly to Zanzibar this Friday night. After we spend a week in Zanzibar, Michelle is going on safari in Tanzania and will climb Kilimanjaro. She will be away from RaDO for three weeks, so she's feeling pressure to put things in place before she leaves.

On Thursday, Michelle and I meet two of her friends: Fasika and Mesele. They are brother and sister (their father was a polygamist, so they have different mothers) who have started a farmers' cooperative as a non-government organization. Fasika is a teacher. She's taken the day off to go to the rural farm with us. We meet at 7:30am and go to a taxi stand. In Ethiopia, they call their van taxis "line taxis." In Kenya, we call them "matatus." Michelle is craving coffee so we stop at a small café-type place. I'm still not hungry or thirsty because of the infection. From the café, we take a regular taxi to the main line taxi stand. We wait for the bus to fill before we head out of Addis, toward Nazareth. It takes two hours to get there.

Fasika's and Mesele's village is actually located 20 kilometers outside Nazareth. It was built by a sugar company; the company operates the mill and provides housing for its employees. Company-run stores offer everything the employee families might need.

To get to the village from Nazareth, we get on a large bus crammed with lots of people. Religious beads, candles and artificial flowers create a shrine around the bus driver. A large painting of mother Mary looks at us from the front. The road is barely a path in some areas and the bus—Mary included—bounces and jolts.

We drive alongside a lovely, curving river until we get to a checkpoint. Since we are officially entering the sugar cane village, everyone must get off the bus and be searched, though I'm not sure what they are looking for. As we move away from the bus, I feel a hand move from my upper back, down over my butt and onto my thighs. I'm taken aback. Turning, I see a female guard and understand this to be the search. Back on the bus, we enter the village built by corporate funds in poor, rural Ethiopia. We pull in front of a few stores constructed of wood and tin, coming to a stop in the dirt parking lot.

There aren't many white people in Ethiopia. In the rural areas, there are fewer still. As we stand in the dirt parking lot waiting for a line taxi to take us to the farmers' plots, all the people in the village stare—especially the children. Some come up to us, touch our arms and run away giggling. Others touch my hair. Although I sometimes tire of being a sideshow, being sick gives me no energy to react, positively or negatively. I just stand, moving as little as possible as adults and children notice me and Michelle. Eventually, we get into a line taxi and head over rough roads and into the bush.

Fasika and Mesele are like many Africans who start NGOs to help their neighbors. They think white people have the money and the means to help them. Michelle has been working with them, helping them write proposals for funding. Now that I'm in town, she wants to expand their network and pull me into it. Although I don't mind, I'm not at all sure how I can help them. I think of Pambazuko's work in Nyalenda. I wonder if I can support more than one organization, also recalling how I've become disappointed in Walter's management of Pambazuko recently. He has been given funds to buy roofing materials, but continues to say the roofer has a broken arm and cannot work yet. I don't understand why there aren't others who can do the job. Walter's stalling concerns me. Will I continue to support Pambazuko? What can I do for any of these organizations?

By the time the taxi stops, we are deep into Ethiopia. Mesele explains how the farmers' cooperative works. Twenty families have joined together, under Mesele's guidance, to help each other farm their plots. It is difficult for a single farmer to own all the tools necessary to sow and reap crops. If the farmers pool their resources, they are better able to cultivate their land and share techniques to increase crop yield. Together, they can accomplish much more. These farmers have rented plows and other equipment. They share oxen to pull the plow. They buy seed and fertilizer at reduced costs because they're buying in bulk. They help each other in tilling or weeding or harvesting if there is illness.

We walk the freshly-plowed fields and meet young men from seven farming families. They take turns leading the oxen pulling a metal plow. They're growing teff, a thin, grass-like plant used to make injera.

After visiting the farmers and their fields, we take the line taxi to Fasika's house. Fasika's and Mesele's father is an employee of the sugar factory. They grew up in this house. Waiting for us are 25 orphans and their guardians.

These children, aged one to 12 years, receive assistance from Fasika and Mesele in the form of food, school fees, school uniforms, shoes and medical care. Just like millions of others in African countries, these children lost their parents to AIDS. Many of these children are probably HIV positive themselves.

The small yard is full of children and their guardians. They've been waiting for us for five hours. Michelle brought bubble gum, lollipops and balloons, but before we take photos and pass out the goodies, I suggest each child tell us his or her name. It's an opportunity for us to meet on a personal level since the language barrier and the size of the crowd makes it difficult to interact. Each child stands and says his or her name. Some speak English. Most are confident. A few are shy but speak up so the whole crowd can hear. Their Amharic names are translated into English for us; Joy, Peace, Hope, Strong, Justice. They smile and we smile. Mesele speaks and they hang on his every word.

We get ready to head back to Addis, so we can arrive by nightfall. Before we leave, I give Fasika US $5. Ethiopia will be celebrating their New Year in a couple of days and she wants to cook for the children. I don't have a lot of money and regret it's in dollars, not birr. However, $5 should buy two chickens. I know Fasika is hoping for much more, enough to buy a goat for slaughtering, but I don't have it and didn't plan to give anything today.

Everywhere we go, shepherds watch goats. Many goats are tagged with green or red markings on their foreheads. Others have their horns wrapped in color-coded scarves, marking the males and females being sold for the New Year's feasts. Ethiopian New Year is a huge celebration. Everyone takes time off from work and gathers with families. They'll slaughter a goat and cook traditional foods. Some men, we notice, have already started celebrating by drinking the local brew. In addition to the men who are drunk on the line taxi, we also share seats with men and women carrying produce and livestock for the local market. One man sits facing me, a chicken with its legs tied together in his grasp. He holds the chicken so its head won't protrude into my face. He and I grin at each other as the chicken protests. He is a skinny old man with a thin jacket. He soon exits the taxi with the others who carry potatoes, grains and handmade goods to market.

We left at 7:30am and arrive at Michelle's house at 8:00pm. I'm tired.

I tell Michelle I'm going to the doctor again tomorrow.

Getnesh, a coworker, insists on taking Michelle and me to lunch. She chooses a traditional Ethiopian restaurant at the Lalibela Hotel. The furnishings are authentic, with hand-carved chairs and carved wooden pictures on the walls. The table is a large woven basket. When the lid is removed, a gorgeous wood tabletop is exposed. A metal tray, the size of the tabletop, sits on the wood surface and is filled with food.

Getnesh orders for us. The waitress spoons out various meat and bean-based dishes and places them on top of a giant injera. Ethiopian food is delicious and it's a beautiful meal, but I still don't have an appetite. I'm beginning to associate injera and the meat sauces with the nausea. It's unfair to the food. Although it's a great meal with truly warm people, all I can think about is getting to the hospital.

Thomas, a RaDO driver, drops me at St. Gabriel's after the meal. Just like the first visit, they move me through the process relatively quickly. Soon, I'm facing a new doctor, one who asks a lot of questions but doesn't give me time to answer. I still like him since he looks into my sinuses and ears and agrees I need antibiotics. I would do a jig of joy but don't have the energy. Instead, I grab the medicine from the pharmacy and call Michelle. She'll meet me at a college near her house in one hour.

I take the little bit of time I have to look for authentic Ethiopian shawls in the shops. It's the end of the rainy season, so I carry Michelle's rather long umbrella, using it as a walking stick since I'm still weak. I don't walk quickly; it's more of a stroll. I have the sticky note in my left hand where Michelle has drawn the map to the college. I pass masses of marked goats tended by men of all ages.

Men with cars the size of shopping carts are giving driving lessons. They call me over, asking if I want instruction.

"No, thank you," I laugh, looking at the ridiculously tiny cars. "But thank you very much any way."

"Of course," one gregarious man says, partly laughing at me and partly at their little bitty cars maneuvering in a little bitty lot.

I keep strolling. A homeless man who mumbles to himself walks next to me. Some people know him and speak, others turn away from him. Small children beg but I don't increase my pace. I just look at them. Eventually the mumbling man tells the chidren to leave me and they do. As I near what looks like the college, a very tall man comes up behind me and speaks to me in Amharic. He appears to be enjoying some pre-New Year's libations. He also appears to be mentally unstable. He continues talking to me and I continue walking slowly with my makeshift walking stick.

The man is bigger than most Ethiopians. He's also making noises that do not sound like any language. His skin is light brown, as are his eyes, and he has them locked on me as I search the street for the college. When I don't pay him any attention, he grabs my left wrist and tries to read the sticky note in my hand. His grip is strong and I don't pull away or yell, for fear he'll react. I just keep moving with him at my side, even though he's holding my wrist and making strange noises as everyone on the street watches. Suddenly, he grabs my arm above my elbow and pulls me to a stop, turning me towards him. I resist and move down the street. He pulls me again.

From five different directions, men step onto the sidewalk and stand between me and the man. Each man who steps in on my behalf is apologetic. They move him away from me, and two of the men insist on walking me to the college. They confirm he has been drinking and is "crazy."

I get to the college safely, where Michelle meets me. We walk back to her place, down the side streets flooded with rainy season showers. We are forced to step on rocks to dodge the mud. At home, we pack for her trip, choosing the best clothes for Kilimanjaro, where the temperature can be close to zero degrees Fahrenheit.

We are ready for our flight to Nairobi, where we'll have a layover for the flight to Zanzibar, but our flight doesn't leave until 2:50am. We walk from Michelle's place to a hotel just across the expressway from the airport. It's 10:00pm. We eat a nice dinner until about midnight, when we leave the hotel, cross the highway and walk the mile or so to the airport. Michelle says Addis is safe. Women can walk alone any time of the night or day. Other people corroborate her story.

That's certainly not the case in Kisumu, where most people are in their homes by 7:30pm.

We get into Nairobi at 5:30am and hang out at the Java House on the international concourse watching CNN coverage of New Orleans. It's hard to watch, and being so far away, I feel impotent. About as impotent as I feel in my abilities to help Kenyans. We contemplate sleeping, but we already know there's no real chance of sleeping in the hard plastic seats.

Our flight to Zanzibar takes us over the top of Kilimanjaro and we get some great photos through the plane window. Michelle is shocked at the barren summit and the sheets of ice. She questions her plans to climb the mountain. I spent seven days there, so looking down on the mountain feels strangely like home to me.

We get to Zanzibar at 9:45am on Saturday, arriving on a plane loaded with white people. Michelle and I both anticipate a week of relaxation, a week during which we can let our guards down.

Oh, boy, are we mistaken.

A visa to enter Tanzania costs US $50. We get our visas at the tiny airport and exchange our money into Tanzanian shillings. Knowing we'll be spending about $10 each night, I've budgeted approximately $100 for our stay: $60 for six nights and $40 for food and souvenirs. I've become accustomed to living off of very small amounts of money, watching what's spent on food, buying only essentials.

The minute we step outside the airport doors, a crowd of men rush toward us, asking if we want a taxi. We've already decided that instead of spending US $10 on a taxi to town, we'll spend about 20 cents and take a dalla dalla, the bus system on Zanzibar Island. It's not really a "bus" in the American sense of the word—it's a truck with a covered back, fitted with a ledge for sitting around the perimeter. As we look for the dalla dalla stand, the men get in our faces and won't back away. Even when we say no, they follow closely, straining to put their faces in ours. We enter a small office at the front of the airport, labeled "Tourist Information," where an air conditioner spits out humid air. The guy points to the dalla dalla stand across the street.

We pull our bags toward the stand as a taxi driver in a striped shirt latches onto me and another tall guy latches onto Michelle. We're having difficulty carrying our luggage across the dirt parking lot and seeing where we're going, so it's rather annoying to have these two men practically hanging off us. The guidebook warns about men who get a kickback from certain hotels. We tell them we know where we're staying and do not need their help, but they do not back down, insisting on knowing where we're staying. Michelle and I have studied the city map in the guidebook and feel if we head toward town, we can easily find our way to the Malindi Annex Guest House, the first place we've decided to check out. The annoying taxi driver finally leaves us because his taxi is at the airport, but the tall guy is still here, climbing into the dalla dalla with us.

"We do not want your assistance," I tell him in front of the other passengers. "If you're getting on here and going to town because of us, we don't need your assistance." He assures me he was going to town anyway.

People continue crowding into the back of the truck until we're smashed against each other. A woman in a burka intentionally presses into me every time the bus brakes. Because I'm against the cab of the truck, the entire line of people crushes me with each movement. When we ask about the best place to get off, the other passengers are vague or act as though they don't understand English. Finally, Michelle and I just pick a place and pull our luggage down from the roof. The tall guy climbs out, too, and tries to help us with our luggage. We refuse him.

We have no idea where we are. The guy keeps saying, "This way, follow me." While we don't want to, because he'll want money, we do follow him slightly. We walk along sandy alleys before coming upon a main road, congested with traffic and market stalls, tiny shack stores and gas stations. The entire island appears to be covered in rough pavement and dragging the luggage is a chore. There is too much noise and too many people staring, trying to sell us things. Cars are honking and the tall guy towers over us, pushing us. At one point, Michelle turns from the main road to get rid of the guy. We end up on quieter city streets, but he's still there.

A small police station sits under huge, spreading trees surrounded by green lawn. When we approach the building, the guy drops back for a block. We sit on a bench under the roof's edge and ask a police officer if he knows where Annex Malindi is. He attempts to give us directions but has to consult with the policewoman behind the counter. We tell them the guy is following us and won't leave us alone, but they don't really care. They point us in the direction toward town, and we again set out with our heavy luggage. The tall guy soon rejoins us.

We turn into the maze of streets that make up Stone Town, an area of stone buildings and houses that create twisting, narrow paths. Michelle is so exasperated, she walks up to a man relaxing outside a store. She's seeking refuge and assistance. When he stands up, I notice his striped shirt. Then I see his face and we both realize it's the taxi driver from the airport, the one who wouldn't leave us alone! It seems fitting that with the thousands of people in town, we approached this guy for help.

We quickly move on, this time following the tall guy's directions. At this point, we don't care what his agenda is, he obviously knows his way around. He leads us straight to the Malindi Guest House, where two men run out to greet us and take us inside. The rate is $15 per night, which is higher than we had anticipated. They offer to show us Annex Malindi, which is only $10 per night. We choose Annex Malindi and settle into our rooms.

The guest house is a stone Swahili building, which means it has mangrove poles as ceiling braces throughout. China bowls are inset into the walls in traditional Swahili fashion. The walls are thick and the ceilings exceedingly high. The staircase leading to the three upper levels is narrow and the steps are deep and uneven. A courtyard is in the center of the building, open to the sky. On the roof are tables and chairs for breakfasting, which is included in the room rate. The Indian Ocean is only a few blocks away.

Keys in Africa are huge, much like the large skeleton keys in old horror movies. My room is on the corner and has two shuttered windows. There are no screens or glass in the windows. Two beds line the walls, both with mosquito nets. A chair sits next to the door, at the bottom of the step into the room, which is deep and dangerous. A ceiling fan does great work in keeping mosquitoes from alighting and the room from becoming stifling in the humidity.

At Annex Malindi, the bath is communal. Each floor has two baths. These are large rooms with a shower head in the corner, a toilet and a sink. Part of the wall is tiled, but the floor is raw cement throughout. One bath has a switch for heating shower water. There is no soap, no towels and often no toilet paper. Travelers in Africa quickly learn to always carry these basics. I have the travel toilet paper roll, but no soap and no towel. I improvise and use shampoo for soap. Luckily, the weather is warm so a towel is not needed. Still, I have to shower in my bathing suit, so I can move from the bath to my room without showing too much before using a t-shirt to dry off.

Living in Africa, I've learned to get by without electricity, to spend a week or more without water and to not bathe or wash my hair regularly. Since electricity is sketchy in all of Africa, I have not invested in a blow dryer. I just comb through my hair and allow it to dry naturally. I've also grown used to not putting on makeup in the mornings. Not having a beauty regimen is a freeing way to live.

After resting, Michelle and I walk to the main harbor in Stone Town, where vendors set up nightly barbecues. Walking the path through the city's main square means walking past table after table piled high with seafood. Each table has a hot grill waiting, a jiko with hot oil for frying chips and a crew to make sure your food is prepared and served promptly. Crew members call out to people walking by, competing with those at the next table. Shark, barracuda, shrimp, lobster, squid, red and white snapper, tuna, mackerel and other fishes are cut into pieces and skewered. Crab claws are stacked next to octopus tentacles. The food is beautiful and especially alluring when lit by kerosene lamps.

Each skewer, which contains about eight pieces of fish, costs 1,000 shillings (US $1), though sometimes they'll drop the price to 800 shillings. Two skewers of fish and chips cost about US $2.50. It's delicious. Set amongst the tables of food are sugarcane juicers. The men run foot-long pieces of sugar cane through the press four or five times, until the cane is dry and splintered. They add a slice of lime to the glass. It tastes almost like lemonade but, amazingly, it isn't overly sweet. One glass costs 20 cents.

We pass through the crowd and are amazed at how many white people there are. Still not used to seeing white faces, Michelle and I find them exotic and interesting. Beyond the tables of seafood stand booths of vendors selling cloth, jewelry, shawls, original oil paintings (Tinga Tinga) and batik. These vendors are aggressive and sometimes desperate, so we walk through and avoid making eye contact. During the day, all these booths and tables of food disappear.

The harbor park is a grassy expanse with a central, round pavilion. Facing the harbor at the grassy edge is the House of Wonder, a massive, restored building that once housed the Sultan of Zanzibar. Now a museum, the building is devoted to the maritime history of Zanzibar. It also explores the Swahili culture found here and along Kenya's coast.

Zanzibar was the oceanic portal through which an estimated two million slaves from East Africa moved on their way to the Middle East. Arab slave traders traveled inland and bought slaves from warring tribes. They brought them to the African coast and then to Zanzibar, where they were sold at open markets and loaded onto ships.

Zanzibar is also called Spice Island; once the slave trade was abolished, spices supported the economy. Monday morning, after a night of deep sleep, Michelle and I join a spice tour. Waiting in the spice tour office with the Muslim men who run the company, we meet Hideaki Suzuki, a young man from Japan who's in Zanzibar to research his dissertation. For eight weeks, Hideaki works every day, researching at the local library, pulling and studying old slave trading documents. His weekends are spent going to beaches on other parts of the island. Today, he's taking the spice tour.

Our spice tour group fills two white vans. We drive out of Stone Town, visiting small houses and large groves of various spices to see the plants up close: ginger, cloves, nutmeg, coriander, cumin, vanilla, black pepper, cocoa, coffee, jackfruit. We learn about the different uses of the spices and the parts they played in Zanzibar's history. Many of the roads we travel are unpaved. Tables line the road and are heaped with small, colorful packets of spices.

One young man in our tour group wears a Kenya t-shirt. He looks to be 30 years old. I finally ask him if he's from Kenya

"Yes," he says, "and I'm proud of Kenya. That's why I'm wearing this shirt!" I ask where he's from and he says, "Kisumu."

"I live in Kisumu," I say to him.

"Oh, so you speak Luo?" he asks and laughs.

"Hericamano," I say (which means "thank you"). We both laugh.

His name is Seba. He's from Kondele, an area of Kisumu near the provincial hospital. He seems happy to talk about Kisumu because he now lives in Tanzania and hasn't been home for a year. Seba is here accompanying an older German woman, who is perhaps 65 years of age. She seems a bit timid, but they sometimes hold hands. Over lunch, they tell us they have spent time in Dar es Salaam, Tanzania's capital. She'll soon go home to Germany, but will return again, to visit Seba. This is her second trip to Tanzania. Older European men and women spending time with young Africans happens quite a bit on the coasts of Kenya and Tanzania.

We head to the beach on a wide, dirt road lined by tiny houses and pine and coconut trees. Along the way, trucks pass. Their large beds are filled with locals dressed in bright green and yellow t-shirts. The national election is coming up next month, and campaigning is in full swing. Truckloads of young people shouting slogans are seen all over the island. As in Ethiopia and other African countries, elections are times of instability. It is the beginning of low season here in Zanzibar for the sole reason that the upcoming elections make it risky for tourists to be on the island.

We turn onto a dirt path with two tire tracks and a line of grass down the center. We're stopping at Zanzibar's slave cave. The structure is not a natural cave, but two rooms dug into the ground, perhaps 15 feet deep. They are topped by a shell and cement roof that protrudes two feet from the ground. A single stairway in the center is the only entrance and exit. The stairs are deep and narrow with nothing to hold as we descend. It's a little scary climbing into the hole on a bright day; I cannot imagine the terror felt by people being herded into the darkness in chains.

A sheltered placard tells the story of this locale: how slaves were brought here in the dark of night when slavery became illegal. Men were crammed into one room and women into the other. They were not fed or cared for, and many died in the sunken caves. This, the slave traders believed, was a way to weed out the weak, leaving only the strongest for trading.

The shell roof covering the rooms is only about 200 feet from the Indian Ocean. Access to the beach made it easy for the slaves to be put into boats and paddled to awaiting ships. We walk the path the slaves took (though they were shackled around their necks, wrists and ankles). The path leads through the thorny shrubs and onto a narrow peaking mound from which a drop of several yards ends in the rocky ocean's edge. Again, the bright sunshine makes it hard to imagine being led to the water through the darkness.

From here, we go to a clearing in the coconut trees and park. A short walk through the bush and we're all catching our breath at the sight of the turquoise Indian Ocean and ancient black cliffs. A few people are already in the water, so we venture to the shade of a cliff and select our spots on the rocky ledge. A guy sits on a cooler next to us. I point and say, "Smart guy!" He smiles.

"Is that yours or are selling those?" I ask.

"I'm selling," he says, standing to open the lid. Inside, nestled amongst large pieces of ice, are glass bottles of Coca-Cola, Sprite, Fanta Orange, and Tusker beer. I get a Coke and relax in the sun, watching Hideaki and Michelle sip their beers in the African heat.

We enter the water and bob around, enjoying the rhythm of the waves and the cooling water. Michelle and I bob next to each other calmly while Hideaki dives nearby wearing goggles, looking for fish. We eventually climb out of the water, Michelle, Hideaki and I, and sit on the sand a few hundred yards down the beach. Somehow, Hideaki and Michelle produce dry cigarettes and a lighter. They enjoy a smoke, Michelle sharing a cigarette from Ethiopia and Hideaki sharing a cigarette from Japan.

Zanzibar. Turquoise water with pure white caps. Scenes from a travel brochure everywhere we look. We're definitely experiencing some of the relaxation we were seeking. It's almost too bad when our guide begins rounding people up, telling us it's time to return to town, but that's just what we do.

We shower, rest and eventually hear Hideaki in the lobby, talking Kiswahili and laughing with the staff, making his way up the narrow stairway to our floor. He brings the promise of the bright and setting sun with him. We all venture out, wondering where we should watch it go down this evening. It becomes routine, walking toward Stone Town's harbor around 5:30pm each evening to watch the sunset. On any stretch of beach, there are locals dividing up into two teams, playing soccer in the angled sunbeams. Tonight, we choose Freddy Mercury's bar. (Freddy was born in Zanzibar but later moved to England before becoming well-known as the lead singer for Queen.)

Freddy's restaurant is a magnet for white people and is always busy. We never eat here, because the food is expensive by Tanzanian standards, but we do sit at tables on the deck's edge, talking and drinking beer or soda, waiting for the sun to be completely gone before we walk the two remaining blocks to the nightly delicious and inexpensive barbecue. Tonight, before we go to the barbecue, while Hideaki is on his third large beer and Michelle isn't far behind, Hideaki tells us about his research on the history of the East African trade routes.

It's not long before he mentions Sir Captain Richard Burton. "Yes!" I agree. "I enjoy reading about Burton, too."

We discuss Burton's accomplishments; how he was the first European to set foot in Harar in Ethiopia. A slave-trading town, Harar was a walled city protected by its Muslim inhabitants. Any white man who ever entered the walled city never left it alive. That is, until Burton arrived. Burton, was able to speak Amharic and Arabic flawlessly and appeared to be Arab when he let his dark hair grow long. By the time he made the trip to Harar, he had already penetrated Mecca, disguised as a Pathan. Burton's linguistic abilities were extensive; he learned to speak more than 30 languages and dialects fluently.

I can't imagine what it must look like for an energetic Japanese man and an excitable American woman to discover they share the same hero. We talk non-stop about Burton and Lamu and Lake Tanganyika and the Mountains of the Moon. Poor Michelle. Most of our revelations about Burton are directed at her, as though Hideaki and I HAVE to inform her about this man or we'll fail as fans. She's interested in the part about Harar in Ethiopia, since she lives there, but her attention soon drifts. Hideaki and I don't notice right away because our enthusiasm nudges us on.

"Oh!" I shout. "Did you know he visited Salt Lake City in the United States and interviewed Brigham Young to learn more about the Mormons' practice of polygamy?"

"No!" Hideaki says, so I tell him about my hobby of studying religions; how I wrote my master's thesis on the Book of Mormon; how, when I found Burton's book, intersecting two of my favorite subjects, I simply floated around Georgia State University for several days.

"And I own the book now!" I exclaim. "I have many of his books, including his book on swords."

"Is it good?" Hideaki asks.

"I don't know," I reply, "I haven't read it. But I will, because I've packed away Burton's book until I return home."

"I have many of his books, too," Hideaki tells me. We just grin at each other across the blue and white tablecloth, in the golden colors of the sunset. We are grinning like happy idiots.

We stroll the path between tables of seafood and watch Hideaki charm the food crews. They all know him because he's been here most nights for the last few weeks. He talks them down to a ridiculously low price. While they grill our selections, we move behind the seafood and sit at a rickety picnic table, next to a harbor wall holding back the ocean. Across the table sits a man who also looks Japanese. We speak to him and learn he's a volunteer who lives in a remote village in Northern Ethiopia. He's in Zanzibar, as Michelle and I are, for a little rest and relaxation, not to mention access to good food and a few of the luxuries unavailable in Ethiopia. After dinner, we stroll along the harbor park with the two men from Japan and talk about development issues and volunteering and the Swahili culture.

The next morning, Michelle and I decide to walk through the narrow streets of Stone Town, to explore the city and photograph its architecture. We enter a part of town obviously designed for wealthy tourists. It's a bit of a mind play to see Italian and French restaurants next to hotels on the water's edge. We walk through hotel lobbies furnished with beautiful antiques, our jaws following us on the floor. We walk on carpets to seaside patio restaurants, wondering what it's like to stay in such luxury. Along these same streets are air-conditioned tourist shops complete with huge, glass counters of Tanzanite jewelry, shelves of African shawls and racks and racks of clothes. We recognize many of the patrons from the spice tour or from Freddy's sunset crowd.

After lunch, Michelle goes to the beach and I go the national museum in the House of Wonder building. The center of the building is open through all three stories. The building is huge and has so much unused space. Dark wood stairs, about 20 feet wide, lead from floor to floor.

Maritime history is displayed on the ground level and artifacts from the Swahili culture are on the second level. As I walk and read, two white men also visit the exhibits. We pass each other, stepping out of each other's way, until I finally say, "There doesn't seem to be a logical system for displaying these items."

The older man, who has dreadlocks, a beard and appears to be in his early 50s, says, "You expected to find logical displays?"

"Yes," I say, "at least organized by locale where the objects were found or by dated periods. These things are from all periods and all locations, jumbled together."

For the next hour, the three of us stand in one spot and talk. And talk. There are no pauses or awkward silences. The older man, Bill, is a retired doctor from the United States. He's of average height and build and seems very normal, except for his dreadlocks. The younger man, Toby, is his son. He's living in Southern Tanzania for three months, studying a community of wood carvers for his bachelor's thesis. Toby is at least 6' 4" with bright red hair and a large football player's build. Bill is visiting Toby for three weeks, and they've just spent time in Dar.

I'm curious about Bill's assessment of Africa. He has donated his services for short periods of time in developing countries in the past. He understands the health needs of rural people. He tells me he has seen the health needs of Africans on this trip, and he remains optimistic about health care access increasing in Africa and other developing countries. He also says he couldn't live in the third world for any length of time. Handing me his card, I notice Bill is now a dance caller.

"Like calling a square dance?" I ask.

"Yes, precisely," he says.

A couple passes us, led by a guide and we half listen to what the guide says about the ceremonial dress display. Soon, Bill, Toby and I realize we must complete our own tours, so we part with handshakes and smiles.

Michelle and I spend sunset at Freddy's, watching the men play soccer and the boys practice gymnastics in the stand. They do handstands and handsprings and run up the wall and flip back onto their feet. At the next table, two women and one man also watch the soccer game. Because they call it soccer instead of football, Michelle is pretty sure they're from North America. Through her eavesdropping, she is able to narrow it down to Canada, at which point she must find out for sure. She asks, and it turns out they are from Canada, from Toronto. They've just arrived in Zanzibar after climbing Kili. Michelle is excited to get the skinny on the climb since she plans to scale the mountain in only two weeks.

When people ask me how the climb is, I'm careful not to make light of it. While it's not a technical climb using ropes and safety harnesses, it is physically challenging, especially because of the risk of high-altitude sickness and the cold. The mountain boasts 10 degree weather, and there is no running into a hotel or lodge and warming oneself by the fire before going back into the elements. On Kili, climbers are in the elements 24 hours a day. Being in a tent, in a sleeping bag, makes it difficult to get warm. I tell prospective climbers that if they can simply focus on putting one foot in front of the other (which means someone else is preparing their food and setting up their tent), then they have a greater chance of making it. Everyone should bring along lots of warm clothes (especially a face cover and gloves), drink lots of liquids and be sure to take Diamoxx to ward off altitude sickness if they aren't allergic to sulfur-based drugs. I would never encourage someone to climb Kili unless they truly wanted to.

Zanzibar is where most folks go to relax when their climb is over. We meet people from all over the world who have just come from Kilimanjaro or safari.

Michelle and I would like to see the northern beaches of Zanzibar, so we seek information. The trip to Nungwe, we're told, will take about two hours. We say goodbye to Hideaki, but I tell him to look for me on Thursday at Annex Malindi.

The road leading from Stone Town soon turns to dirt. We travel for quite awhile before turning off into scrub bush, eventually entering a village with mud houses on the perimeter. We pass through the center of the village and exit on the other side where we see, as if by magic, brick and steel buildings, even shops with glass doors and signs that say "Yes, We're Open" in the windows. They are an incredible contrast to the red mud huts just behind us. The beach is about 500 paces away.

Michelle and I check out the rooms, but the lowest rate is $15 per night, which is more than we budgeted for. We hop back into the van, the only remaining passengers, and take a very bumpy ride through what seems like nowhere until we pull up to a gate. When the doors swing open through the help of the guard inside, we see the little "resort" of Kendwa Rocks. We speak to a large woman through a tiny window. She hands several keys to a man, instructing him to show us the dorm room and the bandas. We pass the bath house, which has four unisex shower/toilet rooms. The sink area is out in the open. It has one mirror and one deep sink for all the resort guests. The dorm room is large and priced at $10 per night. At least 15 people can fit into it. The banda is a small room with a deep, thatched roof and a tiny porch. Two beds with nets make up the furnishings. It's $12 per night, a little more than we had expected, but it's better than being in the unisex dorm.

Other bandas and little cottages sit on tiers leading down to the sand and beach. A restaurant made of wood and thatch serves Kendwa Rocks' guests. We'll eat our free breakfast there each morning.

Michelle goes down to lie out in the sun. I pull out my money and count. I take away the $24 for the banda for two nights. I set aside 10,000 shillings for a room back at Annex Malindi in Stone Town. I then remove 5,000 shillings for the return van trip to Stone Town. That leaves 5,000 shillings for the next three days. I have a pint of water and vow to make it last. Water must be bought in bottles, not taken from taps, so I set aside 450 shillings for buying water in Stone Town. With approximately 4,500 shillings ($4.50) for food, I'm grateful breakfast is free. That only leaves lunch and dinner to buy.

Most of Zanzibar is untouched by development. Local ladies patrol the beach, wrapped from head to toe in their kangas, asking female guests if they'd like a massage or henna paintings. Local men also walk up and down the beach, visiting the three resorts in this area, offering to take people on fishing trips or on dhow rides to Nungwe village. Guys also walk by selling everything from toasted cashews to neckties. I play in the water and walk as far as possible both ways. Kendwa Rocks is not a fancy resort. Every structure is made of wood and woven grass mats, sort of like on Gilligan's Island.

Soon they'll be serving dinner, so we head to the banda for a shower. Because the bath area is unisex, I again take my swimsuit with me to the shower, using shampoo as soap.

At the open-air, thatch-roofed restaurant, a blackboard announces entrees. The food sounds wonderful: red snapper with garlic sauce and Flounder with white wine sauce and rice. Unfortunately, each dish costs 6,000 shillings. That's only US $6, but I have 4,500 shillings that must last for the next three days. The cheapest item on the menu is soup at 1,500. I order the soup—crème spinach—served with chappatti, a flat bread.

When our dishes arrive, the soup bowl is filled only a little more than halfway and next to the bowl sits two small triangles of chappatti. Two tiny triangles! Luckily, my appetite hasn't really returned since being sick, so the soup is plenty and enables me to take another dose of antibiotic.

We're back at the restaurant anticipating breakfast. They bring us five slices of bread, each about two-inches square. Butter and jam are on the table, so I slather both of these on thickly. They also serve unlimited coffee and offer eggs cooked to order. It's not a huge breakfast, but it holds us over.

Michelle finds a spot in the sun with a book and I take a hammock under the eave of the restaurant. Music is always playing here, stuff like James Taylor. It's soothing. I read a book called *Empire: How Britain Made the Modern World* by Niall Ferguson. It has a special focus on Britain's colonization of East Africa. Not light summer reading, but perfect for this trip. We are surrounded by Swedes, Germans, Italians, Dutch, Aussies and Brits who come and go, perching on rope chairs and lathering on sunscreen. Groups of them come to the water's edge and climb into boats, usually on their way to snorkel, dive or parasail. I enjoy the minor sway of the hammock and often drop the book to my chest, enjoying the view of the blue sky melting into blue water against the white, white sand.

A Rasta dude comes up, gives me his hand and says his name is Wiseman. He has a boat tour if I'm interested. I'm not, I tell him gently. We talk about the island, and the conversation eventually turns to my life in Kenya. He has a multitude of questions. When he begins to tell me how hard it is to drum up business, we're interrupted by the knowledge that his favorite soap opera is about to start. He tells me he needs to head home to watch. He doesn't like missing a single episode.

"Wow," I say, "You have a TV."

"Sure," he says.

Mid-afternoon, I walk down the beach. No one else is around until a young man walks up and strolls next to me. He asks the usual questions: "What's your name?" "Where are you from?" "When did you arrive?" "How long will you be here?" "Do you want to visit my shop and look at souvenirs?" Between his questions, I learn his name is King Solomon. He talks non-stop. I answer his questions but don't ask a lot back, though I still learn he used to live here but now lives in Dar. King Solomon travels around Tanzania buying handmade crafts and sells them throughout Tanzania, including Zanzibar.

Eventually, we part at the spot where we first met. I find an unoccupied hammock, shade, James Taylor and a good book. I don't have lunch, but that's okay. I'm not really hungry.

At dinner, Michelle orders the Flounder dish and a glass of wine. I order the soup again, this time potatoes and leeks. It's served with pompano, a thin Indian bread that's usually spicy. When the soup comes, the bowl is once again barely half-filled and the pomp is only two small pieces. I don't want Michelle to know my funds are limited because she would feel obligated to loan me some. And I don't need it, not really. Breakfast tomorrow will be free. I'll be back in Stone Town tomorrow evening, and I'm sure if I ask Tanika, the receptionist at Annex Malindi, she'll give me a room rate of 8,000 instead of the usual 10,000 Tanzanian shillings.

After dinner, Michelle and I tuck under our mosquito nets and try to fall asleep amidst the music war going on between two restaurants. Somehow, falling asleep comes quickly.

After breakfast, we say goodbye. I'm going back to Stone Town for one more night and then my flight to Kisumu. Michelle is spending a few more days here before she climbs Kili.

I meet the 10:00am shuttle. A Swiss couple also climbs on board. They're anxious to make it back to Stone Town by noon, before the bank closes. If they don't, they have no way to get or exchange money for their trip.

We stop at the adjacent resort and fill the van. Everyone speaks English even though they're from all over the world. I feel very lucky that English is so widely spoken. We're all friends by the time we reach Stone Town, so we are happy when the couple makes it to the bank on time. When I return to Annex Malindi, pulling my suitcase through the rocky doorway, Tanika accepts my offer of 8,000 shillings for the night. It's no small triumph; now I have enough money to buy water and a snack this afternoon as well as dinner at the barbecue this evening.

Once I'm settled in and rested, I walk through Stone Town, taking different routes and photographing the architecture. I stroll, really examining the buildings from every angle. A cemetery catches my attention. Although it's enclosed, glimpses of tombstones peer through holes in the wall. As I look and ponder certain shots, three pre-teen boys surround me. Not wanting to appear afraid, I smile at them. One boy holds his hand out and says something. Though I don't know what he's said, I do know he's asking for money. I shake my head "no" and walk on. I don't have any money on me, so I say, "hapana pesa."

The boy then asks me to photograph him. I don't really like to photograph locals because they may expect money. I hesitate. He then insists, so I snap his picture. Again, his hand comes out and again I say, "Pole sana, hapana pesa." In English it means, "I'm very sorry but I have no money." This angers him. The boys walk a few yards away and pick up rocks, which they begin throwing at me, shouting, "Fuck you!" Their pronunciation isn't perfect, but between the rocks and the tone, I understand clearly what they're saying. They walk away but I am unnerved, trying to remain calm. I spot a view of the cemetery wall and Indian Ocean to photograph. Just as I get ready to snap the picture, the boy sticks his head around the corner to shout at me again. He is accidentally caught in the picture.

"Nooooooo," he screams.

I turn to get away from the boys when three teenagers approach me on the path. They're walking with their shoulders back, kicking trash in their path. I take no notice of them, hoping they'll pass without incident. I'm not that lucky. One boy kicks a box that hits my right shin. They bend over laughing, encouraging the second boy to kick a glass soda bottle, which nicks my ankle.

They move away, still laughing, and try to look big and important. This outward hostility is interesting to me. I wonder if it's the way all Zanzibaris feel toward tourists, but only the children have the courage to demonstrate their animosity. Most locals are not kind or warm or respectful. They're attentive when trying to sell something; otherwise they appear cold. Tourists are a necessary evil, it seems.

Michelle and I were wrong to think we could come here and let our guard down. In fact, being on the island has been much more stressful than living in Kisumu. I'm really looking forward to going home.

Back at Annex Malindi, after showering and packing for tomorrow's flight, I hear Hideaki's happy voice ringing up the stairway and reverberating in the center courtyard. He finds me in my old room.

"Ah, you made it back. Excellent," he says.

"Yes, and you're still here," I say.

He spent two days at an archaeological dig on the island, meeting with scientists and having beers with them at a shack bar. He's excited about the dig and tells me if he had seen it a year or two before, he would have become an archaeologist.

Hideaki is interested in cultural exchanges across the Indian Ocean between East Africa, India and Arab countries. Naturally, he wants to learn about inland cultures—and not just the indigenous tribes, but sub-cultures like the Sikh Indian communities, as well.

The sun has set so we walk through the seafood stalls, selecting barracuda, shark, white snapper and chips for dinner. Afterward, we stroll by the merchant stalls and talk to Jumas, a friend of Hideaki's who has a rack of shawls (pareos) and printed kangas. Hideaki is interested in buying kangas to take back to Japan. Jumas models the pieces for us, wrapping his very skinny frame in a black-and-white kanga. Then Jumas wraps Hideaki in a black and turquoise set. Hideaki buys them both.

The shawls are gorgeous and feel silky, even though they're woven of cotton. I've spent all my money on dinner, with reserve for the ride to the airport tucked in my room. I also have 1,300 Kenyan shillings in my wallet, about US $19, but I didn't convert it to Tanzanian shillings because I'll need some Kenyan currency when I re-enter the country.

"Pick a shawl for you, Cindi. I'd like to buy one for you," Hideaki says.

I'm touched by his generosity because I really do want a shawl to take to Kisumu. Of course, I protest. He insists, earnestly, and we look at the shawls, inspecting the color of their weaves. Hideaki has a genuine interest in all things and all people. I enjoy being with him and watching him interact with the Zanzibaris, speaking Kiswahili flawlessly. When he walks me back to Annex Malindi, I'm rather sad our time together on the island is over. I leave tomorrow morning and Hideaki will leave in a week's time to do more research in Oman. We exchange email addresses.

When I enter Annex Malindi, the electricity is off. Candles illuminate the reception room, where the young man on duty has placed a mattress in the center of the floor. He jumps up to welcome me and hands me a candle, leading the way up the stairs. He has placed a candle at the top of the stairs, brightening the entire central courtyard. I leave it burning on the stone step after he's gone downstairs.

There's a mosquito in my net, biting me regularly, and I have difficulty locating and killing it. The taxi will be here at 5:30am and I have no alarm clock, so I sleep lightly.

I'm up before light breaks fully, completing my packing and wondering what time it is. I go downstairs to the reception area to look at the clock above the desk. The mattress is gone from the floor and the front doors are open. Electricity is back on and a small light reveals the time: 5:00am. The taxi is already here.

My flight is at 7:30am. When we pull in front of the airport, a line of white people and their luggage extends to the roadside. Kenya Airways and East African Safari Airways each have a flight leaving this morning. When I check in, the man tells me 12 passengers have been bumped from the overbooked flight to Nairobi, including me. We'll have to travel to Dar es Salaam before moving on to Nairobi. His sharply dressed young manager comes over and explains the process, apologizing. The manager handles my ticketing and baggage himself. Since my flight from Nairobi to Kisumu isn't until 5:30pm, I don't mind the re-routing.

When I approach the immigration desk, on the way to the departure lounge, the officer tells me there is a $25 fee to exit Tanzania. My stomach sinks. I didn't know about an exit fee.

"Well," I say to the guy as I pull out my wallet, "I don't have $25 and my flight leaves in 30 minutes."

The big guy next to him says, "Borrow it from a fellow traveler."

"I'm traveling alone and I wouldn't ask a stranger for money," I say.

I pull out the 1,300 Kenyan Shillings.

"This is all I have," I say.

They point me to the exchange desk and say I may be able to use my bank card to get more money. I go to the exchange window, which is only five steps away, and a large, disagreeable man with 5 o'clock shadow at 5:00am says the Kenyan money is worth US $19 and he cannot get money from my bank card. He points out of the airport and says the bank opens at 8:30am.

I wonder briefly if they'll keep me in the country because I don't have enough money.

I find the helpful East African Safari manager and tell him I don't have the money to get out of the country. He walks over and talks with the immigration officer. When he returns to me, he says, "Give the officer the Kenyan shillings." I do. He places a clearance stamp on my boarding pass and stamps my exit visa. I'm free to leave Zanzibar.

Once I'm at Nairobi's airport, sitting in the departure lounge, I'm excited about being home. I text message Vitalis about a ride from the Kisumu airport. After being away from Kisumu for two weeks, I'm anxious to get home. I'm teaching class tomorrow morning and will instruct students in communication and public speaking.

It is raining when we land in Kisumu, so arriving passengers look for their rides while standing with their backs to the airport wall, just under the eaves, staying dry. John, one of TICH's drivers, runs through the rain and squeezes in next to me, his back against the wall. He smiles down at me. It's wonderful to see a familiar face. TICH's brown van is in the front row.

We run for it.

Chapter Fifteen

I n d e c i s i o n

*I*t's 8:00am and we're in class. Half of the students work for CDC-Kemri (Center for Disease Control-Kenya Medical Research Institute), so they have experience working with programs to assist rural populations. I give them an overview of communication as a field of study, and we work throughout the day, discussing persuasion and rhetoric. In their work with rural communities, they'll need to understand how to communicate ideas and gain compliance from their community partners for teaching new methods of farming or educating about health issues. My job for today and tomorrow is to make their jobs easier.

After class, I go to town to buy groceries and check emails. I call Jaime, my daughter, from the internet café. She sounds wonderful, even though I woke her up by calling. Hearing her voice makes me homesick, and I worry that Jaime and her brother James may need me. It's a recurring theme in our conversations.

"Are you okay, Sweetie?" I ask.

"I'm fine, Mama."

"Do you have everything you need? Have you been well? If there's anything you need, please tell me. There are ways I can do stuff for you, even from Africa." Jaime always reassures me. She's fine, James is fine and Frankie the cat is fine. My footsteps always seem to have a spring in them after I've talked to my children.

Because I want to be home before dark, I rush through the Nakumatt and decide there's enough light to walk home instead of taking a boda boda. I need the exercise. I walk away from town on a busy road recommended as the safest route.

I have a tiny burgundy envelope of a purse tucked under my arm. Normally, I put my purse in the grocery sack when I'm in town, to avoid tempting anyone. Today, I have forgotten to put the purse away. As I approach an intersection, I notice three boys coming from the left. There's something unusual about them. Kenyans are usually quiet and composed in public. These three young men are laughing loudly and actually shouting. I try to estimate their pace and wonder if they'll end up ahead of or behind me. I slow down, allowing them to go ahead, but they stop at a tiny roadside store. I walk straight, looking around to make sure there are other people on the road. Today there are many people, mostly men walking alone or in pairs, heading in both directions. Plus, there are boda bodas passing regularly. I feel safe.

Because there are plenty of people around and it's still daylight, I walk quickly and with my head up, the purse tucked—practically hidden— under my arm. With only three blocks to go, I check again to make sure other people are nearby. I no longer see the three boisterous young men and will be home in time to clean up, cook dinner and prepare exercises for tomorrow's class.

Suddenly, my thoughts disappear as I hear footsteps behind me. This happens often, people running on the street to catch up to me, to talk. When I began living in Kisumu, I had to constantly tell myself not to worry, that the streets are safe and people often run up to simply talk. They want to be friends. So far, most people have been very kind, but a tiny part of my mind still makes me stiffen when I hear running footsteps, causing me to prepare myself. For what, I'm never really sure.

As the footsteps get louder, pounding now, I turn to the left, clamping my arm down over my purse. All of a sudden, I'm hit with a force so strong it knocks me off balance. The guy grabs the purse strap from behind, but my arm is clamped so tightly it doesn't budge. I'm still reeling from being hit when he starts to pull me farther around, grasping the strap. My right hand swings out with the grocery sack and I yell, hoping to alert people on the street. He hits me on the shoulders and chest, grabs me by the arms and throws me to the ground. I tumble into a ditch, at first landing on my knees, but then I keep falling on the sloping ground until my feet are in the air. All the while, I try to keep the groceries from hitting the ground and keep my grasp on the purse. Finally, my feet fall back into the ditch. The young man, persistent, bends over me, holding me down while he grabs at the purse. I hear a rip. He has won.

It takes a few seconds to figure out which way is up. I climb out of the ditch, still holding the groceries aloft, and look around at the men on the street. They stand and look back. My hair has fallen from its clip and my dress is torn.

"Help me," I yell to them as I begin to run. There are men behind me and men on the opposite side of the street. They all just stand, staring, just as they stood and stared while the guy was knocking me around in the ditch. My hair clip strikes my shoulder as I run. I can see the thief's white shirt 30 feet ahead of me and I'm running, wearing Chaco sandals and a sundress, yelling all the way down the street.

A boda boda driver pulls up next to me and peddles at the same rate of my run. He just stares.

"Stop him!" I cry. "He stole my purse!!!"

I know he can understand English. Most boda boda drivers speak English very well. But they do not speak it now. Another boda boda pulls up next to him and they both stare into my face. I turn my sights on this new guy and plead, "Please stop the guy in the white shirt, he stole my purse!" The guy speeds up and heads toward the thief. I urge him on inside my head, chanting "catch him, catch him" with every step of my feet.

When he gets next to the thief, he slows. The thief leaps mid-stride onto the back of the boda boda and the two of them fly toward Nyalenda, the slums. I stop running and look around at all the men on the street, feeling very alone in the world.

A gate opens and a Kenyan pushes his boda boda out. "What has happened?" he demands to know. "I heard screaming."

"That guy in the white shirt on the boda boda stole my purse."

The man immediately pulls his bike onto the road and says, "Twende, Twende!" which means, "Let's go!"

Not feeling particularly trusting of boda bodas now, I say dejectedly, "You really think we can catch them?"

"Let's try," he says. I hop on, not really wanting to chase thieves. I'd rather be in my living room, listening to the BBC and quilting.

"They don't normally rob people this early," he tells me, "it's still day-light."

"Yes," I say, holding the groceries in my lap, trying not to think about the items in my purse. I had also been told they wouldn't rob a white person, or others would jump in and catch the thief. Not today. But I'm so grateful this kind man has offered to help. He's flying, though, really putting an effort into his pedaling. We move quickly, passing people on the street as he rings his tinny bell. I look at each boda boda—at each passenger—but as we near Nyalenda, the streets and sidewalks begin to fill with people. There are too many to see. When the road dead ends into Ring Road and the tiny shacks of Nyalenda spread out in front of us, stretching for miles in either direction, I feel overwhelmed.

Night is beginning to fall. Dusk. Embers light up from charcoal stoves where ladies roast corn on the sidewalk. A large fire burns next to the side-walk. Vendors light kerosene lamps and place them next to their goods.

Points of warm light glow all over Nyalenda, but there's no way we'll find the two thieves. We turn right onto Ring Road, headed toward Pandipiere. As we roll past, I hear a woman scream. I look toward the sidewalk, behind the hundreds of people walking in the street, and see a man grabbing a woman. She screams but no one does anything. The guy hits her across the face and works to get a better grip as she continues to struggle. People walk past without looking at her.

Fire leaps from lamp wicks and roasting corn embers while the woman yells.

'I'm in hell,' I think.

"Please take me home," I ask the man from my seat on the back of his bike, knowing we'll never find the thieves and feeling unable to protect myself, much less the woman being beaten by the man.

I want to be home.

I will not feel safe until I'm behind the locked gates with Samuel. My keys were in the purse, so I'm hoping the Ruprah's have an extra key to the padlock on my front door.

"I want to give you something for helping me," I tell the driver. "However, I'm not sure I'll be able to get into my house. Do you mind waiting a few minutes to see if I can get in and get some money for you?"

"I don't mind," he says. "But you don't have to pay me. If you have the money, that's fine. If you don't, I'll think of it as doing volunteer work."

I smile in the lowing light behind his back.

Volunteer work.

Inside the gate, Samuel tells me that Mr. and Mrs. Ruprah are at temple, but Raju is home. Raju comes out; he and Samuel are both dismayed to hear what happened. Samuel keeps shaking his head, tsking and saying, "So sorry this happened, very sorry. Pole sana." Raju doesn't know if there's an extra key, but he gives me 20 shillings to give to the boda boda driver. I return to the gate and thank him for helping me. Samuel thanks him, too, and shakes his hand. The driver gives me a copy of his ID card, complete with his photo. His name is Erick Otieno. A good man.

Because I can't get into my house, Raju invites me to sit with him and his grandmother. He tells her in Punjabi what happened, and she's visibly saddened, shaking her head and saying things I don't understand. Her knee is bothering her so she doesn't get up. Raju brings me a cup of tea, which is very thoughtful, and asks if I'd like sugar. I notice my knee is hurting and lift my skirt to find my knees raw and bleeding. Mama's face scrunches up when she sees the wounds. She calls to Raju. Soon, he's bringing me cotton and disinfectant. They take good care of me as we wait for Raju's mom. Raju won't be picking her up from the temple for two hours, so they encourage me to sit back and watch television. It's on an Indian station and a soap-opera-like show is playing.

I get lost for minutes in the show, but it's not long before I return to my reality in Kenya. I'm in Kisumu. I've been robbed. I'm sitting with the Ruprahs, the closest thing to family I have here. Tears flow and I turn so Mama won't see.

They took my cell phone, which I've had for less than a month. My blood pressure medicine was in the purse. There were keys to the house and to my office at TICH. About 1,700 shillings (US $21): a lot of money to me and more than I usually carry. I never take credit cards with me and typically hide my "valuables" in zippered shirt pockets rather than carrying a purse. Today I broke that protocol.

Most painful to think about is the memory stick, which held many precious documents and pictures. I try not to think about that right now, focusing instead on the silly actors.

After a while, Mama starts talking to me in Punjabi and Kiswahili, neither of which I understand. But I know what she's saying. She's trying to comfort me. Raju comfirms this. Looking at my knees, it occurs to me I want to be back in the United States before they heal. I want to run away, get out of Kenya, go to where it's safe and there are people who love me, who would want to smash the face of the guy who robbed me. But I'm not in the United States: I'm in Kisumu and I can't even get into my house.

When Raju does return with Mrs. Ruprah, she's upset and anxious to make sure I'm okay. She looks for a spare key to my house in every cabinet and drawer. We make several trips to my front door, trying various keys in the lock. No luck.

Well, she says, we'll have to wait for Mr. Ruprah. He'll be home around 11:30pm. Mrs. Ruprah encourages me to take the lounge chair in front of the television in case I want to sleep before he arrives. I take the lounge chair and sit back against the cushions, trying not to get my dirty sandals on her furniture. I wonder where Mr. Ruprah is before realizing he's probably out drinking.

An Indian movie is on and it's quite good, even though I have no idea what they're saying. There's a strong, silent Muslim man who wins the heart of a beautiful girl who has been used by men. They borrow a man's car, none of them aware that someone has planted a bomb in the car. We watch, wondering when the bomb will go off and if they'll be in the car. The Muslim man is in the doorway of a jewelry store, where he's selected a bejeweled necklace for the woman (did I mention he's also rich and handsome?). He's trying to entice her into the jewelry store with the necklace and it works. But as she closes the car door, her long, gorgeous scarf gets caught. Before she can free her scarf, the car blows up, annihilating her. For the rest of the movie, the strong, silent Muslim man lives with a Hindu family, where he has a contentious relationship with the wife and mother of the family while he seeks revenge against the men who killed his girlfriend. He does get revenge, although he, too, dies in the last scene of the movie. By this time, the Hindu wife/mother has grown to love and appreciate him. She mourns and wails the loudest over his dying body.

The handsome, rich, silent Muslim man does a great job of easing my mind for two hours. Then Mr. Ruprah arrives. He is drunk and doesn't have a spare key or anything else strong enough to break the lock. He decides to unscrew the padlock base, allowing us into the house.

We stand on the patio at my front door: Mr. Ruprah, Samuel, Mrs. Ruprah and me (Raju floats in and out of the scene). Mr. Rurprah can't see well enough to handle the screwdriver, even with the candle Samuel is holding for him. He needs another screwdriver, so he sends Mrs. Ruprah to the trunk of his tan Mercedes, instructing her to pull out a tool kit. It's dark and she's having trouble locating the kit.

"It's on the left," he yells across the compound. "Stupid woman! You can't do anything right!"

"Hey, hey, hey," I whisper while touching his arm. "She's a good woman and a good wife. Don't say those things to her."

She finds the tool and brings it, but Mr. Ruprah is too drunk to operate the screwdriver and he doesn't trust Samuel to do it correctly. He hands the tool to me. Getting to the screws is difficult because the padlock is in the way. It takes pressure and concentration to turn the screw even the tiniest distance. Mr. Ruprah holds the candle for me to see, but he holds it directly over my hand and hot wax drips on me. I yell and push his hand back, telling him not to burn me.

"Turn it, that's it, and unscrew it," he's saying, "just unscrew it."

"Okay," I answer. But he repeats it over and over and the hot wax continues to drip on my hand. Mrs. Ruprah has a large knife with a wide blade. She thinks if she can slide the knife blade behind the padlock base, it'll come out of the door faster. But first, I must get the screws loosened and that takes awhile. I move from screw to screw while Mr. Ruprah tells me to "Just unscrew them!" Mrs. Ruprah occasionally sticks the knife behind the base and twists it.

"Don't," he yells at her, pushing the knife away and nearly burning me with the candle. I unscrew some more, gritting my teeth all the while. Samuel is behind us the whole time repeating what Mr. Ruprah says. It's like a dance: Mrs. Ruprah inserts the knife, Mr. Ruprah yells and pushes it away and I try to keep from being burned by the candle.

"How long are these screws?" I ask in desperation.

"About two inches," Mr. Ruprahs says.

They're only out about an inch. Mrs. Ruprah slides the knife into place and twists it, trying to leverage the plate off the door. Mr. Ruprah barks one final time, "Don't do that!" He grabs the knife from her, right across the front of my face, and throws it on the cement patio with all his might, just behind his right leg. The knife hits the ground, and the wooden handle immediately pops off. Mrs. Ruprah retrieves the pieces and takes them into the house. I try to concentrate on the screws, knowing as soon as the door is open I'll have a little peace and quiet.

No locks. No security. But peace.

Finally, I can turn the screws between my thumb and forefinger. The plate is loosened; the padlock is off the building. They tell me the lock will be replaced tomorrow.

Goodnight.

I'm in bed by 1:00am but don't sleep. Instead I think about the hot wax and Mr. Ruprah breaking the knife and how I want to see my children before my skinned knees heal.

It's 8:00am and we're in class once again. I try to push away thoughts of the robbery, of leaving TICH, of leaving Kisumu, of getting on a plane and flying away, watching Lake Victoria recede into the background. But I can't help but think how nice it would be to see the London airport, filled with white people with "soft" hair. Or the Schipol airport in Amsterdam, knowing with one more leg of the journey I'd be riding up the escalator at Atlanta's airport, looking for my children's waiting faces.

I love this school, these students, the work we're doing. The thought of leaving because I'm scared saddens me. And tires me.

I tell no one what happened the day before. I'm still processing it. Class goes smoothly, and we have several exercises where the students prepare and present short speeches. We go over pointers for preparing and delivering great presentations. We talk about how they communicate in their jobs and within their families, how their communication can be improved using the techniques we're discussing. The students are open and responsive and we make it through the day. I'm honored to have been a tiny part of their journeys toward a degree and toward making a difference for the many Kenyans living in rural poverty. I tell them this. I wonder if I'll leave and not see them progress through their curriculum.

I mustn't think about that. I need to just get home and chill, where no one can make any more demands on me.

The question of whether I should stay or go wears me down. I've committed to two years and have been here eight months.

I go to work on Monday morning and fight with Charles in accounting. We have two men waiting to be paid for work they've completed, work I've approved, but Charles wants to see more paperwork. I'm yelling, which is something I rarely do. And I'm yelling in front of others.

"Don't you care, Charles, that these men are here to collect money owed to them, money that's been approved for payment?"

"Yes, Cindi," Charles says calmly, "I care, but we also have a process here."

"Well," I shout, "it's wonderful that you can hide behind your processes, Charles, while people aren't paid and things aren't completed."

Walter, a member of our IT team, stands next to me, speaking softly, interjecting reason between each of my angry statements. I walk out and leave him to deal with the situation. I realize the stress of dealing with the robbery, of not facing the deep decision of staying in Kenya (where I feel increasingly less safe) or going home, is getting to me. I have no desire to hear about issues related to IT, and I feel incapable of managing the decision process. I stop to see Director Dan Keseje, to tell him what I've been feeling and thinking. He's at his desk, but apparently busy; two people behind me are also waiting to speak with Dan. I tell him I'll talk with him tomorrow.

Stress mounts. I send Chris, our VSO program manager, a long email. I tell him what has happened, informing him that the robbery is causing me to rethink my purpose for being in Kenya. I also tell him I want to work through the trauma of the robbery without losing time at work, but the stress is getting to me and I need to talk to someone. Chris suggests the VSO counselor, but she's in Nairobi, and I absolutely do not have the strength to ride on a bus for six hours to switch to a taxi to find this woman's office. Visiting VSO's counselor would require a night's stay in Nairobi and, because of the city's high crime rate, I can't even imagine being there.

The last few days, all I've wanted to do is to stay behind the gate at home or the gate at TICH. When I step outside those gates, even on a sunny day, I don't want to see people on the street. Don't want to look them in the eye. Don't want them speaking to me. I resent them. They only want to take from me. I'm here to help them, yet they won't help me. I can't face them.

"What about Dr. Sokwala?" Chris asks.

"That's perfect," I say, having forgotten about her. "I'll talk to her. She won't let me get away with any bullshit."

We agree I should take the rest of the week off to talk to Dr. Sokwala. To heal. Chris is aware I'm thinking about leaving Kenya, but he wears two hats in his role with VSO. The first is to take care of me as his volunteer, to make sure I am mentally and emotionally well. The second is to act as guardian of the VSO/TICH partnership, which I will put in jeopardy if I leave.

I mustn't think about these things as I make my decision. Everyone has a personal stake in me staying, or going, so I can't view things from their perspectives. I must do what comes from my head and heart. Toward this end, I decide not to tell my family or friends in the United States what has happened, at least until I make a decision.

Mostly, I don't want to be a quitter.

It's only fair that Director Dan Keseje knows where my head is these days, so I return to his office to talk with him. He listens while I tell about the robbery and my thoughts of going home, of needing to speak to a professional and taking time to heal. He graciously agrees I should take the next three days off. He keeps shaking his head, saying, "Terrible, terrible."

Wednesday morning, my first day off, I'm not strong enough to go into town. It would require walking or taking a boda boda, being around people and noise and traffic. I can't bear it. I'll go tomorrow. Today will be a free day. I'll stay inside and sew and lick my wounds.

"Sandy!" Mrs. Ruprah sings through the open windows of my house. "Sandy, are you okay?" It always makes me smile to hear the way she pronounces my name.

"Yes," I say, opening the door.

"I'm going to my friend's house. You come! It's not far, we'll walk and we won't stay long." She's pointing toward the gate, toward the street.

I'm scared.

"It's not far?"

"No," she says, "come!"

"We'll walk?" I ask, still unsure.

"Yes, it's very close."

She's so authoritative, I agree to go.

We walk two city blocks and enter the drive of the house with the huge "B" painted on the front. I've seen this house many times and wondered about the kind of people who would paint their initial on their home. Inside, three Kenyans tend to the yard, the gate and the poodles running around. Only Sikhs have pets in Kisumu. No one else can afford to feed animals they're not going to sell or eat, unless the dog is for security. These poodles have tiny poodle puppies rolling over each other on the green lawn.

I walk closely to Mrs. Ruprah as we go to the back of the house. It looks like a hotel, with its deep veranda full of cushioned furniture. The kitchen is open to the backyard, too, and two young ladies I've never met are there, wearing jeans and t-shirts, their dark hair in ponytails, tending to boiling pots. It's a lovely surprise to see the elder Sikh priest here. The younger priest, Lucky, is here, too. They're going to read scripture over lunch.

I still feel a bit raw. A bit open. I just want to melt into the background and watch the ladies interact. It's soothing to watch women converse effortlessly and comfortingly, without cares. Mrs. Ruprah, however, immediately tells them about the robbery.

They respond with logic rather than compassion. That's okay.

They tell me what I should have done differently. That's okay, too.

Mrs. Ruprah is talking and talking in Punjabi. A lady next to me tells me Mrs. Ruprah is worried that I will shut myself away in my house and become depressed and want to go back to the United States. Mrs. Ruprah is right. She's a very smart, very caring woman.

They serve us sodas and snacks—delicious handmade crackers. When I comment on the tasty crackers, an older woman tells me cooking is the first thing a Sikh woman learns for her husband. The older women sit and visit while the younger women, daughters and daughters-in-law, serve us.

One young woman has sewn a gorgeous red silk jewelry case with white trim. It's quite elaborate, with a zippered pocket and a tube for holding rings. We admire her handiwork. Mrs. Ruprah wants to duplicate it, so they put the silk case in a zippered bag for her to take home. It feels awkward to sit under this lovely pavilion, the young ladies serving us while Kenyans walk about the yard, carrying water, tending to the plants and unloading groceries from a truck. Five families live in this house. The standard giant picture of the original Sikh guru hangs on the back wall.

When it's time to go, another visitor offers to drive us. Instead of going home, however, we drive to another house—the Sokhi's—which also looks like a hotel. Their name is on the gate and garage. Inside, just beyond the open kitchen (where several ladies are busy cooking chappatti), is a huge living room with a wide circular staircase. Three families live here. The living room is divided into six seating areas. Six! Like a hotel lobby, each seating area contains three couches facing in, a center table and a rug. Down the center of the room, large ceramic pots hold green plants.

Mrs. Sokhi sells fabrics sent by her mother and sister from India. We look at the fabrics and everyone talks. Once again, Mrs. Ruprah tells them about the robbery. They tell me what I should have done differently. I'm starting to feel less sensitive about it, learning to let things roll off.

We return home. As I enter my house, Mrs. Ruprah says, "Come. Come. Help me make lunch. I'm going to a friend's later. You come."

"Okay," I say and smile, "I'll come."

In the large kitchen, with Grace washing dishes in a big plastic tub outside the window, Mrs. Ruprah places a metal bowl in front of me. Opening a bag of meal, she tells me how to mix the chappatti dough. I sprinkle water and knead. More water, more kneading. The consistency makes the bones in my right hand ache. Mrs. Ruprah is busy cooking rice and heating stuffed peppers, and I'm totally concentrating on mixing the dough, enjoying the process, noticing how calming it is to be in a kitchen preparing food. I watch Mrs. Ruprah prepare the pans for cooking chappatti and marvel at her ability to have three dishes going at once. Her goal is to have lunch on the table at 1:00pm when Mr. Ruprah and Raju arrive from the workshop. Food is spooned into bowls and I carry them to the table. Grace has set out drinking glasses and plates and small bowls for dahl.

Mr. Ruprah arrives promptly and sits at the table, next to the back door. Raju drives home in his own car and sits at the other end of the table. Food is passed and placed on plates. Chappatti is torn to scoop up dahl and mixed vegetables of varying spiciness. No one talks. By 1:15pm, Mr. Ruprah rises, takes two steps to the sink on the wall, washes his hands and leaves.

After every meal, I try to clear the dishes, at least to carry them to the back patio where Grace will wash them, but the elder Mrs. Ruprah always yells, "No!" It doesn't feel right eating their food and not contributing in some way.

After lunch, we visit Mrs. Ruprah's Sikh friends who live only two blocks away. Nonni is very pretty and seems much younger than her husband. She came from India 14 years ago to marry in Kisumu. Their house is large and the living room immense. Shelves contain wooden African sculptures, elephant figurines and photos of their children. Each chair and sofa section is covered by an embroidered doily, as are the chair arms. Everything is very neat. Our hostess makes tea and brings in homemade crackers. She serves us one at a time, passing the cup and saucer and offering the crackers. They exchange cake recipes and talk in Punjabi. I enjoy the tea and crackers and imagine what life trapped inside this house would feel like. It's cozy, but it's not a good sensation.

It is often hard to watch the Sikh women in their daily roles. Their schedule is set around their husband's work schedules. Rarely do the women work outside the home. They keep house, entertain guests, cook food, work on handicrafts and attend temple, where they cook for the entire group in the temple's kitchen.

Some of the ladies drive, but most do not. Their primary concern each day is feeding their husband and children. Very few seek higher education or build careers. These women often do not fulfill any of their own personal talents, skills or interests. Society is much the poorer from this lack of self-actualization. Women in many cultures cannot venture beyond their roles as wives and mothers. A large percentage of women the world over could be contributing to research, business, medicine, the arts and many other areas of knowledge. But they don't. Aren't allowed to. In 1950s America, it was called the feminine mystique, this strange ailment from which women suffered; this urge and desire to do more. They felt trapped and miserable, useless and depressed, and didn't understand why. Though the United States has largely moved on, it is the life of women in countries around the world even today.

Mrs. Ruprah cries often. A few days ago, she sat next to me on her couch as I ate the lunch she prepared. She was crocheting a black scarf for her daughter in London, when she turned to me and said, "I'll make one for you. What color do you like?"

"You don't have to do that," I said. "I know how much work it is. But I really like white!" I smiled and she laughed.

"Would you really make one for me?" I asked, not believing how generous she was—always is.

"You are like my daughter," she said, her eyes tearing up. Soon, her whole face was red and wet.

"Ah," I said, touching her shoulder. She put the scarf and crochet hook in front of her face and cried. In the next moment, she removed my hand and said, "Eat! Eat!" She used the ball of her hands to dry the tears.

Every time I've seen her cry, she puts both hands to her face and strokes downward from her red eyes. It tugs at my heart.

Mrs. Ruprah is lonely.

Today, I psyche myself up to take a boda boda into town, asking him to drop me at Dr. Sokwala's office. Once there, I'm sent right in.

Dr. Sokwala sits behind her desk. I tell her I'm struggling with the decision to stay in Kisumu or return to the United States. That it's weighing on me and I'd like to talk with someone.

"Do you provide counseling?" I ask.

"I do, but not during regular hours. This office is not the right environment. I usually like to go to lunch or dinner, and then talk in a relaxed environment, as friends."

We decide to meet at 12:30pm for lunch.

"I'll try to leave here at 12:30pm," she says, "but sometimes it's hard and I don't get out until 1:00pm."

I don't tell Dr. Sokwala why I'm thinking of leaving Kenya. That can come later. She senses the stress and says, "That's a wonderful problem to have, isn't it?"

I look confused, so she says, "Good things will happen whichever decision you make. If you decide to stay, you and I will get to see each other more and if you decide to go, you'll be with your family or friends." I'm grateful to her for framing the situation in such a positive light.

"See you at 12:30pm," I say.

With two hours to spend, I go to the internet café. There's one very important email I must send today, so I spend time crafting it carefully only to discover, upon trying to send it, that the net is down. I look around and notice the owner at the front desk on his cell phone. He's calling the service provider. The problem isn't the service provider but the phone line. Soon, two men from the phone company show up, declaring a bill hasn't been paid.

People leave because the internet is down. I have no way of saving the email, and I'm desperate to send it. The phone company men argue with the owner as we all watch. If he paid the bill, they say, then all he has to do is produce proof the payment went through the phone company's account. He can do this by faxing the proof with a form. It'll take him hours to produce the proof and fax it over. He's not the only one upset; I'm frustrated at not being able to send the note after spending so much time on it. I'm frustrated at not being able to save it. I must leave to meet Dr. Sokwala, so I tell myself to take a deep breath. Let it go. These glitches occur regularly in Kisumu. Either the electricity is out or the phone lines are down. We must be flexible.

Still slightly frustrated, I rush through the busy streets to Dr. Sokwala's office, only to see the door closed and padlocked. My heart drops. A guy strapping vegetables to the back of his bike says, "She just left." I know I must be late but still can't believe she'd leave me. Tears are working their way up as I cross the street in the bright sunshine. I feel like I've thrown my lifeline out only to have it avoided.

I suddenly remember an incident six months earlier, another time that I was leaving Dr. Sokwala's office. She told me then not to be a victim.

My head goes up. I'm not a victim. I wanted to speak with Dr. Sokwala today to get an objective perspective about my decision to either stay or leave Kenya. Because everyone else has a stake in what I do, I thought she was the one person who could provide a neutral opinion.

But I wonder. Deep down, don't I already know what my decision is? Don't I truly want to go back to the United States, where I'll feel safe and will be able to pursue other options in promoting TICH?

Yes.

I already have my answer.

I've been afraid to bring it out into the light for fear it will look like I'm running away. I admit this truth and feel lighter. I go to another internet café and email Chris at VSO in Nairobi, saying I've made up my mind. I'll be returning to the United States.

Walking through Kisumu on my way home, I'm not happy. I'm not thrilled. It feels like things are unfinished here. I already know the hardest part about leaving will be telling Dan Keseje, and the Ruprahs, and my co-workers at TICH. It makes my stomach hurt to think about telling them.

At the top of Oginga Odinga Street, the main street through Kisumu, police are moving street vendors from the sidewalks. Arguments and chaos ensue as vendors pack up their wares. Boda bodas, too, have been forbidden to congregate on the street where they normally wait for passengers. Kisumu is cleaning up its image because a conference is coming to town; with it come top executives from sugar companies as well as ministers of parliament from several African countries.

They're painting the curb of Oginga Odinga and the curbs on the roundabouts in town. They're sweeping the street clean and spraying for mosquitoes in the parts of town where the MPs might go during their two week conference. Milimani, the neighborhood I live in, is the nicest residential area. Of course, it gets sprayed for bugs. I notice immediately there are no mosquitoes in my house—before, I had to burn a repellant coil just to sit in my living room. If I had to guess the number of bites I get while living in Kisumu, I'd say it's about 10 bites a day. Now, suddenly, there are no mosquitoes.

When Ed visits, I ask if he's noticed the same thing.

"No," Ed says, "as a matter of fact, there have been many more bugs lately."

When they sprayed Milimani, the mosquitoes went to Nyalenda, a slum area two blocks from my house.

As I watch the improvements taking place in town, all done to impress our very important visitors, I wonder why Kisumu doesn't sweep the main street free of vendors and boda bodas all the time. I wonder why they don't clean the streets and paint the curbs as a matter of city maintenance. When Priscah, the mayor of Kisumu, visited the TICH campus to pass out certificates at the end of an entrepreneurship workshop, she gave a short speech on how great and safe Kisumu is. She wouldn't allow anyone to even suggest Kisumu is less than perfect.

There are advantages to being positive about your work, but not if it means sweeping the true situation under the rug. Mayor Priscah was sweeping Kisumu's less palatable features out of sight. In truth, cars and trucks emit masses of pollutants. Street boys are beaten by the police. Everyone—individuals and businesses—is afraid of being robbed by thugs.

As I walk home from town with the sad knowledge I'll be leaving Kisumu, the boda boda drivers call out to me, "We go, White Lady?"

I just shake my head.

Walter Odede comes to the Ruprah's gate. He heard about my mugging from Tonny, and it's evident he's upset. He thinks it might be Victor, the guy who was stalking me after I first arrived, but I tell Walter it was just a random thief.

"Please don't go back home because of this," Walter says.

"I've already decided," I say, "to go home."

He drops his head into his hands and makes a tsking sound.

"A few days ago," Walter says, "the five orphans sponsored by the medical students had school fees due. They can't attend school until the fees are paid."

I go into my house and get 4,000 shillings (about US $50). It's a lot of money and the last money I'll give Walter. I've been disappointed in the Pambazuko building that stands without a roof, even though he's received monies for roofing supplies. Now is not the time to discuss it with him, however, because there is so much going on related to my departure. I will eventually communicate my misgivings to Walter.

On her way home from work, Dina stops by to check on me. She's with Pam, another coworker, who parks her car across the street. They're in a hurry and don't have time to come in, so we stand in the Ruprah's driveway talking. As we chat, Reverend Obondi drives by and parks behind Pam. He crosses the street. I'm very happy to see him, since he's been away from campus all week. Reverend Obondi has heard what happened, and he says what everyone else has said, "Pole sana, pole sana."

The reverend is also in a hurry, saying he's on his way to see his niece, Amelia. Thugs have been terrorizing her. Earlier in the week, they broke into her home while she was at work and held a knife to the nanny's throat, demanding money. They were convinced there was money in the house and took everything apart looking for it. They even went into the light fixtures in the ceiling. This morning, they came into her compound and were hiding in the back, waiting for her to leave her house. She saw them and called her coworkers, who came to get her. I find it odd she didn't call the police.

Or maybe I don't.

"Why has no one told me to go to the police to report the robbery?" I ask the three of them. Their faces are blank.

"Why waste your time?" Dina asks.

"They won't do anything," Pam says. "Well, they'll probably laugh at you."

"I don't expect them to find the guy and get my stuff back," I say. "But it seems the police would want an accurate picture of the crime in Kisumu. If people report crimes, then the police will know the types of crimes being committed, the victims, what's taken, where it happens, the time of day. That would help them develop crime prevention programs."

They all just look at me like I'm crazy.

In Kenya and other African countries, there's a thing called "mob justice." It happens because the police are corrupt. They'll fill out reports and investigate crimes, but only if the victims pay bribes. This sort of practice is why the reverend's niece called her coworkers instead of the police.

Residents across Africa have taken criminals in hand through mob justice. If a thief is caught in public, the crowd will beat him or burn him, usually until he is dead. People do not want criminals in their neighborhoods, so they catch them and kill them. Just this week, a thief was shot in Nyalenda by an off-duty security guard after the crowd caught him stealing. Another guy stole a 15-cent toothbrush from a vendor's shack in Nyalenda; the crowd beat him to death.

This evening, as we talk in the driveway, I learn the reverend is anxious to move Amelia somewhere the thugs can't bother her and her adopted baby girl. Amelia, a college graduate working for an NGO, recently had visitors from the UK in her home. The thugs saw white people at her house, decided Amelia must have money and began their campaign of terror.

"Okay, now I'm getting scared," Pam says. "I'm not going out tonight, I'm going straight home."

Reverend Obondi, Pam and Dina leave. It'll be dark in about 30 minutes. I walk back into the gate and Samuel shuts it, securing the padlock through the heavy chain. I feel somewhat safe.

Arriving on campus Monday morning, I talk to Sister Masheti, a manager at TICH, telling her of my anguished decision to return to the United States.

"Cindi," says Sister Masheti in her forthright way, "I support your decision. You must decide what's best for you and not worry about others. TICH is an institution and it will continue without you and without me and without others. But your safety and peace of mind is of utmost importance now."

I'm taken aback by her level of understanding and grateful to her for realizing how hard this has been. She says my perspective is unique, for I come from another culture. While everyone here may think it's normal to expect to be robbed, I am taking a stand in letting them know it's not.

She tells me a story about Dan's Christmas Eve party, an incident that happened only three months before I arrived in Kenya.

Dan had 30 guests from around the world dancing in his living room. Fred, the guard at TICH's gate, was working the gate at Dan's house during the party. Thugs cut the chain and were inside the gate before Fred knew it. One guy hit Fred on the head with a gun, knocking him to the ground and dazing him. They then took Fred to the front door and pushed him ahead of them into the living room. Sister Masheti was across the room when she saw Fred stumbling through the door. She thought someone was drunk and giving Fred a hard time. When Sister Masheti stood up to go to him, the men shot their guns. A bullet went over Sister Masheti's head and stuck in the wall. The guests were commanded to get down on the floor. They were all robbed.

Sister Masheti also told me that sometime in 2003, Dan was awakened in the night by men holding AK-47s in his face while they robbed his house. Dan could live in safer places around the world, but he chooses to stay and grow the university.

"Every year for the last six years," Sister tells me, "Dan has been robbed. So I can't tell you something like that won't happen to you."

Everyone I speak with has a very recent crime story to share, sometimes two recent stories. Some people say it's just the way things are and I must accept the risks. Others say I'm doing the right thing by going home.

I've made my decision.

But I'm torn.

I drop my resignation off for Director Dan Keseje. Throughout the day, I talk with people and tell them about my decision to leave. When I see Kikoli, a student from the Congo, and tell him, he frowns. Kikoli is an incredibly kind man and an earnest student. I admire how hard he works to learn English and can appreciate the difficulty of having to do his thesis research and writing in a language he hasn't yet mastered.

We're in the library on the second floor, exchanging email addresses when Kikoli says, "You made the right decision." I'm rather surprised by his attitude until he tells me his story. He shares an apartment in a 13-unit building in Nyalenda. In July, at around 9:00pm, Kikoli and his two Congolese roommates were relaxing in their living room when 17 thugs burst through their front door. The men had guns and knives and took just about everything of value.

"We are Congolese," Kikoli says, "and because we live in Kenya to go to school, they think we have money."

With each new person I tell about my decision to leave, I hear of personal experiences with crime—whether it happened to them, their family members or their friends. Crime in Kisumu is much worse than both VSO and I had realized. It's worse because people consider these incidences normal. They don't report them to the police and don't tell people in warning. If I had heard some of these stories before, I might have been more cautious and better prepared.

After work, I walk to the end of the road where I live and meet Dawn, a fellow VSO volunteer, at the Tom Mboya Labor College. Dawn is from Texas and she's serving as a volunteer in Kitui, a village southeast of Nairobi. Dawn will stay with me while she's in Kisumu to attend a nurse's conference this week. She's shocked to hear about the robbery and understands why I am returning to the United States.

Instead of attending the second day of the nursing conference, Dawn tours TICH, meets the people and checks out the library. She is impressed with the school's curriculum, the medical books in the library and with the education and experience of the staff members.

"Seeing TICH and meeting the people is worth the trip to Kisumu," Dawn says.

We walk home after work and meet Dr. Sokwala a block from my house. She's walking with her cousin, who happens to be a self-described ambassador of the neem tree. Every part of the neem tree—bark, leaves and seeds—is used for such diverse things as candle wax, tummy soothers and a cure for malaria and skin rashes. This is the first time I've seen Dr. Sokwala since missing our lunch date, so I tell her why I was thinking about leaving Kisumu. I want to tell her I've made the decision to return to the United States but don't feel the roadside is the right place to deliver the news.

When I tell her about the robbery, she immediately says, "1994!" in a dramatic television voice with a suspenseful pause.

"It's 10:00am and two men burst into my office. They have guns and force me onto the floor. One sits on my chest and chokes me until I pass out. When I wake up hours later, they've stolen money and drugs."

"How horrible," I say. She then tells me how she and her husband, along with a female neighbor, were walking in this neighborhood recently, taking a Sunday stroll. Her husband commented on three guys walking toward them. Dr. Sokwala didn't notice anything unusual about the men, but listened to her husband. The three of them stopped in the driveway of a house, as though they were about to enter. They waited for the three guys to pass and decided to return home. As they walked, Dr. Sokwala said they heard footsteps pounding toward them and turned to see the men raising large rocks overhead. Between herself, her husband and their friend, they were able to fight them off.

"This is how it's been since I began telling people what happened," I tell Dawn. "I hear at least two stories from each person about how they, too, were robbed."

Even Grace, the Ruprah's housekeeper, was robbed. She told her story in Kiswahili with Raju translating. She was in her home in Nyalenda with two other female relatives when more than 20 men burst in with knives. One man grabbed Grace from behind and held a knife to her throat, demanding money. Grace told them she had no money but suggested they take her television, which they did. Grace does not have a lot of money. She lives in a mud house in the slums. She has electricity, though, and that might have been why they thought she had money. Also, she works for an Indian family, so they think she has access to lots of cash.

Tonny has lived in Nyalenda most of his life. Because he's completed college and has a good job at TICH, he's improved his home by adding piped water and electricity. He says he is robbed regularly. He constantly hears doors being knocked in and robberies taking place. Yet he refuses to move away. He wants to stay and act as a role model for the children. When they see him walk through the slums each morning, pushing his mountain bike while wearing dress slacks and a long-sleeved dress shirt, they get a first-hand glimpse that just because they live in Nyalenda doesn't mean they cannot excel.

The more people I talk with about crime, the more I'm convinced living in Kisumu is much riskier than I had bargained for. Just the same, I begin to develop plans to continue supporting TICH after I return home. I talk with Director Dan Keseje about spreading awareness of TICH as well as development issues in general by starting a non-profit. It will be a way to promote TICH and their programs to feed orphans and train Community Health Workers. I might even be able to do more for TICH from the United States than I'd ever be able to accomplish in Kisumu.

I know I cannot simply leave the school and the students and my friends and not look back. I plan to be constantly looking back to pull them forward.

I give away clothes and possessions. Preparing to leave means saying goodbye to friends, collecting email addresses, closing my bank account and packing.

During my last day at TICH, I work hard to burn CDs of files and documents and photos. I want to make sure everything is transitioned to Tonny and explained thoroughly. Walter Odede comes by to visit. I'm a little stressed for time, but try not to show it. Walter is also stressed and keeps rubbing his forehead.

"My landlord," he says, hesitating, "is on my neck about the rent."

I watch Walter shaking his head and looking down. Just last Friday I gave him 4,000 shillings and vowed that would be the last he'd ever get from me. So I say nothing when he repeats the statement. He says it a third time.

"I can't help you with your rent, Walter," I say, and he immediately sits up straight.

"Oh, no," he says, "I wasn't asking that."

But he is asking in his own way, and I feel horrible not being able to make it right for him.

After Walter leaves, other people visit to say goodbye and to make sure I'll be at the student hostel for the going-away party. It's a bit humbling, having a party. First, they don't normally throw parties for people who leave. Second, I feel badly about not being here for the full two years.

The catering crew has prepared a full dinner, including chicken, beef and liver with ugali, rice and sukuma wiki. Bernard and Tonny arrive in Bernard's VW bug to unload two cases of beer. The party has begun. There are warm and touching speeches. Dr. Ngode talks about how I drove everyone across Rwanda. He calls me "Nyaloka," which in Kiswahili means beloved daughter from across the sea.

After dinner and after the speeches, after they've given me a wrapped gift (to be opened later), we dance to traditional music. The party goes on until 11:00pm. My IT team members have grown close through our regular meetings and recent accomplishments. We're the last to leave.

First thing the following morning, Grace taps on my front door. She stands outside my bedroom window and speaks to me in Dholuo. Eventually, I climb out from under the mosquito net and open the door. I'm wearing only a t-shirt, and Grace giggles when she sees my bare legs. She's pointing to the gate so I look out to see a man. From this distance, I can't tell who it is. He waves. I put on pants and walk slowly to the gate, still sleepy. It's Walter.

"Walter!" I whine. "Man, it's too early to be visiting."

"Sorry, sorry," he says as I open the gate.

"Look, I'm going to use my coffee maker for the next three mornings, so I'll leave it with Tonny at TICH for you on Monday." Walter had asked for my coffee maker, even though he doesn't have electricity in his house.

"That's okay, that's fine," he says, pacing with his hands in his pockets.

"What's wrong?" I ask.

"I've been evicted," he says, looking at the ground, acting agitated.

"Oh, dear, Walter. I'm sorry. Have you been out all night?"

"I stayed with a friend last night," he says, "but I haven't changed clothes."

I feel badly for Walter, he's obviously in mental distress, not knowing what to do. I've been telling him for months to find additional donor streams for Pambazuko if he wants to make a living from the organization. I want him to understand that if he cannot manage to pay his own rent, it will make it difficult for him to manage an organization. And if I give him money every time he asks for it, he won't learn to provide for himself and Vincent, the former street boy. Instead, I say nothing, and simply watch as Walter paces across the top of the drive.

"What are you going to do?" I ask.

"I guess I'll go to town and see if I can get the money. If I can get 1,000 shillings, that'd be enough."

I stand, looking at him.

"Well, I'm going to go," he says, not looking at me, tsking his tongue. He appears helpless. I think of the times he stood up for me, talked me through some emotional down times. I want to return the favor. But handing Walter money doesn't seem like the best way to help him. I just can't bring myself to give him 1,000 shillings.

He walks away without looking back, his hands deep in his pockets.

During my last five days in Kisumu, there is no water. Every day I awake and hope to shower and wash my hair. Every day, the tap simply drip-drips.

These last few days, I buy a few souvenirs for family members and friends. I email everyone from my favorite cyber café. The day before I leave Kisumu, I'm at the café when a man named Jacob begins talking to me. He's sitting in the waiting area but never gets on a computer. I suspect he's there to find white people to fund whatever his project might be. He is sharply dressed and well-groomed, wearing nice, new shoes and a shiny leather belt. Within the first three minutes of our conversation, he has asked me three times if I have a husband and children in the United States. Jacob is an architectural student, but he has a briefcase NGO, called Garden of Hope, which focuses on orphans in the slums.

"Would you like to hear about Garden of Hope?" he asks.

"Actually, I've worked with individuals who have organizations assisting the needy and I've been disappointed by each of them. They seem to be in it for the money they can get for themselves, so I have no interest in learning about Garden of Hope. Sorry for being so blunt."

"That's okay, I appreciate your honesty," he says. He goes on to talk about his architectural aspirations. He tells me that he's been offered two software applications so new they're not even on the market in Kenya yet. He can get them from a friend for only 5,000 shillings each. I know he's suggesting I buy them for him, but I ignore his implication.

The following day, my last day in Kenya, I go to the cyber café in the morning. My flight is at 6:30pm, so I have the whole day to finalize things. I've spent a great deal of time in this building over the last eight months and have become friends with Johnson, a technical assistant who works here. He's in his mid-20s, tall and lean. He wants to travel as a missionary for his church. We talk briefly and I notice Jacob sitting in the waiting area, scoping out people to approach. Jacob asks to speak with me but I say I don't have time.

After an hour on the internet, Johnson and I step outside. I ask him about Jacob. He confirms that Jacob hangs out at the café waiting to befriend white people. Many Kenyans have learned the easiest way to get money from white people is in the name of orphans and widows. Johnson thinks it's the worst sin of all. I suggest they talk to the guy and make him stop hanging around.

"Excuse me," Jacob says, "sorry to interrupt, but do you have a minute to talk with me?"

"I'm sorry," I say, "not right now, I'm talking with Johnson."

Johnson continues to educate me on how individuals like Jacob will act as though everything they do goes to helping impoverished children, when in reality, they often keep the monies they collect and build houses and buy cars. Johnson is confirming my recent observations. Many people travel to Africa with open hearts, wanting to help. When they meet someone like Jacob with a direct connection to rural people in need, they contribute the best way they know how—with money. That's not always a good idea. I've learned the hard way that funneling resources, money and connections through an established institution like TICH is the best way to promote long-term and effective development.

Johnson and I agree to stay in touch. I leave, in a hurry to get home and to the airport. As I turn in front of the Nakumatt, someone from behind calls my name. Twice. I turn to see Jacob running to catch up.

"Listen, Cindi, I'll let you know whether or not I buy the architectural software. But what I'd really like is a laptop for my work."

I'm outraged that he thinks I'll buy him a laptop after I've already told him I'm sick of people approaching me for things because I'm white.

"Good for you," I say biting each word, "I hope you get that laptop one day. Goodbye!"

I spin and walk away, calling Jacob a jerk under my breath. It is my last day in Kenya and this man—a man I don't know—is chasing me through the streets to ask for a laptop, when even he has told me about the widows and children without parents who are in greater need. I stomp on angrily and approach the top of the hill where boda boda drivers wait for passengers. They call out to me with big smiles, offering a ride, accepting my rejection good-naturedly. Their open and sincere faces hold no malice.

Suddenly, my anger subsides as I realize I cannot take things so personally. I cannot be a victim. I must look beyond the surface to see the true forces of poverty driving the desperate, including the guy who robbed me. Looking into these friendly faces, I know there is far more goodness and rightness in Kenya than men who rob or ask for things.

The guy who robbed me didn't know my motives for being in Kenya. It probably never occurred to him that his attack might make me want to leave the country. He obviously didn't consider how his action could cause deep and powerful reactions. Likewise, Jacob hasn't bothered to ask why I'm here; he simply started asking for things. When I think about my coworkers at TICH, I realize not one of them treated me like a source of money or a ticket to America. They are far too busy advancing their educations and careers, working to pull Kenya and other African countries out of poverty's vicious cycle.

With my anger toward Jacob fading, and with a little more understanding of why I was robbed, I no longer feel like I'm running away. In fact, I choose to leave and continue my work for TICH in a more secure environment. I know it's not a totally secure environment, because there is certainly crime in the United States, but it's an environment where I am used to the forces that drive us. I am not leaving TICH or the Community Health Workers in the villages behind, because TICH and the Community Health Workers are my reasons for resettling in the United States and working hard to spread the word about development issues.

"Hey, white lady," a boda boda calls to me, "let's go."

I keep walking but smile a big, wide smile at him. I want to remember his face. The promise of his call, his good-naturedness. I do not want to be bitter; I do not want to be angry at the robbers and the Jacobs. I want to carry the good of Kenya with me—the good, open and sincere faces of Kenya so full of promise.

Mrs. Ruprah cries as the reverend loads my bags into the car. She uses the balls of her palms to wipe away tears. I wear the earrings she just gave me, elegant clusters of copper droplets that tinkle when my head moves. The sun skips off the silver ring I just gave her as she wipes her eyes.

I feel guilty leaving Mrs. Ruprah in Kenya.

Traveling home takes 23 hours. I fly from Kisumu to Nairobi to London to Atlanta. Along the way, I see the Sahara desert, the Alps and more and more white people. I have not bathed properly in five days and wear my hiking books to save packing space. I am grungy.

London's Gatwick Airport is overwhelming.

I'm going home.

Conclusion

*R*emarkable people all over the world are working hard to make life better in developing countries by building schools and orphanages; by providing food to the malnourished. They're not all rock n' rollers or movie stars—most of them are just ordinary people with passions. They want to do work that matters to others. Organizations as diverse as CARE, Oxfam, the Carter Center, Rotary International, VSO and Lions Clubs work on the ground in developing countries, creating food security and access to clean water to ensure individuals and communities are lifted out of poverty. High profilers like Bill and Melinda Gates and Warren Buffet are putting their hard-earned and highly-sought-after money where their heads and hearts are to eradicate disease and promote education for all: two factors that will push countries up the development ladder.

Many people are throwing light about them instead of darkness, including my fellow VSO volunteers. After their volunteer roles ended, most continued their work in development.

Ed Yarrow, from the UK, returned home and began working with Practical Action, an organization that employs 100 people in the UK and 400 people in overseas offices. The aims of Practical Action are the broad principles of sustainable development; helping people to help themselves with the use of appropriate technologies. Ed says the principle of sustainable development encouraged his interest in becoming a VSO volunteer. Now that he's back in the UK, finding a similar credo in another organization and getting paid for the work he does is music to his ears.

Ed writes, "Last week we had a global get together for all of our Finance Managers (FM). It was a real melting pot of cultures with four FMs coming from the Horn of Africa plus Zimbabwe; three from Bangladesh, Nepal and Sri Lanka and one from Peru. We were running a weeklong workshop for this group with me facilitating a couple of the all day sessions. Once upon a time, the idea of running all day workshops would have been enough to send me into a self-conscious bundle of shyness, but now it just seems second nature, with a little twinge of anxiousness to get the adrenaline flowing."

Tom Craven, also a volunteer from the UK, was working in Mombasa at the Bombolulu Workshop, which Ed Yarrow and I visited during our trip to the Kenyan coast. Tom writes to say, "I'm now a school teacher in the UK, working in a small state primary school. I took my postgraduate in Education when I returned from Kenya. So, I'm not in the development field anymore, but have a future goal of going back to Kenya in ten years or so and starting a school, once I've gained experience and training here in inner city London schools. Our student population is very diverse; 55% of my students speak English as a second language. I have been thinking about what advice I would give to anyone wanting to work in development. First, they must ask what is motivating them to work in development, and where does that motivation come from. Second, they must understand there are different definitions of development. Third, I would advise them to speak to people who have done it or are doing it. Fourth, having realistic expectations is crucial to a successful volunteer experience, for the volunteer and the people they work with. Fifth, I would tell them not to see themselves as the solution to other people's needs; they should facilitate only."

Frank van der Looij from the Netherlands was a volunteer administrator at a hospital in Ndhiwa in Western Kenya. He is home again and working for CORDAID, one of the biggest private charities working in health care in Africa. He is responsible for CORDAID's health care program in Tanzania. Frank writes, "My base is in the Netherlands, but I am traveling to Tanzania quite often. It is a strange job, completely different from my VSO experience. Although I am still living in this small apartment in the Netherlands, I also get special treatment when in Tanzania. Of course, I am the donor, and people expect money, so they pick me up anywhere, drive me around and have me sleep in their house, which means I rarely interact with real life in Africa.

"Fortunately, I was able to visit my old project in Ndhiwa a few weeks ago, which meant riding in completely run-down Matatus again, hours of waiting at junctions where no cars pass, etc. Nevertheless, I was very surprised by what I found in Ndhiwa. People are really doing their best, the most important administrative systems are still in place, the accountant is making adjustments in the systems all by herself and the management committee is active. The hospital now has about 250 people on Anti-Retrovirals (ARV) for AIDS, which is a fabulous achievement. Really, I only expected about 30 percent of the things to be still in place, but what has happened in Ndhiwa is just amazing. It is also a good example that development can work, if done correctly. Investing in people and their skills and capacities is most important. One of the things that really made a difference in Ndhiwa is that I showed them how things could be done in a different way, and change can occur, even without financial support from a donor.

"There is a lot of criticism about development work, but my experience with Ndhiwa shows there is hope. Of course, things take time and careful planning. I know many development agencies that are aiming for fast results. They are in obvious places (like Tsunami areas and post conflict areas in Africa), because being in those areas 'sells,' while the common places (like relatively stable rural areas in Tanzania) are forgotten. More important, though, is that by going for the fast results, they often lure good health professionals with high salaries who then migrate to these projects which are mostly just handling a small issue in health care. At the same time, the regular health care system in a country collapses.

"CORDAID still has many programs aiming at health systems in rural areas and we have a problem in selling our achievements in these areas, which means our finances are continuously under pressure."

Pusparaj Mohanty, VSO's first volunteer from India, was working in Mombasa when I arrived in Kenya. When he finished his VSO stint, Pusparaj began working with CARE International and spent six months in South Sudan, one of the most dangerous places on earth. He's contemplating working with CARE in Afghanistan.

Sandra, from the Philippines, completed her role with the Catholic Diocese of Kitale. She writes, "I have succeeded in installing an appropriate accounting system for the Diocesan Accounting Office, which includes development and social services, handicap support (for the physically and mentally challenged), women and gender, water and sanitation and health, youth and vocational training.

"I went home after my placement and came back to work with the Little Sisters of St. Francis of Assisi in the Western Region, an indigenous congregation founded in 1923 in Uganda. My work as Organization Capacity Builder involves the installation of financial systems in the programmes they operate, including a hospital, health center, nursery schools, primary school, a bookshop, vocational school and agriculture project. Donors are responding very well. By next year, we will fully implement an HIV/AIDS programme that will include livelihood support to our target clients. They came to the hospital for treatment of other diseases but accepted positively when the Sister managing the hospital suggested they be tested for HIV. Bungoma town is generally a Luhya community and their cultural practices of old are still very much 'in' today, like wife inheritance, but we are trying to penetrate the core of the matter. At least now, girls have equal opportunity to an education."

Mila is also from the Philippines. She spent two years in a rural village working with the Ngolanya Community Aid Programme (NGOCAP) as a fundraiser and capacity builder. Mila then extended her role for another year and continues to seek donors for the organization. She writes, "Imagine, when I came here, I spent my own money on stationery and solicited used paper from other agencies to recycle. Whew! I am sometimes ashamed but have to do it for the organization to be able to move on. Why are we volunteers? When we give up, nothing will happen with the issues VSO is fighting for. Even with all the hardships, things have been good because within one year of starting my job, we were awarded three years of continuous funding, which is tremendous. It is hard to work in this arid place without electricity and water, but with God's grace, I was able to survive all those trying times. When I came to the NGO, other organizations immediately wanted to collaborate with us.

"We are running an integrated community development programme in health, education, income generating activities, food security, and water, and we are implementing a programme on Early Childhood Education focusing on capacity building for ECD teachers. Another partner will support the construction of ECD classrooms. When I leave, I am sure the organization will go a long way towards realization of their goals to reduce poverty at the household level and I can say I have done something for this organization and the community."

Ces Villamena, also from the Philippines, volunteered as a small business adviser in Mumias. She now works in the VSO Bahaginan Recruitment office in the Philippines where they select volunteers to send to other countries. VSO is discontinuing their program of placing foreign volunteers in the Philippines.

Ces writes that she "started at VSO Bahaginan in June of 2007. I ended my term in Kenya in March 2006 on quite a sad note. Although I enjoyed my stay there and found it fulfilling and significant, the motorcycle accident I had the last week of January 2006, abruptly ended the last leg of training I was conducting. I'm happy I contributed something to my organization in Kenya and to the Special Education concerns in the District. I am being given updates by my colleagues from time to time.

"I am currently working as a Volunteer and Program Adviser (VPA) and training coordinator. I am in charge of the pool of volunteers specializing in business management (small business adviser, project management, accountant, human resource specialist, etc.) and technical people (engineers, lawyers and human rights specialists, journalists, communication specialists, fundraiser, and special educators). I enjoy my work and understand the volunteers' concerns and anxieties and get to address them realistically from volunteering realities. Aside from having to attend to the pool of volunteers, I get to do all pre-departure training coordination and arrangements. I also arrange work focus courses like motorcycle riding, computer literacy and HIV and AIDS immersion awareness for volunteers who need these skills. I'm especially excited about being in a Masters' program on Development Management. My hands are full, but I do not complain as I enjoy working in volunteering concerns, especially with people who are into it."

Paul Watts, from Canada, was in our VSO training group before he left to work as a marine biologist in the Philippines and I went to Kenya. Paul writes about beginning his work, "I found myself with an opportunity to contribute to indigenous peoples, sustainable fisheries and development along the shores of the North Philippine Sea. Similar to you, Cindi, my work is through an academic institution; Aurora State College of Technology. When you were experiencing Philippine volunteers in Kenya, I was meeting the Kenyan volunteers in the Philippines; we were all contributing to circles of change - patterns of development, exchanges of people and perspectives, sharing positive values as we work for a world based on human equity. I remember so well my VSO Annual Volunteer Conference in the Philippines, dancing with friends to the music of Africa.

"I continue to work in this surprising environment, and serendipity smiled upon me. On my way to the Philippines, I went to Vancouver for training on Philippine fisheries and met another Ethnoecologist doing her doctorate on Philippine Marine Protected Areas. We communicated across the Pacific; a Canadian in the Philippines and a Filipino in Canada. Recently we were married and have started an endeavor called Daluhay, or flow of life, a Filipino term derived from daloy (flow) and buhay (life). We hope to work together on sustainable livelihoods within sustainable environments, building upon our backgrounds with indigenous peoples and fisherfolk, wherever we can connect and partner.

"I read about the Somali current flowing along the shores of Kenya and Tanzania and wonder about the project stirring inside me. For now I continue with the North Philippine Sea and Aurora State College as I move towards the end of my term and the end of VSO bringing volunteers to the Philippines. What I remember most from my time in the philippines is the relationships, and that includes relationships with other volunteers who landed in other parts of the world. Perhaps some day we will meet again… and perhaps, through our efforts, the world is just a tiny bit better."

Wendy Foster, the VSO volunteer Ed and I visited in Mombasa, is back home in the UK and has assisted in setting up a charity for Ethiopia called Alchemy World. Her organization establishes training schools to teach young people business and IT skills to set up their own businesses. Wendy is happy she still gets to travel to Ethiopia occasionally. She and I share a similar experience. When her volunteer stint was completed, before she went back to the UK, Wendy wanted to travel around Kenya. When she visited Kisumu, she was robbed on the street. She writes, "I was really shocked about being robbed in Kisumu as it was the last place I expected it to happen. However, I could see the build up, but there was nothing I could do to stop it. The thing which annoyed me most was that they took my credit cards, which were useless to them, and I was flying home a week later through Dubai and had no money. It was painful!" Wendy hasn't allowed the mugging to keep her from working in Africa.

Hilary Whitwell, also from the UK, was my roommate during our training in Nairobi. When her two-year stint ended, she extended her stay for one more year. Hilary plans to return to the UK to acquire more physiotherapy skills, but her long term plan is to go back to Africa and continue her work.

Dawn Surrat and Vini Bhansali, volunteers in Kitui, Kenya, returned to the United States and relocated to the San Francisco Bay area. Dawn, who is a nurse by training and who visited me in Kisumu near the end of my term, now works as a clinical manager for a clinical trials program at San Francisco General Hospital. Vini works for a youth development non-profit called Juma Ventures. Interestingly, "Juma" translates to "work" in Kiswahili. Juma Ventures develops and operates bussinesses, called "social enterprises," where economically disadvantaged teens are given employment opportunities. "In Kitui," Vini says, "I worked with three youth polytechnic schools to increase their efficiencies, funding and standing in the communities. Without my VSO volunteer experience in polytechnics, I wouldn't be working for a youth development company right now. It's challenging, but fullfilling."

Parham Rasoulinejad, the medical student from Canada who took me on rounds at the provincial hospital in Kisumu, has started his residency in orthopedic surgery in London, Ontario.

Karen Okrainec, the other medical student on attachment to TICH, is in her first year residency in Internal Medicine.

"In other words," Karen writes, "I am in my first of five years' training in the specialty of Adult Medicine. Infectious Disease is one of the many subspecialties I can choose to study during my fourth and fifth years of residency, for example, or Cardiology (heart), Nephrology (kidneys), Neurology (brain), etc. I'm not quite sure what I'll choose to do in the next few years, but I'd like to chose a specialty that allows me to continue to work with people from all walks of life.

"I've always had a thirst to meet people from different parts of the world and see how they live. It was this thirst that took me to Africa. During my second trip to Africa, in Kisumu, Kenya, I experienced both the good and bad of working in a foreign place. I was a medical student at the time, full of enthusiasm and will to change what I could. I knew so little. There's a feeling of wanting to 'make a difference' which many people traveling to these parts of the world arrive with. Then there's the feeling of disappointment, and also shame, when I realized how presumptuous it was to think I knew better than my hosts. I was in a state of constant comparison. Perhaps it was my way of coming to terms with all the new sounds, tastes, smells and sights. Yet, I was more in shock when I came back to Canada. I went to Kenya to work in the hospitals and communities. I saw diseases we had eradicated in Canada decades ago. I saw poverty and the limitations to basic food, water and medicine. I saw how poverty can lead to corruption and how poverty can lead some people to do wonderful things. How little people can do big things. And how little things can be big.

"I continue to be inspired by the stories of people from all professions who have traveled to parts of the world and done beautiful things. Journalists, soldiers, local people, teachers, engineers, nurses, families.

"I returned to Africa, this time in a completely different setting as part of a team of 20 health professionals who brought essential medicines to two of the poorest communities in Benin, Western Africa. As a fourth year medical student, I worked in the pharmacy, triage, the medical clinic, the obstetrical-gynecology clinic, the schools teaching on HIV and AIDS and in homes doing house calls. It was hectic and the hours were long. We slept in the clinic quarters on old hospital beds covered with garbage bags we had found in our storage bins. There were at least a hundred people every morning by 5:00am gathered outside the clinic and who had walked miles to receive the free health care and medicine. The people who inspired me most in this group were the volunteers, many from other impoverished African communities, who wanted to join the work.

"I live in Montreal now, a multicultural town full of newly arrived immigrants and refugees. I'm not sure of what I'm going to do. I'm still open to the world and what it has to offer. I believe there is so much to learn from our very own community. Medicine, in itself, opens up a unique portrait."

Sandra was kind enough to write, "I think the work you are doing for TICH in the United States is more productive than when you were here. However, you could not have reached that resolve if you were not here to see the 'real story.'" She is right. In the United States, with access to reliable technology, I am better able to spread the word about TICH and development issues in general. I am mainly continuing my work with TICH through the non-profit, Just One Voice (www.justonevoice.org), and by supporting TICH and its programs that help rural communities use their own resources and newly acquired skills to increase crop yields, improve health care and educate their children. This book, too, is a tool for sharing the work in developing countries, to raise awareness and inspire someone to care enough to do something. Anything. Every little thing makes a huge difference. Believe me, I've seen it.

Many people are throwing light about them instead of darkness, including people born in developing countries. In Kenya, I volunteered at a college founded by Kenyans, managed by Kenyans and attended by students from many African countries. They will become leaders, showing their countries the way to development and prosperity. The college has since received the letter of interim authority from the Commission of Higher Education, giving TICH university status. They are calling the new university, under the umbrella of TICH, the Great Lakes University of Kisumu (GLUK). GLUK's core business is to produce a new generation of leaders, managers and workers concerned with changing the situation of the poor, the disadvantaged and vulnerable people at the community level. To this end, TICH offers a graduate program in Community Health and Development and is developing an undergraduate course in Development studies that will include Anthropology and other Social Sciences.

TICH's Health Sciences department offers a degree in Nursing and is working on other programs in Pharmacy and Microbiology. The Science department has undergraduate programs in Agribusiness, Community Nutrition, and Information Technology, and is currently working on an MBA in Agribusiness and Applied Engineering Sciences. The Humanities department has courses in Pastoral Theology, Education and Music.

TICH has graduated more than 300 students with diplomas and certificates and 85 students with Masters in Community Health and Development. A number of graduates are working for international institutions and NGOs in Kenya and abroad, while others head various institutions within the country and elsewhere. Currently, 310 students are enrolled at TICH. They hail from Kenya, Rwanda, Tanzania, DRC, Malawi, Uganda, Nigeria, Swaziland, Sudan and Ethiopia.

TICH continues to build its student exchange program with universities around the world. The latest addition is the National Cheng Kung University in Taiwan. Other student exchange partners are:

University of Amsterdam (The Netherlands), University of Ottawa (Canada), Free State University (South Africa), Universite' Libre Des Pays Des Grand Lacs (DRC), London School of Hygiene and Tropical Medicine (UK), University of Nairobi (Kenya), Moi University (Kenya), Kenya Methodist University, The University Cheikh Anta Diop (Senegal), Makerere University (Kenya), Jimma University (Ethiopia), University of Dar-es-salaam (Tanzania), University of Kwazulu Natal (South Africa), and Emory University (USA).

Sister Margaret Nduta, a traveling companion to the Congo who received her master's degree, is in the United States working toward her PhD. She plans to return to TICH and continue her work in the partnership department once she's received her PhD.

Ogutu Owii, a coworker from TICH's partnership department, is still working with TICH and building the university's student exchange program with National Cheng Kung University of Taiwan. He was on our trip to the Congo and received his master's degree. Of his experience as a student and staff member at TICH/GLUK, Ogutu writes, "GLUK has contributed enormously to making me what I am today. I have acquired administrative, management and leadership skills, can handle complex situations, recognize and accept unity in diversity across the globe and am persistent, passionate, and commited to all endeavors of community work. I've learned to provide services and understand every community can be involved in doing something for their life. Health issues are not just about diseases but come from poverty and inequity."

Maureen Kimani, who also graduated on our trip to the Congo, still works in research at TICH's Nairobi campus.

Reverend Obondi is now the university Chaplain at GLUK. He writes, "In addition to my Chaplaincy duties, I also lecture on sociology and management courses. When the Commission for Higher Education approves the Bachelor of Arts in pastoral theology, I will have a lot more to teach, including Biblical languages (Greek or Hebrew), theology, and ethics. It's important to me to address people by name, so they know they are valued. As the Bible teaches, a good shepherd (in the manner of Jesus) is one who knows the sheep by name and the sheep also know him/her. GLUK is growing so fast, I must work hard to keep up with all the new names!"

Dina, our coworker who lost her sister-in-law when I first arrived in Kenya, has started an organization to help the people in her community. The organization is called Alice Visionary Foundation Project and Dina's sister, Beldina, who lives in the United States, is part of the program to house, feed and educate orphans in their home village. Dina continues her work at TICH and is also studying for her Community Health and Development degree.

Tonny Bolo, my fellow IT team member, now works for AfriAfya, an organization that has absorbed several other TICH veterans. AfriAfya is a consortium of health NGOs who bring communication technology to rural and marginalized communities. They have several sites in Kenya and a few in

Somalia, so Tonny travels to set up resource centers and teach villagers how to use a computer, printer, digital camera, etc. The organization uses a combination of satellite, radio, video, print, email, text messages, CD ROMs, telephone, post, folksongs and traditional media to provide access to health and development information. Many of the communities do not have electricity, but because Kenya and Somalia are on the equator, they receive lots solar power.

Tonny, like most TICH staff and students, is committed to helping others. He writes, "To be selfless is to dedicates one's life to helping the marginalized and giving them a reason to believe there is always hope and a good life at the end of the tunnel. I chose this path many years ago and no matter how challenging life has been, I stick to the journey. I may never gain much. I may never change much. But that does not stop my dream, because I know it is POSSIBLE to change and improve the life of another. I would be happier to not have anything in my pocket, but know I changed someone's life for the better.

"Why would I struggle to make my life more comfortable if someone else has no basic needs met? Why try to be different from others when we want to believe we were all created equal?"

After I've been home a while, Walter emails to tell me the landlord sold the piece of land with the Pambazuko building on it, next to the slums' water source. The roof was never completed, but when the landlord sold the land, the building was dismantled, just as Tonny had feared. Walter writes, "Some of the materials I kept in case I get a new site. I will use the materials for constructing the new office block."

My advice to Walter, since he's now running Pambazuko from the room he rents in the slums, is to get training in community development. He will continue to stumble by keeping Pambazuko in a briefcase. His work is selfless, for sure. And his heart is golden, for sure. He just needs training in mobilizing the slums and in organizing development projects. I hope Walter listens.

I'm haunted by Walter, what he's going through living in the slums, somehow still thinking I pulled out and left him stranded. Sometimes, when I'm writing marketing materials or picking out apples at the grocery store or driving through the desert, I'm haunted by images of Michael, the 14-year-old, whose ear infection turned into a brain infection. I'm haunted by young

Vincent, the boy paralyzed from the waist down who rode to school on his mother's back. I'm haunted by the aged mamas with tiny grandchildren to care for, and the burn victims who lost their sight or their fingers. When I least expect it, these images come to me and I wish I could have done more for each of these people. And I ache because I know there have been many others since my visit and many others who are still in pain.

I will return soon and will do all the things for people I regretted not doing before. The thought of giving comfort brings me solace. For now.

Recollections

*B*efore I leave Kisumu, the moon partially eclipses the sun. Visible in Spain and Portugal, the eclipse then makes its way to Algeria, Somalia, and out over the Indian Ocean. In Kisumu, the day is yellow and then deepens to orange as the moon creeps over the sun. Students and staff gather in the front yard at TICH, taking turns looking through three blank 35m photo negatives. The film is tripled to block harmful rays.

More and more people come out of the academic building to see the eclipse. Their desire to learn is immense. They buzz and laugh and speculate. They gather shoulder to shoulder, holding the film strips high so they can peer up, to see the sun and moon tangoing. They gather shoulder to shoulder, men and women of all ages and all heights, and they laugh as though they don't have a care in the world; as though life in Kenya has not embittered them.

Trees cast yellow and orange shadows in duplicate and triplicate and the shadows dance on the schoolyard and on our shoulders, though the wind is still.

My colleagues and classmates share their joy as they pass the negatives to the next small group, who stand shoulder to shoulder to admire the heavens. They, too, are not bitter, but laugh and see promise in this schoolyard, under the yellow glow.

Acknowledgments

*T*here are so many wonderful people who touched this journey with their grace and intelligence and kindness. Unlimited thanks go to Dr. Dan Keseje and my colleagues at TICH who allowed me to be me, but more importantly, they shared themselves as they are. People like Sister Margaret Nduta and George Nyamor with their graceful spirits, and Sister Masheti with her unabashed energy.

Elizabeth Ochieng, Beldina (Dina) Opiyo, Bavon Mupenda, Charles Wafula, Pamela Juma, Jecinter (Jessie) Oketch, Lynette Oyucho, Rose Olayo, Dr. Lucas Ngode, Ogutu Owii, Florence Obiero, Bernard Owuor, Herman Jaoko, Dennis Ochieng, Grace Were, Henry Oyugi, Mitch Odero and Caroline Musita all shared their warmth and knowledge and soft laughter when it was needed most. Reverend Obondi was a constant, a comfort. Tonny Bolo, Elias Ojwang and Apollo Odhiambo gave me more than team support in our department, they gave from their guts and their hearts, continually. George Owino, Paul Ramogi, Fred Ochuodho, Vitalis Matengo, Erik Okwengu and John Ochieng keep the school safe and clean and moving; they are all golden. It is no secret Dr. Dan Keseje is a hero in my eyes. As is Dr. Stephen Okeyo.

The Ruprahs provided much more than a home when I was seeking connection. I cannot begin to reciprocate their tenderness. But I will try.

I thank my mother, Kathryn Bohannon, for her belief in me. I hope she continues to believe and find delight in my endeavors.

Kate Yandoh is a wonder, a powerhouse of new ideas and new sensations. Thanks to Kate for her generous proofreading and support and brilliance. Pushkaraj Parangpe, too, lent his creative forces to proofreading while pursuing his own filmmaking dreams. Thank you, Raj, for your transcendent view.

Thanks to Richard Down, Louise and Paul Mell, Richelle and Kevin McPherson, Jennifer and Glenn Miller, Deedee and Tony Johnson, Gail Joyner, Marsha Johnson, Kourtney Bryant, Sherri and Shane Aycoth, Rich Millett, Steve Shelnut, Susan Tallant, Sarah Moore, the inspiring Dunwoody Optimist Club members, Ed Sutton, Rose Szymanski, Penny Levine, Kevin McClafferty, Bill Jackson, Maureen Gilroy, Cynthia Hatcher, Nan Lewellyn, Dana and Lee Brown, Gail Wetzel, Martin O'Connor, Greta Garcia, Jill Kramer, Pamlea Harris-Efurd, Eddie Sheffield, Hugh Hunt, Kelly Jo Crantas, Larry Thiesen, Richard Welsh, Mike Todd, Jennifer and Mike Benson, Julia Versteegh, Richard and Sandra Bohannon, Sonua and Rick Bohannon and all others in the Great Bohannon Clan for your loving hearts. You cared…about everything… and I am thankful for your friendship, guidance and unconditional love. You buoy me.

Much appreciation goes to VSO, a group of forward thinkers who make amazing things happen around the world, and to all VSO volunteers, especially those who shared their experiences, humor and insight as we all made our clumsy and inquisitive way into international development.

To Brent Fisher, Jaime Coleman and James Coleman, the truest loves of my life, I say thank you for your understanding, your flexibility, your consistent lifting up and your pure love. You are my rock, my joy and my conscience. Brent, your constant singing and morning jigs kept my spirits up and make my world go around. Jaime, since before you were born, I knew you would be precious and sweet and grounded. It is so. And, my sweet baby James, you show us the world through a different lens and make us think. You enrich me.

I am grateful to Brenda Schmidt, who makes a great mentor without even trying, and to Kristi Williams, who aligns her mind with her heart to spread love and goodness.

I thank the people of Kenya who give so much when they have so little. They still have faith, in others and in themselves, and they are my motivators, our motivators. They are a treasure, each one, and I celebrate them every day.

Ignacio Pintos, thank you for your perpetual optimism and stellar style. Tamara Berry, your love of Africa and your wordsmithing talents added immensely to this book's essence. A million thanks to you two for your dedication and passion.

Many incredible people touched this journey along the way and I am grateful; their smiles, sighs and actions have made all the difference.

Give the Gift of a Journey into the heart of Africa and Kenyans!

If you've enjoyed this book and know of others who might like it, please order more copies! As usual, 100% of the proceeds will go to Just One Voice to feed children and educate adults in agribusinesses in Western Kenya.

Yes, I want _____ copies of *Poverty and Promise: One Volunteer's Experience of Kenya* at 18.95 to $4.50 shipping and $1 per book handling.

Allow 15 days for delivery. _____ My check or money order for $_____ is enclosed.

Please charge my credit card

Mastercard ☐   Visa ☐   American Express ☐   Discover ☐

Card # [   ]   Expiration date: [   ]

Signature: _____

Name _____

Address _____

City/State/Zip _____

Phone _____ E-mail _____

Please make your check payable to AtlasBooks, and return to:

AtlasBooks
30 Amberwood Parkway
Ashland, OH 44805

Or order by:

Visiting www.justonevoice.org

Email: orders@bookmasters.com

Phone: Toll-free 1-800-BOOK-LOG or 1-800-247-6553

Fax: 419-281-6883